red - Fatally shot in front of
uring an altercation over room
Fred Scott, who, on 3/30/21
w n 22.   1/18/22 Joliet Pen - 1 yr. to life - Fitch

lly shot July 6, 1921, in her
chigan Ave., by her brother-in-law
who boarded with her, during a
nd board. Frank committed
him self. 10 P.M.

Body found in river at Maywood,
n thrown by Harvey W. Church
in the basement of his home,
killed Carl A. Ausmus in same way).
h confessed to the two murders
his desire to gain possession
nuto which they had brought to
1/16/22 Sentenced to hang 2/17/22 - Caverly
d re-sentenced to hang on 3/3/22 - Scanlan
Jail.

ck and fatal   4. 4 - 1921
and North curb, while crossing
unidentified driver recommended by

Murder City

Michael Lesy

MURDER CITY

The Bloody History of Chicago in the Twenties

W. W. Norton & Company
New York · London

Murder City: The Bloody History of Chicago in the Twenties
Michael Lesy

The text of this book is composed in Century 731
with the display in Berber and Clarion.

Book design and composition by Laura Lindgren.

Manufacturing by R. R. Donnelley.

Publication of this book was partially underwritten by a grant from Furthermore, a program of the J. M. Kaplan Fund.

Library of Congress Cataloging-in-Publication Data
Lesy, Michael, 1945–
   Murder city : the bloody history of Chicago in the twenties / Michael Lesy. — 1st ed.
344   p.   cm.
   Includes index.
   ISBN-13: 978-0-393-06030-0 (hardcover)
   ISBN-10: 0-393-06030-6 (hardcover)
   1. Homicide—Illinois—Chicago—Case studies. 2. Murder—Illinois—Chicago—Case studies. 3. Chicago (Ill.)—Social conditions. I. Title.
HV6534.C4L47 2007
364.152'3097731109042—dc22   2006030788

W. W. Norton & Company, Inc.   W. W. Norton & Company Ltd.
500 Fifth Avenue   Castle House
New York, N.Y. 10110   75/76 Wells Street
www.wwnorton.com   London W1T 3QT

1 2 3 4 5 6 7 8 9 0

It is impossible to leaf through any newspaper, from any day or month or year, without finding in each and every line the signs of the most appalling human perversity, together with the most astonishing boasts of probity, kindness, charity and the most shameless assertions concerning progress and civilization.

Every newspaper, from the first line to the last, is nothing but a tissue of horrors. Wars, crimes, thefts, licentiousness, torture, crimes of princes, crimes of nations, crimes of ordinary individuals, an intoxicating brew of universal atrocity.

And it is this disgusting apéritif that the civilized man takes with his morning meal. Everything in this world oozes crime: the newspaper, the street wall and the human countenance.

I cannot comprehend how an unsullied hand could touch a newspaper without a convulsion of disgust.

Charles Baudelaire,
from "My Heart Laid Bare,"
in the *Intimate Journals*
translated by Luke Bouvier
© Luke Bouvier 2006

Lieutenant Carl W. Wanderer

1 · Carl Wanderer

Carl never lied. He never drank, never smoked, never chewed gum. Everyone knew. Worked in his father's butcher shop. The ladies liked him. Worked there, then went in the Army. Joined up in 1914. About the time his mother started acting crazy. "Used to preach around," Carl said. She had a vision that wouldn't let her rest. Said she'd seen Carl lynched, hanging from the limb of a tree. One of Carl's sisters—his older one, not his twin—said, "It made her despondent." Some people say that's why she killed herself. Slit her own throat. "Bumped herself off," Carl said. "I was in the Army, then. I liked the Army."

Later, when Dr. Hickson heard that, he said, "We can now add latent homosexuality to the complications." Dr. Hickson was head of the city's Psychopathic Laboratory. "Psychoanalysis has revealed," he said, "that a mania for Army life is one of the inevitably distinguishing characteristics of women haters. . . . I have observed several such cases while in the Army, myself."[1]

Carl was nineteen when he joined up. The Army made him a machine gunner. Then it made him a sergeant; then it promoted him to second lieutenant. People respected him. His own lieutenant said, "I was with him under shell fire in the Alsace sector for months. He was alert, intelligent, very competent, brave, a good soldier. As sane as any man I have ever known."[2]

Carl never gambled. "In the Army, I never spent my money. . . . I saved $800." (That $800 would be worth at least ten times as much today.) Carl came home in October 1919, and married Ruth Johnson a few weeks later. They'd known each other since they were kids. "I never kissed a woman until Ruth came along and never anybody else." Ruth had sung in the choir of Holy Trinity, Lutheran for eight years.[3] When Carl enlisted, she resigned from the choir. She said she didn't want to give any other man the opportunity to ask to escort her home after practice.

A month after Carl married her, Ruth announced she was expecting. Carl was back at work at his father's shop. He and Ruth were living in a room in her parents' apartment. They were saving their money so they could buy a home of their own. By June 1920, they'd saved $1,500. (All dollar amounts cited in this chapter are equivalent to ten times their value today. Please see note 10 in the Afterword.) Ruth was eight months pregnant. She'd been buying little things for the baby. Kept a list in her dresser. One day, she told Carl it was time to get their money out of the bank so they could buy a house. That's what Carl said, anyway.

"We never quarreled," he said. "A man's duty is to keep his wife happy. . . . I've always done what was exactly right and never done wrong."[4]

Once Dr. Hickson heard that, he was ready to make a diagnosis. The city's Municipal Court referred all sorts of cases to Dr. Hickson. His job was to evaluate people before they went to trial. "Dementia praecox catatonia," Dr. Hickson said. "A very well defined case. A mind geometrically moral but emotionally 'unmoral.' Preoccupied mechanically with ideas of right and wrong . . ."[5]

Of course, if things had worked out differently—worked out as Carl had planned—Dr. Hickson wouldn't have said that.

What happened, according to Carl, was that he and Ruth went to her bank and withdrew all but $70 of her savings. They took the money home with them. Ruth put the cash in her dresser, next to her baby list.

Carl said he stayed home the next day, all day Sunday, to guard the money. And—to guard Ruth.

That's because, Carl said, Ruth had told him she'd noticed a strange man, "a raggedy stranger," eyeing her. "Suspiciously." Carl was ready for him, though. He had his side arm from the Army. An automatic. A .45.

Monday came and Carl went shopping for a new knife for his father. He worked behind the counter all afternoon. That night, after dinner, he and Ruth decided it'd be nice to go to a movie. They went to see *Sea Wolf*. They left the show early.

As they were walking home—it must have been almost nine-thirty by then—Carl said he noticed a man—a raggedy bum—following them. The man didn't just follow them. He came up right behind them; he came up right beside them. The city was infested with bums: homeless men, men out of the Army, men out of work. Carl and Ruth kept walking. The man followed them right up the steps into the front hall of their building.

"My wife was opening the door," Carl said, "but she was having trouble with the key. I spoke to her about it. She said she was going to turn on the light. The man said, 'Don't do that.' He said, 'No you don't. How about the money.' "

Carl was ready. He reached for his gun. The man shot Ruth. Carl shot the man. In the dark. In that little hallway. Ten shots. Ruth collapsed. Carl lunged at the man. He knew he'd shot him, but Carl grabbed his head and beat it into the floor. Then he swept up his wife. She was bleeding. He carried her upstairs and told her mother to get help.

Ruth was dead. The raggedy stranger was dead. The police lieutenant who interrogated Carl said, "I thought he was entitled to a medal for bravery after I listened to his version."[6]

The newspapers thought so, too. WAR HERO IN DEADLY BATTLE. "I got him, honey. I got him," the papers wrote Carl had murmured as he cradled Ruth's body. There were reports about how Carl had mowed down Germans in the Argonne. How he'd been awarded the Distinguished Service Cross. How the French had honored him with the Croix de Guerre. Later, much later, his commanding officer was asked about this. "He was not in the Argonne and did not mow down Germans. . . . He was in officer candidate school behind the lines when the battalion was in the Argonne."[7]

Carl had fought it out with the stranger exactly nine months after he'd come home from the Army.

A week passed. Lieutenant Wanderer, Heartbroken Hero. Mourns. Etc. Then the papers found other stories to tell. Carl went back to work behind the counter of his father's shop.

About the time Carl was mustered out of the Army, the Chicago Police Department established its first Homicide Bureau: its brightest and best detectives, specialists in murder. The department chose a sergeant named John Norton to head the squad. Norton read the papers along with everyone else. If Wanderer was a hero, who was the dead man? There was something else: the dead man had a revolver—a heavy-duty Army Colt that fired .45s. Two big guns blazing away in a foyer. Two shots in Ruth. Three shots in the bum. One hole in the floor. Four holes in the walls. Not a scratch on Wanderer. How come?

Everyone knew who Wanderer was, but the bum didn't have a name. He'd been in his twenties, about the same age as Wanderer. He was frail, dirty, dressed in rags. He was going bald. The strange thing was that he'd just gotten a haircut. And a manicure. Norton had only two pieces of evidence that could identify the man.

The first was a meal ticket—a commissary card—issued by a circus—in Kansas City to a man named Masters.[8] Norton sent a photograph of his John Doe to the circus. A commissary agent there identified the man as a roustabout named Mahoney. Mahoney had disappeared—but not before stealing Masters's meal ticket. The good news was that Mahoney had killed a man in New Hampshire—clubbed him to death after a bar fight. He'd been sentenced to ten years, then been pardoned and released. The bad news was that Mahoney was twenty years older and six inches taller than Norton's corpse.[9]

People began visiting the morgue to view the body. The more visitors, the more identities: An elevator operator at a theater identified the man as a fellow she'd met in a military hospital in England during the war. He'd been a member of the Canadian Expeditionary Force. He'd told her his father was a "wealthy New York turfman who had everything money could buy and heart desire."[10] Norton's squad contacted the police in New York, but they couldn't even find the "turfman" father.

The head of a Catholic boys' orphanage, the Working Boys' Home, said he was sure he'd seen the dead man's face before. He took some of his boys back to the morgue with him. "All the boys recognize him as a former resident of the home," said the priest, "but none of them can recall his name."

A cop whose beat was the city's Skid Row thought the dead man was a homeless veteran everyone called "Snuffy."[11]

A fellow named Pryor thought the corpse belonged to a childhood friend of his named Bill. "I haven't seen Bill for eight or nine years . . . he ran away from home to join the circus. Gentry Brothers. He . . . did odd jobs, made himself useful. Everybody liked him. . . . Bill didn't have any freckles though, but of course, freckles come easily. . . ."[12]

Norton kept the body cold and turned to the only other piece of evidence he had: the dead man's gun. Police had found it lying next to him. An Army Colt .45. Serial number C2282.[13]

(In 1920, forensic ballistics relied on cartridge calibers and weapon serial numbers. The marks left by firing pins and by the rifling of barrels—all that and the parallel-viewing microscopes that made comparisons possible—came later in the decade.)

The Colt Company told Norton that it had sold the weapon to a well-known sporting goods store in Chicago. A clerk in the store told Norton he'd sold the revolver to a man named John Hoffman. There were plenty of John Hoffmans in Chicago. But this John Hoffman—what a coincidence!—

this John Hoffman was a brother-in-law of Carl Wanderer. John Hoffman told Norton he'd sold the weapon to Fred Wanderer. Fred was—another coincidence!—Carl's cousin.

The newspapers kept writing little stories about the different people who thought they knew who John Doe was. Sergeant Norton decided it was time for Lieutenant Wanderer to tell him more about himself.

Norton had Wanderer brought in. Wanderer may not have known about habeas corpus, but the attorney his family hired did. Norton knew the clock was running.

For two days, three men from the State's Attorney's office, three detectives, including Norton, from Homicide, and two men from the coroner's office, including the coroner himself, played good cop/bad cop with Wanderer. They showed him pictures of his dead wife; reminded him she was looking down at him from heaven; accused him of killing her because he wanted her money or because—fool!—he thought she was cuckolding him. They bellowed and shook their fists at him, pushed him around and stomped his feet, talked to him quietly, man-to-man, with their arms around his shoulders, asked him, over and over again, to play out the scene in the front hall of his apartment building.

Wanderer smiled little smiles at them and spoke calmly, when he spoke at all. He told them eighteen different stories. His favorite story, the one he told most convincingly, had to do with how Fred's gun got in the hands of the dead man.

"Now my wife tells me," Wanderer said, "she hasn't got the key. Then I start looking for mine—but it's under my cousin's automatic, which I have in my hip pocket. I borrowed it because Fred could have gotten into trouble for having a gun like that. While I'm reaching for it, the other man reached in and grabbed it. He shot my wife twice with it, and I shot back." Wanderer had carried two guns to the movie.[14]

As for the $1,500 Ruth had withdrawn from her bank: Sometimes Wanderer said he didn't know anything about it; sometimes he said he'd told Ruth to withdraw it; sometimes he said she'd withdrawn it on her own and he didn't know where it was until his mother-in-law found it in Ruth's dresser after she died. Sometimes he wondered out loud why people were making such a fuss about the money—half of it was his, from the Army.

At two o'clock in the morning of the third day, police woke him up and began sixteen hours of what they called "the third degree." Bellows, shouts, pushes—and punches. More provocations, accusations, consolations. They wouldn't let him rest, then they gave him a big steak for lunch. His attorney threatened to file a writ of habeas corpus unless they either charged him or released him.

At six o' clock that night, Wanderer leaned over to one of the interrogation team's "good cops"—a secretary named George Kennedy—and said, "Let me get policed-up and I'll tell you the whole thing."[15] They hadn't let Wanderer wash or shave for three days. Kennedy ran out to find some soap and a razor. Wanderer shaved himself calmly, a nice clean job, without a nick or a scratch. The police brought in a stenographer. Since whatever confession Wanderer might make had to be presented to a coroner's jury, Coroner Peter Hoffman, a middle-aged man with a distinguished gray mustache, asked Wanderer nearly all the questions.

Wanderer's confession was twenty pages long. Some of what he said sounded strangely matter-of-fact, hollow and inexplicable, the reasonings of a crazy man. Much of it, though, sounded cold-blooded, clear-minded, and very sane. As his fellow inmates in the county jail later said, "Wanderer's either innocent or crazy or he's not human. And he doesn't seem crazy."[16]

Wanderer said—to the police and later to the newspapers—that it took him a week to make up his mind to kill his wife. "I just thought of killing her—and decided I had to do it quick while I was wanting to or pretty soon I'd lose the idea of doing it . . . A man's place is with his wife and I was always at home. I was always kind to her—but I got this Army idea in my head and decided to follow up on it. . . . See, I was just tired of her. I didn't want her any more. I killed her so no one else would have her. I never thought of going in the Army until two days before I killed her. . . .[17]

"The thought of killing anybody doesn't bother me as much as it would the average person. I've put a lot of time in my father's butcher shop; the idea of shedding blood doesn't offend me much. Besides that, there's my Army experience. That taught me not to mind killing. . . .[18]

"Now, I want to be hanged. I want to join my wife in death. . . . Her lying in that vestibule after I shot her . . . haunts me. I wonder if she will forgive me. I loved her too much to let another man have her. I didn't want her, myself. It was the Army I wanted. . . ."[19]

When the coroner asked Wanderer why he'd borrowed his cousin's gun, Wanderer answered, "To make out like it was a stickup job." He knew Fred's gun was the same caliber as his, so he "planned to leave it, lay it there on the floor to make out like it was the other man's gun." When Hoffman asked,

"Did you think this gun could be traced?" Wanderer answered, "I did after a while." "Is that the reason you didn't leave your own gun there?" "Yes," answered Wanderer. "Because you thought your own gun could be traced?" "Yes," said Wanderer.

The longest part—the most unnerving part—of Wanderer's confession concerned the course of his relationship with the man he used to murder his wife. Wanderer used that man's hunger to serve his own. The cheapest whores worked for better wages. Later, the newspapers described the dead man as "the poor fool who hired himself out to be killed."

On Monday morning Wanderer went shopping for a new butcher knife; he also went shopping for a man. After he bought the knife, he told his interrogators, he "went for a walk." He said he crossed Lasalle Street to Madison, then kept on Madison, walking west, across the river. He was headed for a neighborhood that the newspapers called "notorious . . . a resort for mendicants, bums, and derelicts." At the corner of Madison and Halstead, Wanderer spotted what he was looking for. Standing in front of a cigar store. Young and hungry. Wanderer asked the man if he wanted a job. "He says, 'What kind?' I says, 'Driving a truck, working in our business.' He says, 'How much do you pay?' I told him, 'Twenty-five dollars a week.' He says 'Alright.' "[20]

(Twenty-five dollars a week was a good wage in a good year, but 1920 was not a good year. A depression began in 1920, a severe depression, that would last two years.)

"He says, 'When can I get the job.' I says, 'Meet me at Logan and Western at half past 6:00.' I gave him car fare—a quarter." The corner of Logan and Western was one block from the Wanderers' butcher shop. It was also the first in a series of rendezvous points that Wanderer would arrange, like a hunter leaving bits of food along a path that led to a pit he'd dug and camouflaged. Times, itineraries, and meetings—Wanderer described them clearly and carefully throughout the rest of his confession.[21]

At six-thirty, the man showed up as Wanderer had instructed; Wanderer told him to follow him. They climbed onto a streetcar. The man didn't ask any questions; Wanderer told the man to follow him off the car. He told him to wait on the corner. He said he'd be back.

Wanderer walked to his cousin's house and asked to borrow his gun. Fred asked why. Wanderer told him he needed it for a bet—a bet about how quickly he could take it apart, then reassemble it. Fred believed him. Wanderer walked back to the man with the weapon in his pocket. They got back on another streetcar; it was too crowded for them to talk. At Lawrence and

Lincoln, "right by the restaurant, one door from the corner,"[22] Wanderer signaled the man to climb off with him. The corner of Lawrence and Lincoln was two and a half blocks from where Ruth and Wanderer lived.

"Did you talk after you got off the car?" asked the coroner. "Yes," said Wanderer. "For five or ten minutes." "What was said between you and him at the time?" "I asked him if he wanted to make some money. He says, 'Yes.' I says, 'You just carry out my instructions. When I get to a certain place, just ask for the money. I will give it to you. You just get it as quick as you can.'" The coroner asked what that "certain place" was. "Up in the vestibule," answered Wanderer. "In the vestibule of what?" asked the coroner. "My house," said Wanderer. "Then," said Wanderer, "I gave him a dollar for to buy his supper and I left him there. I told him I would meet him. I told him I would meet him there between 9:00 and half past 9:00."[23] It was almost eight o' clock in the evening by then.

Wanderer went home and ate his own supper with Ruth. They decided it would be nice to see a movie. On the way to the show, Wanderer made sure they didn't walk a route that would take them past the man. On the way home, Wanderer steered them to the rendezvous point.

At the corner of Lincoln and Lawrence, by the drugstore, the two men spotted each other. "I nodded my head to him. He began following us. Sometimes along side us, sometimes a couple of steps behind us." Up into the vestibule. The key, the lock, the light . . .

The coroner asked, "Then what happened?" "He says, 'No you don't. How about the money.' That's what he said." "Is that what you told him to say, previously?" "Yes." "Where was he when you told him that?" "Lincoln and Lawrence."

"Then what did you do?" asked the coroner. "Then I drew out my gun. First shot accidentally hit the floor." "Yes?" "We did not have no money. I saw I had made a blunder, not taking the money with me. I knew . . . I had to do something—he might squeal. I drew my [other] gun and shot in both directions." "Did you want to shoot this man?" "Yes . . . I did not have the money on me there. I knew he would squeal if I did not carry out my plans." The coroner wanted to be sure. "Why were you going to kill him?" "Well," Wanderer said, "just to make it look as if he had done the job." "What job?" "Killing my wife."[24]

After everyone was satisfied—coroner's office, detectives, prosecutors—Wanderer ordered pork and beans for supper. Coroner Hoffman had his confession transcribed. Police called in reporters and photographers. Wanderer's interrogators gathered around him as he prepared to sign his statement. Hoffman pointed at the spot where Wanderer was to sign. George Kennedy, the "good cop"/secretary, sat next to Wanderer, hunched and attentive, like an attaché at a treaty ceremony. Norton stood behind them, calm, watchful, somber, a man in his prime, the broad brim of his boater as dark and proper as his suit. And Wanderer? He sat placidly, watching his right hand lightly move a pen across the page in front of him.[25]

Lieutenant Carl W. Wanderer

Everyone in the city began talking about what had happened to "the facts." "The facts" being what everyone had been told—and agreed and believed—was true. A violent, vicious bum turned out to be an innocent victim. A noble man—a war hero!—was really an ice-blooded killer. No one said it, but everyone thought it: a man who'd kill his pretty, young, innocent wife *and* the child she carried in her womb—that man *had to be* crazy. "Nobody knows me or anything about me unless I tell them," Wanderer said to a reporter who interviewed him.

"I should never have believed it," said Ruth's mother, "if Carl had not confessed. If I had seen it with my own eyes, I should not have believed it." She shuddered as she spoke. "Night after night, I have seen them together, happy, loving, talking about the baby. . . . And, after my darling was dead, I tried to help Carl bear the blow. I would throw my arms about him. . . . He seemed always to be greatly affected when I tried to comfort him. And now—how could he have done this thing?!"[26]

Dr. Hickson from the Psychopath Lab had his theories. "A 'shut-in personality,'" he said. "No contact—that is emotional contact—with his parents or his wife. Lives like a man in a cave . . . conceals his cold bloodedness or non interest in life by methodically doing everything that is right. He inherited from his mother—an out-and-out case of dementia praecox who herself committed suicide—a moral mania. He utilizes it as a sort of code. Behind the code lives the real Wanderer."[27]

Three days after the newspapers published Wanderer's confession, a pretty, seventeen-year-old stenographer named Julia Schmitt contacted Sergeant Norton. She said she lived with her family across the street from the Wanderers' butcher shop. That's how she'd first met Carl. They became friends. "He wrote me wonderful letters. I showed them to my mother." She said she didn't know Carl was married until she read about his wife's death in the newspapers. "I was out with him six times," she said. Four times before his wife died. "We either went on taxicab rides or to Riverview [amusement park]. He was a nice fellow and a good friend. He never said he loved me. We had our pictures taken, once. He always acted like a gentleman. I thought he was a fine chap until I read in the paper about his wife's death. The fact that he was married was a great shock to me. I was greatly disappointed with him. He continued to write. He became more affectionate in the tone of his letters. He said I was his only friend. I told him I could never think the same way of him. I saw him twice after that. To say good-bye. He told me he was going back in the Army."[28]

Miss Schmitt gave Sergeant Norton two of Wanderer's letters. Norton asked her if Wanderer had ever kissed her. "Yes," she said. "But he was always very gentlemanly like."

Norton was delighted. Finally! A familiar, venal—sane—motive. Detectives searched Wanderer's room and found a single letter he'd written to Miss Schmitt, but never mailed. It began, "Sweet-heart—I am lonesome." He'd torn it up, but he'd kept it.

Norton took Miss Schmitt to visit Wanderer to see what would happen. Wanderer was polite, but indifferent. "She was just like a lot of other girls who came into the butcher shop," he said. "I just happened to like her better than the rest—liked to go out with her. I liked a lot of others, too. . . . I never told her I was going to marry her. I had no bad intentions. I just liked her better than the rest."[29] His only regret, he said, was all the money he'd spent—$40 wasted!—on taxicab rides to take her out.[30]

Wanderer's father and his sisters visited him the next day. They brought him a Bible and a prayer book. They prayed with him and they wept.[31] Even the guards were moved. Not Wanderer. "A man's got to take his medicine," he said. "I'll plead guilty. . . . I'll ask him to hang me as soon as possible."[32] Sergeant Norton wasn't impressed. "A man without a soul," he said as he locked Wanderer in his cell that night.

A week passed.

One of Wanderer's guards tipped off a reporter. Wanderer had told him: He'd changed his mind. He'd decided to plead not guilty. "They will have to fight to hang me," he'd told the guard. "I've got a swell lawyer and we'll beat the case yet."[33] His lawyer had told him to change his plea.

Three months passed. The day before his trial—on the charge of killing his wife (no mention of their child)—Wanderer gave an interview to a group of reporters. They asked the obvious: Wasn't he denying his own confession? How could he do that? Wasn't he denying everything he'd told everyone—press, police, family—for months?

"Life is sweet and I'm fighting," Wanderer answered. He ended the interview. "I can't talk anymore now. You'll get it all tomorrow."[34] He stood up and walked away. As he strode down the corridor, the reporter could hear him whistling, softly, "There's a Long, Long Trail A-Winding."[35]

Lieutenant Wanderer was back. He'd told eighteen different stories before he'd confessed. He had a new one, now.

Wanderer's trial opened on October 4, 1920. There were no women on the jury. (The Nineteenth Amendment, the one that enfranchised women, had become law in late August—too soon for women to become part of any jury pool. Amendment or no amendment, there were no women on any of the juries who heard any of the cases described in this book.) But from the first day of Wanderer's trial to its last, the courtroom was crowded with women. "Court regulars" were a scruffy lot—an unkempt crew of men, has-beens, pensioners, and rumormongers. Wanderer's spectators were different: "Women attired in the latest fashions . . . corpulent dowagers . . . mothers holding the hands of boys and girls."[36] The women who came early and stayed late brought sandwiches to eat so they could keep their seats during the noon recess. The judge was offended. "This court is no lunchroom," he said, then ordered the ladies to eat in the corridor. The women did as they were told but they kept coming: Ruth had been young, pretty, innocent, and pregnant. Eating in the hallway was a small price to pay for justice.

The prosecution took two weeks to present its evidence: Fred's Colt and its serial number, Ruth's money and the timing of its withdrawal. The prosecution rested its case by reading aloud Wanderer's confession. Wanderer's lawyers confided their strategy to the press: they would argue that Wanderer was insane; that his so-called confession had been coerced; that even if Wanderer had shot his wife, it had been an accident. Reasonable doubt joined with mental incapacity.

On October 20, the defense called Wanderer's family and friends to testify about his mental health: Carl was the son of a mother who had been insane for at least five years before she committed suicide; when Carl was a boy, he'd tried to commit suicide after he'd caught scarlet fever and been quarantined. In France, in the Army, he'd somehow or other been hit in the head with a baseball bat and been unconscious for three hours. Another time, he'd fallen off a horse and been hospitalized for three weeks.

The next day, the defense called Wanderer to the stand. His lead attorney began by asking him if he'd shot his wife. "No," he said. Then what about his confession? "They bullied and beat me," Carl said. A detective sergeant had come into his cell and, while he was still in his underwear, had beaten him up. Coroner Hoffman, himself, had shaken his fist in Carl's face and then punched him in the head "several times." "It was all forced out of me," Wanderer said. He repudiated everything as calmly as he'd once admitted it. All that talk about "taking his medicine" and wanting to be hanged—he denied he'd ever said it. Whatever it was the press, the police, his family said he'd said—he denied it all.[37]

More and more people pressed into the courtroom as Wanderer held forth. "Old women, young girls, politicians who knew bailiffs, a noted orchestra leader, an artist, several leading criminal attorneys."[38] "Let no one else in," ordered the judge.

The prosecution called five people to bear witness to Wanderer's sanity. Two of them were the parents of his dead wife.[39] The prosecution pressed on. What about Julia Schmitt? the prosecutor asked Wanderer. (Miss Schmitt's age dropped from seventeen to sixteen by the time the prosecution ended its cross-examination.) What about the love letters and the taxicab rides and the trips to the amusement park? prosecutors asked Wanderer. Wanderer said such things had never happened or, if they had, he didn't recall them.

"Kisses for Julia; bullets for Ruth"[40] stormed the prosecutor in his summation. The prosecutor was an old pro. He'd worn a red tie for the occasion. "The most remarkable story ever told in the history of Cook County," replied Wanderer's lead attorney. Dramatic or not, said the attorney, the facts remained: Carl didn't kill Ruth; his confession had been extorted; if Carl had shot Ruth, her death had been an accident. Most important: Carl "was not mentally perfect, but an insane man, suffering from dementia praecox." Thank you, Dr. Hickson.

The jury took twenty-three hours to make up its mind. "We decided," the foreman later said, "that his confession was forced out of him" by Homicide Detective Norton. "We did not for a minute believe the story told in the confession. . . . The state did not present enough evidence in regards the ownership of the two [weapons]. We had difficulty deciding whether Wanderer or the stranger owned them. We finally decided Wanderer owned both of them. Some of us were afraid that if we found him insane, he would be committed to an asylum for a year or two and then be released. We didn't want that. We finally decided he was sane. Some thought fourteen years would be sufficient. Some wanted life. We compromised on twenty-five years."[41]

Wanderer was jubilant. "I knew they couldn't crack me. . . . I knew I'd never swing." Was this the same man who'd said he wanted to join his wife in death?

His defense attorneys expressed surprise. The newspapers described his lead attorney as "astonished."

The prosecutor, who'd told reporters throughout the trial that he was certain Wanderer would hang, said he was "dumbfounded. What absurdity! What ineptitude! What fallacy! What foolishness!"

"You have erred," said the judge to the jury. "You told me that you believed him insane, but that an insanity verdict would not keep him locked-up. Now you find him sane. Why, men, I would have sent him away for so long a time that he would never again kill. . . . A grievous error. A regrettable error."[42]

Sergeant Norton was a bit more insightful. "They should have a woman's jury try that wife killer. Women would certainly have done no worse and chances are they would have done much better. That bird should swing, if ever a man should."[43]

The jury's official verdict was "manslaughter." Manslaughter was (and is) defined as "a crime without malice, express or implied. This may be voluntary, upon sudden heat or excitement of anger, or involuntary, but during the commission of some unlawful act." If Wanderer behaved himself while he was in jail at Joliet, he could be out in "thirteen years and nine months." The state decided that this would never happen. If Ruth's death had been a lethal accident, the state still had "the commission of some [other] unlawful act" to use against "the butcher boy Lieutenant." Carl had shot two people.

The prosecutors still had Mr. Doe.

Or, at least, they thought they did.

The same day the jury made up its mind, a visitor to the city's morgue gave John Doe his fourth—or was it his fifth?—new identity.

"I'd know him in hell," said Herbert Potter. "He's an ex-Canadian soldier named John Barrett. He stayed at the old Ironsides Hotel." The Ironsides was a Skid Row flophouse, much like the place where Mr. Potter, himself a Canadian, down on his luck, currently lived. "I loaned him $15 last February on a couple of baggage checks he had."

Potter was certain Mr. Doe was John Barrett because both men had a protruding front tooth. Better yet: Barrett had signed his name, big and bold, in the Ironsides hotel register, every day, as the hotel required, until the day John Doe was shot. One day, "John Barrett," the next day, nothing. "Do you think I'd loan money to a man and not know him again," Potter said. "I'm not that easy."[44] Potter's story held—until a new set of visitors claimed Mr. Doe as their own.

Police continued to keep the stranger cold and on view for more than sentimental reasons: no one had ever prosecuted a John Doe case in Cook County before.

The newspapers began to refer to John Doe as "that poor boob." The state decided its best hope of hanging Wanderer was to prove him sane. Sane and guilty of killing Mr. Doe. Wanderer's new attorneys—a man named

Bartholomew and a "lady attorney" named Lefkow—decided their only chance was to prove the opposite.

The governor appointed a "Special Board" of experts[45] (including a psychiatrist employed by the Public Welfare Department named Singer) to evaluate Wanderer (yet again) and testify as to his sanity. Wanderer's new trial judge ordered the experts to conduct their exams in the presence of both the defense and the prosecution.

Although the state's specialists hadn't released their findings by the time Wanderer's John Doe trial began, his lead attorney, Mr. Bartholomew, declared to the jury: "Results show conclusively that Carl Wanderer had the mentality of a child of eleven. We shall prove this by four alienists [psychiatrists], none of whom is paid by us, that Carl Wanderer is and has been insane for some time. We will not ask you to acquit him, but we shall ask you to send him where he belongs—to a hospital for the criminally insane."

The state's mental hospitals were notoriously overcrowded and understaffed; their escape rates were as high as 25 percent. The primary reason Wanderer's first jury had—finally—voted him sane was to keep him locked up for more than a few years. But proving Wanderer sane implicitly meant that "sanity" had to be redefined. How could a man be sane and still have done what Wanderer did? Wanderer's defense attorneys were risking the same pragmatic "public safety" verdict as before. Wanderer's prosecutors were risking something more abstract—and profound: If sane men were crazy enough to fight the "Great War," then a man like Wanderer (Lieutenant Wanderer!) might be judged as normal. Normal and culpable. If Wanderer was sane—then who was crazy?

The courtroom was as crowded as it had been during the first trial. Wanderer's new judge (an incisive man named Joseph David, a German Jew born in Louisville, Kentucky, from the same milieu as Louis Brandeis) intervened quickly: no men were to be admitted to the room until all the women who wanted to see the trial had been seated.[46] Most important: wives of the jurors (once again, all the jurors were men) were welcome to attend the trial; if these women wanted to sit and watch as their husbands decided the fate of Wanderer—the wife killer—that was their privilege.

On the second day of the trial, as the defense and prosecution were presenting opening arguments, a mother and a daughter announced that John Doe was really Joseph Ahrens, their missing son and brother. Twelve men, including Ahrens's old boss at a tannery, signed an affidavit attesting to that.

A week later, Ahrens himself came to the morgue to identify his own body. "He resembles me, remarkably," Ahrens said. "I can understand how the mistake occurred. There is a resemblance in the eyes and hair. I am going to buy the poor fellow a wreath. I hope they identify him."[47]

Back in court, the alienists, criminologists, and psychologists began their debate. Dr. William Hickson, the head of the city's Psychopathic Lab, reiterated the diagnosis he'd made the day after Wanderer's arrest: the accused suffered from dementia praecox catatonia; it was a disease he'd had since birth. The defendant was the insane son of an insane mother. During cross-examination, Dr. Hickson added something of general interest; it was his belief, he said, that 90 percent of all criminals were insane.[48]

A state psychologist from Evanston followed Dr. Hickson. "Did you examine the defendant? . . . What did you find out?" "That he was only eleven years old, mentally."[49] Judge David interrupted: "What do you mean by 'standard tests' . . . are they the same for everybody? Suppose a man has lived on the mountains all his life. . . . Would you ask him the same questions you asked Wanderer?" "Yes," answered the psychologist.

In their first day of questioning, Wanderer's defense had opened a Pandora's box: Treatment vs. Punishment. Standard tests that were not standard.

The prosecution countered with its own experts. The superintendent of the state's psychiatric hospital testified that Wanderer was sane. "I should diagnose his case as a bad man, a criminal who ought to be cared for by the law."[50] The prosecution didn't ask what the superintendent meant by "cared for." Dr. Singer, the Department of Public Welfare's staff psychiatrist, testified next. He said Wanderer had told him that his wife visited him every night in his dreams. That didn't prove he was crazy, though. "Sane," declared Dr. Singer. Finally, Dr. Krohn, the only specialist in private practice on the governor's board, took the stand. "I have examined Wanderer in court and shortly after his confession and, in my opinion, he is faking insanity."[51] "Faking insanity" was a wonderful possibility: Faking required cunning. Cunning implied sanity. (Krohn and Singer would both testify again, four years later, during another, even more unsettling murder trial—the trial of Nathan Leopold and Richard Loeb.)

Prosecutors followed up with two civilians: Julia Schmitt, the girl Wanderer took on taxi rides; and Lieutenant Lester Atkins, Wanderer's superior officer in France. Miss Schmitt testified that Wanderer had kissed her "Almost every time I was with him." Nothing indecent? asked the prosecution. Nothing odd? Nothing strange? No, said Miss Schmitt. "Sane," she said. Lieutenant Atkins said he'd met Wanderer in training camp. Then he'd been sent to

France with him. He'd been with him in combat. In camp, Wanderer "was pointed out to me by a captain . . . as an efficient machine gunner." "As sane a man as I've ever met," said the lieutenant. Sane, efficient, flirtatious, mildly adulterous. Not as moral as Wanderer had said he was. But recognizably sane.

The defense called its last two experts: one was Dr. James Whitney Hall, president of the Cook County Insanity Commission (Like Krohn and Singer, Hall would also testify, four years later, during the Leopold and Loeb trial); the other was Dr. Florence Fowler, a colleague of Dr. Hickson in the city's Psych Lab. Hall testified that Wanderer had been hearing voices since he was a child. Fowler simply reaffirmed Dr. Hickson's diagnosis.

Wanderer's John Doe jury took twelve minutes to reach a verdict. On its first ballot, it elected a foreman. Its second ballot determined Wanderer to be sane. Its third agreed on his guilt. Its fourth ordered him to be hung. The jury's foreman wept as he delivered the verdict.[52] Wanderer tried to smile as a flashbulb went off in his face. "I hope my mother-in-law is satisfied," he said. "If she is, I am."[53]

Of course, that wasn't so.

Back in Joliet, Wanderer began to frantically pace his cell. "He's been extremely nervous since the verdict was returned," said his jailer. "He's been morose and irritable and will not talk to anyone. . . . He stops his pacing once in a while to listen for his wife's ghost." The jailer placed Wanderer under a suicide watch.

Two months passed.

Wanderer said the Devil—and his wife—had been visiting him. The judge ordered a Chicago psychologist named William Herschfield to reevaluate Wanderer. "Dementia praecox paranoia," declared Herschfield. Judge David was skeptical: Just because he's visited by spirits doesn't mean he's crazy, said the judge. All sorts of people believe in spirits. Arthur Conan Doyle—grieving the loss of his son during the war—was the most public of many—widows, mothers, sisters, brothers—who'd lost men during the war and now attended on the spirit world. "Does that mean Arthur Conan Doyle is insane?" asked Judge David. No one knew the truth about such things, said Herschfield. No matter: Wanderer was now insane.

Agreement about Wanderer's sanity seemed to change as often as John Doe's identity. Doubts, possibilities, certainties—everything about the two men kept shifting. Like a magic show or a chemistry experiment, from solid to liquid, from liquid to gas. The public watched and waited for the next shape to appear in the next episode.

State law required Judge David to order a sanity trial, complete with lawyers, expert witnesses, and an entirely new jury. If that jury decided that Wanderer was, indeed, crazy, he had to be hospitalized. If the jury decided he was, for better or worse, sane, then, according to a recent State Supreme Court ruling, he was to be hung within forty-eight hours.

Ten days of psychiatric point and counterpoint played out in front of a jury. The only surprise: Dr. Singer, a member of the governor's original "Special Board," changed his diagnosis. Three months before, during the John Doe trial, Singer had pronounced Wanderer sane. Not this time. "Dementia praecox catatonia," said Singer.

The jury took less than an hour to reach its verdict. "Sane." Once again Wanderer rubbed his face and yawned.

July 28, 1921, was supposed to be his last day alive. Wanderer released a thirteen-page statement: He hadn't killed Ruth; he and Ruth had always been happy; the police knew he had no motive to kill her, so they kept him awake for three days and three nights until he confessed to something he'd never done. "I die loving everyone. . . . I would be a poor soldier if I could not stand to be put to death by the people I fought for. . . ."

The "soldier" part must have had an effect.

The Illinois Commander of the American Legion (the legion had been founded in Paris in 1919 by U.S. veterans of World War I; it had been incorporated that same year, by an act of Congress) appealed to the governor to grant Wanderer a sixty-day reprieve. The commander asked the governor to appoint a "new commission of alienists" to determine if Wanderer was sane. The commander said that Dr. James Whitney Hall had presented new information to him. According to Dr. Hall, "the horrors of war" had deranged Lieutenant Wanderer's mind.[54] No one asked the commander or Dr. Hall why Wanderer had said, over and over again, that all he'd ever wanted was to reenlist in the Army. "Horrors of war? I was happy in the Army," the lieutenant said.

The governor granted the commander's request.

Wanderer smiled when he heard the news. "I guess my wife will just have to wait awhile before she sees me."[55] That night, his jailer reported, he started acting crazy again.

Wanderer's lead attorney, Mr. Bartholomew, announced he was optimistic. In fact, he said, he had new information that would reveal the true identity of "the ragged stranger. He was a notorious gunman and his identity can be proved."[56]

Mr. Bartholomew never had a chance to prove anything.

On August 6, 1921, a homeless washerwoman named Nellie Ryan told the world the truth:

John Doe was her long-lost son, Eddie. Mrs. Ryan and her two daughters, Agnes and Marie, had known it was Eddie for months.

"I hadn't seen him since he was a boy until I came upon him in the county morgue," Mrs. Ryan said. "Eighteen long years that was, filled with thinking of him and praying for him and trying to find him.

"My husband died when Eddie was six years old. There were six children and it broke my heart but I couldn't support them. Sure, I wept like it was a funeral when I said goodbye to the curly haired darling eighteen years ago. He went to a farmer named Alexander Anglin in Redfield, South Dakota. . . . The other boys went other places. . . . The girls I kept with me despite everything.

"I used to write Eddie often. He stayed on the farm until he was about sixteen and then he set out to see the world. I heard many a time he was in Chicago. But it's such a big city. I looked for him everywhere, but I never could find him.

"I read in the paper long ago about the homeless body that had been killed by Wanderer and many the prayer I said for him. I was down in St. Mary's on last Holy Thursday and I said a prayer for him and for my own homeless boy and I burned some candles for both of them.

"Then I determined to go to the morgue and look at the boy who had been killed and whose body had lain there so long without a woman to weep over it. I went and it was Eddie. I hadn't seen him in eighteen years since he was a little boy. But I knew him at once. He looked so much like Marie, so much like myself."[57]

The governor never appointed a new sanity commission. Sixty days came and went.

"I ain't afraid to die," Wanderer said. "I fought in France."[58]

On the scaffold, the hangman asked him if he had any last words. Wanderer began to sing. He had a baritone voice.

> *Old gal—old pal*
> *You left me all alone.*
> *Old pal—why don't you*
> *Answer me. . . .*[59]

Down he went.

Mrs. Cora Isabelle Orthwein

2 · Cora Isabelle Orthwein

Cora and Herbert went out drinking that night. Nothing unusual. Herbert's chauffeur said he used to drive his boss and Mrs. Orthwein to clubs—the Green Mill, Colosimo's, the Rainbo Gardens—five nights a week. Dinner and drinks, dancing and drinks, drinks and drinks. His boss and Mrs. Orthwein used to argue, the driver said. Sometimes Mr. Ziegler would get rough, lose his temper, slap Mrs. Orthwein around; sometimes Mrs. Orthwein would get upset and say things. About what she'd do if she ever caught Mr. Ziegler with someone else. About what she'd do if Mr. Ziegler ever left her. Mr. Ziegler was thirty-eight; Mrs. Orthwein was forty-nine. Drivers hear things.

That night, Cora and Herbert went out separately, then met up later. When Herbert came home from work that evening—Herbert was a big shot, a district manager for Goodyear—Cora was in the kitchen. Cora had a maid, but tonight she was making dinner herself. Herbert's favorite. "Herbert," she said, "I have bean soup and I want you to have dinner at home tonight."[1] Cora was worried about him. Herbert hadn't been eating much lately. He had a complicated life: a wife and a daughter; a business that wasn't doing as well as it had been. Goodyear stock had gone down. Herbert owned too much of it. Way too much of it. Worse yet, booze was now illegal. Herb had leveled with Cora: he needed $1,000; he needed to stock up, but he didn't have the cash. Cora pawned one of her diamond rings for him. She'd never ever done anything like that before. But when the man you love asks you . . . Herbert took the $500 Cora got and bought booze with it. Scotch, gin, and champagne. Cases of it. Stacked up in Cora's pantry.

"Herbert," said Cora, "I want you to stay home so we can have dinner together." Herbert went straight to the pantry and refilled his flask with gin. "No," he said, "I can't. I have an appointment with some of the boys on important business."[2]

A broker friend of Herbert's, a nice young man named Parsons, was in the living room. "You go have dinner with Parsons," Herbert said. He poured himself a drink, offered Parsons one. Parsons declined. "I'll meet you at ten at the Green Mill," Herbert said as he left.

Herbert had once been a cop. A detective, no less. Herbert's father was a retired police sergeant. Father and son were well thought of in the department. Peter Hoffman—the coroner who'd interrogated Carl Wanderer—was a family friend.

Somehow or other, back in 1916, Herbert had been offered a big job by Goodyear. He had a salary of $25,000 (worth ten times as much today), owned a Pierce Arrow, bought stock. People who'd never owned cars were buying them. Every truck, ambulance, and scout car the government bought for the war needed tires. Once the war ended, Goodyear stock plummeted. Herbert almost went down with it. Buying on margin and drinking too much took their toll.

Young Mr. Parsons took Cora out for dinner. They ate; they drank. Cora ordered a gin and ginger ale. Ten o'clock came; she had another; eleven o'clock; she had one more. Twelve o'clock; she ordered another. Parsons sat with her. Herbert didn't come.

A friend of Cora's, a woman named Viola Dockery, noticed Cora was alone. "Where's Herbert?" Miss Dockery asked. "Downtown on business," Cora said. "Oh no he's not," said Miss Dockery. "You're a sucker if you think he's on the square. I saw him with a blonde at the Rainbo Gardens tonight. He kissed her. They danced right past me. He was hugging her close. He was having an awfully good time."[3] "My God!" said Cora. "He did that?" Miss Dockery told Cora again. For her own good. When Cora thought about it later, she said, "That was like putting a dagger in my heart."[4]

The woman—Mrs. Charlotte Lewinsky—with whom Herbert had danced that night remembered things differently. First of all, Mrs. Lewinsky was a brunette, not a blonde. Second: She was an acquaintance of Cora's. She thought she'd be meeting Cora and Herbert for drinks that night. And, finally: Herbert was so drunk that, when he did ask Mrs. Lewinsky to dance, he could barely stand. After three minutes on the dance floor, Herbert's knees buckled.[5] Mrs. Lewinsky asked Herbert to have his driver take her home.

Emma Lewis

Herbert told his driver to drop him off at the Green Mill, then take Mrs. Lewinsky wherever she wanted to go.

Several people saw Herbert when he walked into the club. The Green Mill's owner, Tom Chambales; a regular named "Handsome Jack" Berry; a young lady friend of Mr. Parsons—they all saw Herbert stumble in. Cora saw him, too. Herbert headed straight for the dressing room of "an entertainer" named Emma Lewis.

"So that's where you are!" Cora said as Herbert walked out of Miss Lewis's dressing room. He looked refreshed, rejuvenated, bright-eyed, a new man with a spring in his step. A man who could dance all night.

Everyone noticed. A waiter said: "Mr. Ziegler danced alone near his table; he danced the shimmy alone." Herbert attracted so much attention that Mr. Chambales, the owner, asked him to sit down.[6]

"What are you trying to do?" Cora asked Herbert. "Where were you?" "Working," Herbert said. "You are a liar," Cora said.

That's when Herbert started throwing things at Cora. Saltshakers, glasses, a water bottle. Cora threw her drink in his face. Herbert emptied a glass of what Mr. Chambales called "water" over Cora's head.[7]

"Ziegler was noisy and drunker than I'd ever seen him," said Mr. Chambales. "Mrs. Orthwein got up and left the table several times, but always went back."

Herbert grabbed Cora's purse. Her keys were in it. "I asked Ziegler for Mrs. Orthwein's purse," said Mr. Chambales, "but he said he didn't have it. Then I found her purse—he was holding it between his knees."

A friend of Herbert's—another broker—offered to take Cora home. "I could smell the fumes on her as we sat in the cab," the broker said.[8]

The phone started ringing almost as soon as Cora walked through her door. It was Herbert. Cora poured herself a drink. It was two o'clock in the morning. "I drank gin 'til I could drink no more. It fired me, inflamed me, made me crazy. I didn't know what I was doing. . . ."[9]

The phone kept ringing. Herbert, Herbert, Herbert. By then it was four o'clock. "Mr. Ziegler used terrible language. . . . He called me names . . ."[10] "I said, 'You can't talk to me like that.' I asked the operator not to call me anymore. In about fifteen minutes, I heard him at the door. He tore the whole molding off the hinges. I don't know how. It was locked and bolted. He tore the bolt right off."[11]

Cora ran back to her bedroom and locked herself in. Herbert began pounding on the door and yelling. Cora's neighbors were already upset with her: the noise, the late-night parties, the sight of Cora's maid hanging Herbert's underwear on the same clothesline as Cora's clothes. Cora's neighbors wanted her evicted.

"Herbert, Herbert don't," Cora called to him from behind the door. "I don't want people to move me out of the apartment."[12]

Cora opened the door. "Herbert, please be quiet." Herbert hit her in the face, knocked her backwards. He picked up a settee. There was a gun on the night table. Cora grabbed it. It was a cute, little blue steel revolver. A lady's gun. One of a matched set. Peter Hoffman, the coroner, had given it to Herbert. Herbert had given it to Cora.

"I picked up the gun," Cora said. "If you hit me again, I'll shoot."[13] "You ain't game," Herbert said. "Please, Herbert, don't come near me."

He charged her. She fired. The shot went wild. A warning. "He looked like he was crazy," Cora said. "His eyes were wild. He came towards me. . . . I wanted to shoot past him, but he swerved[14] and was hit. . . . I was so frightened. . . . He staggered and fell on the bed. I saw he was wounded. . . . I ran over and I picked him up and I kissed him."[15]

Police found Cora, sitting on the bench of her baby grand piano, eyes closed, swaying from side to side.[16] "I shot him," she said. Her clothes were bloody. "I loved him and I killed him. It was all I could do."[17]

A police sergeant named Moffit asked Cora if the dead man was a burglar. "Damn him," said Cora. "He's no burglar. He's my sweetheart. I loved him. . . . When I knew he was cheating, I was through with him. Give me that gun so I can kill myself. I'm glad he's dead. Oh! Why do they make guns, anyway?"[18]

The shooting made the front pages of every paper in the city. It was March 1, 1921. The opening day of Lieutenant Carl Wanderer's second homicide trial was less than a week away. Wanderer had been sentenced to twenty-five years for killing his wife and the child in her womb. The state was determined to find a way to execute him. Prosecutors were eager to try him again—this time for killing the raggedy stranger known as John Doe.

The sequence of the crimes—a man murders his wife, then a woman kills her lover—and the sequence of the trials—Wanderer's first trial, Cora Isabelle's impending inquest, then Wanderer's second trial, then Cora's actual trial, then yet another sanity trial for Wanderer—were too thought-provoking, too loaded with meaning for the papers to ignore. Progress reports about Cora Isabelle and Lieutenant Wanderer began to appear as if their stories were being sung in counterpoint: Gilbert and Sullivan mixed with Verdi.

"Police found Mrs. Cora Isabelle Orthwein, former St. Louis society woman . . . sobbing over the body of Herbert P. Ziegler, the married man for whom she had sacrificed husbands, family, and friends. A revolver with two empty chambers lay nearby."[19]

"Close at hand was a bottle of crème de menthe. A few feet away was an open bottle of gin."[20]

"A copy of Robert W. Service's 'The Spell of the Yukon' lay on a table by Mrs. Orthwein's bed. 'The Harpy' up at the police who'd burst into the disordered apartment."[21]

All the papers quoted the poem:

"I paint my cheeks for they are white and cheeks
of chalk men hate;
Mine eyes with wine I make them shine that men may seek and sate . . .

"Midway through . . . was a stanza that she had regarded as wise enough to underscore heavily:

"From love's close kiss to hell's abyss is one sheer
flight I trow,
And wedding ring and bridal bell are will-'o-wisps of woe,
And 'tis not wise to love too well, and this all
Women know."[22]

The story—and the writing—became more graphic:

"Ziegler had bled to death while the frantic Mrs. Orthwein lay across his chest, calling to him. Detectives found evidence of the strange nocturnal life Mrs. Orthwein had led. Her dressing table was littered with bits of paper, marking engagements with manicurists, masseurs, all the curious craftsmen of the boudoir."[23]

The facts of Cora's life—the personal history of the woman who'd loved unwisely and too well—varied, depending on which newspaper "reported" them. Within a few days of the crime, Cora had as many identities as the raggedy stranger Carl Wanderer had killed.

According to the *Chicago Daily News*:

"Her own love story, starting with the day in 1903 when as Miss Cora Landin, of an old Kentucky family, she sacrificed a brilliant social career to marry a professional baseball player, was an epitome of the dangers of unleashed love. . . .

"Her first husband was Jack O'Connor, manager of the St. Louis Browns. From him, she turned to Ralph Orthwein, the owner of the baseball team itself. She divorced her first husband in 1907. . . . This repaired her social fortunes. As the 'Belle of the Grandstand,' a title she acquired by her striking appearance and her constant attendance at baseball games, Mrs. Orthwein gained . . . social standing. . . .

"Then came Ziegler and, in 1915, the woman again strayed into the tangled loveways which seemed to always lure her. There was a $350,000 settlement, a divorce, and Mrs. Orthwein came to Chicago. . . ."[24]

The "dangers of unleashed love"!

The "tangled loveways which seemed to always lure her"!

A divorce settlement that would have been worth $3.5 million today!

The *Chicago Herald Examiner* told an even better story:

"She came out of the West and married a man of the Plains. The great outdoors held few attractions for her, however, and she next found herself the wife of Jack O'Connor, manager of the St. Louis team of the American League.

"She met millionaire oil man Ralph Orthwein, known as a 'sport' and a 'spender.' She divorced O'Connor and married Orthwein. Her new husband purchased an investment in the baseball team. . . .

"Six years ago, the Orthweins were divorced, and Mrs. Orthwein received a settlement which, she told police, totaled $350,000. She knew Ziegler then and moved to Chicago. During the past five years, she had taken $150 a month from him and used his Pierce Arrow when she chose. . . ."[25]

The *Chicago Herald Examiner* didn't explain why a woman with the twenty-first-century equivalent of $3.5 million in the bank would want or need her lover to give her a monthly allowance.

The *Chicago Tribune* summed up everything:

"Booze and a woman's kisses, the swift nightlife of old, persisted-in despite the law's edicts, open brawling, gin rickeys splashed in the faces of angry quarrelers . . . there [sat] Mrs. Cora Orthwein . . . unemployed divorcée and devotee of poetry whose clandestine affair with Herbert Ziegler was a 'long, long trail' that ended with a smoking pistol in her hand and the body of her lover, dead across her bed. . . ."[26]

The facts of Cora's life were a bit less dramatic than the stories the papers told about her.

Cora had been born in Ohio, near Columbus. Not in old Kentucky. Not west of Chicago. She had no bloodline—Hunt was her maiden name. She'd sacrificed no brilliant social career when she'd married Jack O'Connor.

In fact: Cora's marriage to Jack O'Connor gave her a social career. The St. Louis Browns—the team Jack managed—were a glamorous team—the late-nineteenth-, early-twentieth-century equivalent of an NBA team like the L.A. Lakers.

Cora's second husband was the millionaire son of a millionaire father: Orthwein senior was a grain merchant. The Orthweins moved in the same St. Louis social circles as the Busches (the Budweiser people). An Orthwein cousin had married a Busch. Money married money.

The facts about Cora's divorce from her baseball manager husband were these:

While Jack O'Connor was on the road with the Browns, Ralph Orthwein seduced Jack's wife. Ralph spent so much money on Cora that his father cut his allowance. One day in 1905, after a home game, O'Connor went out for drinks. When he walked into his favorite roadhouse, he discovered his boss was already there. Having a very good time with Cora. Jack sued Ralph; Ralph's wife sued Ralph. Ralph asked Cora to marry him. Their marriage lasted almost ten years. It's not certain who betrayed the other. First. Herbert Ziegler was named in the divorce petition Ralph filed.

As to the $350,000 settlement:

Cora received $15,000, plus alimony payments of $250 per month. St. Louis papers reported that Cora immediately "took flight to New York to test her wings on Broadway." Cora would have been forty-three by then. Too old for liftoff. But $15,000 in cash and $250 every month would have feathered a comfortable nest.

Herb followed her to New York. He threw a big party at a fancy restaurant called Churchill's to announce their engagement. Cora didn't know that Herb was married at the time. She also didn't know that Herb was a mean drunk. She found that out only after they were living together. Only after Cora took Herb's advice and invested $10,000—most of her savings—in Goodyear stock.

One day after Cora shot Herbert, Coroner Hoffman convened an inquest. The papers had just published their stories about Cora—"The Harlot," the cluttered dressing table and the crème de menthe, the baby grand, and the bloody clothes. All this along with Cora's $350,000 divorce settlement.

Herbert Ziegler's widow hired a former assistant state's attorney named Dwight McKay to represent her. Mr. McKay was as much a part of the city's Establishment as Coroner Hoffman. Mr. McKay threw a few more pieces of wood on the bonfire that was being prepared for Cora:

"Mrs. Orthwein was insanely infatuated with Ziegler. She was insanely jealous of any attention he paid to other women. It is very probable that he was telling her he was through with her when she shot him. . . . It was the old, old story of selfish, insane love—if she couldn't have him, no one could have him. She clung to him like a leech. . . . She killed him before he could return to his home as husband and father. . . ."[27]

Cora was three times "insane." An insane, jealous leech.

Sackcloth and ashes might have been a useful costume for Cora to have worn when she appeared, under guard, at Coroner Hoffman's inquest. The pleasure produced by the misfortunes of privileged people—who turn out to be as foolish, helpless, and sad as everyone else—guaranteed that whatever Cora did and didn't do, said or didn't say at the inquest would be closely watched.

Instead of wearing rags, Cora dressed as she usually did:

"Deeper and deeper into the flesh of the third finger of her left hand, Mrs. Cora Orthwein digs the narrow platinum band decorated with its motif of orange blossoms.

"With a shiver, she draws more tightly about her shoulder a luxurious mink cape, a birthday gift from the man she has slain, as others in the stuffy courtroom move to open windows to get a breath of air.

"Next to her, Mrs. Mary Shea, policewoman for detention home No. 1, drops her shabby brown cloak from her arms and fans herself with a worn, black cotton glove. . . .

"When a particularly graphic bit of testimony causes Mrs. Orthwein to sit forward, the fur cape, bought for her by another woman's husband, slips from her shoulders, revealing a plain, black velvet suit. . . .

"Her hands were ungloved and covered with gems. A dinner ring in platinum, set off with a cluster of diamonds and sapphires, blazes on her right hand. Near it are several smaller rings, platinum set, and a huge diamond solitaire. On her left hand is a very large, very heavy jewel on her little finger, and the simple platinum wedding band."[28]

Coroner Hoffman concluded his inquest by questioning the physician who'd autopsied Herbert. The *Chicago Herald Examiner* reproduced the doctor's testimony next to its description of Cora's boudoir.

Said the doctor: "I found the bullet [entry] wound on the right side of the body, two inches to the left of the posterior side of the right arm. I found the man fully dressed. . . . I found no powder marks on the overcoat or suit coat. . . . On opening the body, I found the bullet had passed through the right lung from the right side, through the right lung to the blood vessel, and through the left lung, passing in an upward course and lodging in the left arm. In doing so, it struck . . . the arm . . . dislocating the arm. . . . To receive the bullet, he had [to have] stood up."[29]

Coroner Hoffman questioned the doctor more closely.

"Was he struck from the back?" asked Hoffman. "The bullet was fired from the side," said the doctor. "It passed through the center of the body."[30]

Herbert was buried the next day.

"A crowd of more than 2000 persons, representatives of the great mob of the monstrously curious, fought for entrance [to the funeral home] with a special police squad."[31] A Methodist Episcopal priest delivered the eulogy: "The makers of illicit liquor might take unto themselves a full measure of responsibility."[32]

The Masonic Lodge to which Herbert belonged sent bouquets and floral tributes. Wreathes from Goodyear Company offices in Chicago and Milwaukee adorned Herbert's casket.

Everyone with eyes could see:

A well-respected man—a stalwart of the community—had been put to death (shot in cold blood; shot before he could return to his hearth and home) by a bejeweled (insanely jealous) woman, dressed (shamelessly) in furs that her lover had given her.

The only thing that prevented Cora from being burnt at the stake before she went on trial was the city of Chicago's own, rather unusual legal history.

"Cook County juries," wrote the *Chicago Tribune* (in the same article that included "the smoking gun in her hand"), "have been regardful of woman defendants." By "regardful," the *Tribune* meant that "Cook County prosecutors convicted [only] 16 of the 102 women who killed their husbands in the city between 1875 and 1920."[33] This rather modest rate of criminal conviction occurred despite the fact that "the rate of husband killing spiked between 1875–1920. . . . The husband killing rate increased three-fold, whereas the overall rate for the city doubled in the same period."[34]

One day after Ziegler was buried (and two days after Cora wore the wrong costume to the inquest), Cora began to use Cook County's history of "regardfulness" to save her own life. She began by giving the *Herald Examiner* an interview. The *Herald*'s reporter noticed her "almost Spanish beauty," and "her dark eyes" filled "with sorrow."

"From time to time," wrote the reporter, "she touched a scar on her lip—a scar she says was made by Ziegler when he struck her. . . .

" 'That was part of what I had to endure,' she said, mournfully. 'I was forced into a strange position. It was not the life I was made for, or the life I planned. I am a very domestic woman. I love to fix things around the house. . . .

" 'I never drank as much as I have, lately. [Herbert] kept wanting me to drink. Friends argued with him not to keep piling the liquor into me. Even he noticed it was hurting my complexion.

" 'We planned some day to go West and get a bungalow and live quietly. That was after I had begged him to return to his wife . . . he told me he loved only me and would not leave me. . . .

" 'If he planned to stop drinking, it was because I asked him to. I pleaded with him. . . . I told him he must stop. I said, "You are ruining your health, your position, and me." He put his head in my shoulder and cried like a baby.' "[35]

The president of an automobile company posted Cora's $25,000 bail. He pledged $300,000 worth of real estate to raise the cash Cora needed. The "Belle of the Grandstand" could still stir a rich man's heart.

Three months passed.

The state and its allies on the editorial board of the *Tribune* decided to ignore Herbert's autopsy report. The day before Cora's trial began, the *Tribune*'s editors wrote:

"Under cross examination, Mrs. Orthwein will have one insistent question to answer: 'Why—if you shot . . . in self defense, did you shoot Ziegler in the back?' "[36]

On the second day of Cora's trial, Lloyd Heth, the chief prosecutor, outlined the state's case. In front of a judge, a jury, a courtroom full of spectators, and a courthouse packed, three floors of people, with the same sort of "monstrously curious" crowd that had mobbed Herbert's funeral, prosecutor Heth declared for all to hear: "She shot him in the back."[37]

Meanwhile, in Joliet, Carl Wanderer had begun to act crazy. He said the Devil and his wife had begun to appear to him. News reports about "the butcher boy" lieutenant's sanity began to coincide with news reports about Cora's guilt and innocence. By the end of June, as Cora's trial entered its final days, Carl Wanderer's attorneys began opening arguments (for a sanity hearing) before Judge Joseph David. In the same courthouse—and in the same newspapers—a parallel set of questions began to be asked: Was Lieutenant Wanderer responsible for what he did? Was he a victim of insanity? Was Cora responsible for what she did? Was she a victim of passion, inflamed by drink? Was Carl Wanderer a lunatic or was he a fiend? Was Cora Isabelle a victim—or had she brought disaster down on her own head? Victim or vamp? Cora's and Carl's stories—and the legal, moral, medical, and philosophical questions their stories raised—played off each other in public view.

Cora's defense attorneys moved quickly to prove the prosecution wrong. They began by proving that the blonde who'd danced with Herbert at the Rainbo Gardens was a brunette, and that Herbert had been so drunk, he couldn't stay on his feet. No one suggested that Cora's friend Miss Dockery had committed the private, personal version of yelling "Fire!" in a crowded theater.

After calling Mrs. Lewinsky to the stand, Cora's attorneys produced a "surprise eyewitness." "An attractive young woman" named Miss Rosamond Dove.

Miss Dove.

Miss Dove said that she and her boyfriend and another couple had been driving back to the city, late one night. They were driving along a deserted stretch of highway called the "Milwaukee Road." Just after midnight, Miss Dove and her friends spotted a woman, her hair down, her face cut and bleeding, her mink wrap torn; she was standing alone, in the dark in the middle of the road, frantically waving her handkerchief, calling for help. "Save me!" the woman cried. "Save me or he'll kill me. Please take me home. He's drunk and he has a high-powered car. Hurry."

That woman was Cora. Miss Dove and her friends drove off with her. A big, powerful car pulled up beside them. They slowed down, then stopped. A man climbed out of the other car and walked over to Miss Dove. He leaned over and said, "You think you're smart. I'll fix you." One of the young men with Miss Dove got out. The man's chauffeur grabbed him so his boss could beat him up. "Herby, Herby," Cora cried. "Please don't."[38] Cora climbed into Ziegler's car. It roared off.

Cora's sister and Cora's brother-in-law took the stand after Miss Dove. They testified that Cora had stumbled into their apartment that night: her face, bruised; her lip, bleeding. She stayed in bed for a week. Then she went back to Herbert. That happened in March 1920, a year before Ziegler kicked in Cora's front door. Three other times, Cora's sister testified, Ziegler had beaten Cora. Each time, Cora ran away, then recovered, then returned to him.[39]

Rosamond Dove

Cora's attorney called her to the stand.

"Our first quarrel," Cora said, "was in the fall of 1917. . . ."[40]

"Every corner of the courtroom was filled," reported the *Chicago Tribune*.[41]

"Gaily dressed women crowded the space set aside for the clerk. Scores of chairs, borrowed from other rooms, crowded the narrow space set aside for reporters, the defendant, and trial lawyers. The jurors in shirtsleeves leaned forward as Mrs. Orthwein began to talk. The twelve men listened intently to her every word. Graphically, she described Ziegler's attacks on her.

"She saw him drunk for the first time . . . barely a year from the date they become engaged, she said. [Engaged? A bigamist and a liar was he.] She said she was in her sitting room when an altercation in the kitchen attracted her attention. Running into the room, she saw Ziegler in the act of striking her maid. She remonstrated and—he struck her. Screaming, she ran into her room and tried to pick up the telephone to call for help. He tore the telephone from her grasp and . . . 'He was drunk,' she said. 'He beat me cruelly. It was the first time I had ever been struck. . . . He was so sorry afterwards, I forgave him.' "[42]

Cora described the other times Ziegler had abused her. Once, when he was drunk, he'd insisted on driving his car himself. (Driving drunk was as new an experience for Herbert as it was for every other first-time driver in Chicago—or anywhere else in the U.S. during the twenties.) Herbert drove himself and Cora into a ditch. Cora was injured; once again, she forgave him.

Finally, Cora's attorney asked her to describe the night she shot Herbert.

Cora's version of events sounded like a retelling of the story of the Big Bad Wolf:

"Herbert said, 'Let me in.' He called me all kinds of names. I said, 'Go home and go to bed.' He said, 'When I get in, I'll kill you.' I said, 'I'll not let you in.' He tried to break the chain. He pushed and pushed with all his might. . . . I said, 'Herb, please go away. You can't get in.' He said, 'Damn it, I'll kill you. I'll show you if I can't get in.' He threw himself against the door and I saw the door start to give. . . . I said, 'For God's sake, Herb. Go away.' He said, 'I'll kill you.' "

After hearing these three "I'll kill yous," Cora said, "I ran down the hall and closed the bedroom door and locked myself in. He broke the [front] door and I heard him pounding on the second. . . . He was pounding and hammering and I knew . . . that he would break that [second] door open. So—I opened it. As I did, he hit me and knocked me back over a bench.

"I picked up the gun and said, 'If you hit me again, I'll shoot.' He said, 'You ain't game.' I said, 'Please, Herb, don't come near me.' . . . He looked like he was crazy. . . . His eyes were wild. He came towards me. I had the gun and I fired."

Her first shot did nothing but make him angrier. "He stooped over to pick up the bench and said, 'I'll brain you.' I guess I fired again. He staggered over and fell on the bed. I saw he was wounded. . . . I ran over and pleaded with him to talk with me."

Cora sobbed as she told this to the jury. Her attorney asked her a few

Mrs. Cora Orthwein's bedroom, where the shooting of Herbert Ziegler took place.

more questions. "At the time you fired the shot, what was your intention?" "I was so frightened," Cora said, "I didn't know what I was doing." "What frightened you?" her attorney asked. "He did. He picked up the stand and I thought he was going to brain me."[43]

It's likely that, over the years, the men in shirtsleeves who leaned forward to listen to Cora had read other stories about other drunks who'd abused—and then killed—their wives. In fact, between 1875 and 1920, "more than four white wives were killed by their husbands for every white husband killed by his wife."[44]

By 1905, a judge, presiding over the trial of a husband killer named Jesse Hoffman, told the jury, before it withdrew to deliberate: "A woman, by marrying, does not become a slave or a chattel of her husband. She has the right to kill her husband in self-defense if she is in imminent danger of bodily harm." Other Chicago judges agreed. In public. On the record.

Said one: "A . . . wife has the absolute right of defending herself, even to the extent of taking a life." [45]

Cora's defense had one more piece of evidence to use against Ziegler. All the papers had described Cora as a woman who'd taken gifts (a mink coat *and* a sealskin coat) and money from the man she'd killed. With $15,000 in the bank and $250 alimony, why—other than greed and extravagance— did she take Herbert's money?

"Did you have any money when you came to New York?" Cora's attorney asked her. "Yes," she said. "About $10,800. I kept it in cash, in the house. But Herb said, 'Chicago's a tough town. Better invest it in Goodyear Tire and Rubber stock. It'll pay you a 12 percent dividend and it's safe. All my money is in that stock . . . that's why I have as much as I have.' "[46]

Cora did as Herbert advised her. "Have you that stock now?" asked her attorney. "It paid dividends," Cora said, "but the company got into difficulties and Mr. Ziegler needed more collateral to put up with his bank. He asked me if he could use my stock. I told him to take it and—I never saw it again." "Is that all the money you had?" asked her attorney. "Yes," said Cora. "But I gave it to him willingly. Everything was his because I loved him dearly. . . ."

A drunk, a liar, a leech, and a failure: Herbert's reputation had changed since his funeral.

The prosecution pressed ahead.

It had the murder weapon; it had Cora's confession; it had Ziegler's corpse. It was certain it had enough to convict her. The prosecutor cross-examined Cora.

What a mistake.

"With tears streaming down her cheeks, [Mrs. Orthwein retold] the story of Ziegler the lover, Ziegler the brute. Introduced in July, engaged in August . . . and beaten before the year [1917] was out—such was her story."[47] In a voice that quivered and sometimes seemed almost a whisper, the black-clad divorcée swept swiftly through three of her five years' relationship with Ziegler. Again and again, she seemed on the verge of collapse. Gathering new strength, her eyes flashed and her voice became sharp and vindictive. . . .

" 'Why,' demanded [the prosecutor], 'why if he beat you and drank himself into a frenzy, time and time again, why did you continue to go out with him?'

"She flashed a pitying glance at him—a glance which seemed to say he could never understand.

" 'I went with him,' she whispered, 'because I always did everything he wanted me to do.'

" 'Everything?' repeated [the prosecutor].

" 'Everything,' she whispered. 'I always did just as he wanted me to—because I loved him.' "

The prosecutor dug his own grave deeper: "Picking up . . . the revolver with which Mrs. Orthwein had killed Ziegler, [the prosecutor] demanded, 'Is this the gun with which you killed him?'

"She flinched as the weapon was thrust in her face.

" 'Yes. That's it,' she replied.

" 'Take it,' snapped [the prosecutor]. 'Show the jurors how you killed him.'

"Trembling as if uncertain of her power to rise, she slowly stood up. She held the weapon, limply. Turning toward the jurors, she began a halting sentence, then sank weakly into her chair. 'I can't,' she cried. 'I don't remember.' "

The prosecutor seemed pleased. At last! He had her where he wanted her! "Don't remember"?! He turned to the jury and proclaimed the facts:

"She lied and lied and lied to protect her reputation for chastity. What lies wouldn't she tell to protect her life? This penniless woman lived in luxury for five years—in an expensive apartment. When Herbert Ziegler entered that apartment, he had a perfect right to enter it because he was supporting it. . . .

"I ask you not to give Cora Orthwein a monopoly on your sympathy. Think of the women—the great number of women!—who may be contemplating a similar violation of the law. If you find this woman guilty of murder, you will extend sympathy not only to the victims of the many women slayers in Cook County criminal records—but to the potential murderesses who may be deterred from such acts by your verdict. . . ."[48]

Whatever effect the prosecutor thought his argument on behalf of deterrence might have had on the jury, he hadn't counted on the effect Cora's fluctuating blood pressure (such a storm-driven, frail flower of femininity she was!) might have on them:

"Mrs. Orthwein . . . sank into her seat at the prisoner's table . . . and, a moment later, leaned forward, fluttering her handkerchief, and attempting, apparently, to warn [her attorneys] that she felt faint. Then she fell forward and her head sank on the table."[49]

The judge ordered an adjournment.

The prosecution took the opportunity to withdraw its murder charge. It announced that a verdict of "manslaughter" would be satisfactory.

In the afternoon, the prosecutor did his best to save what remained of his case.

"I do not stand here," he said, "as a champion of Herbert Ziegler, the man who left the company of his wife and daughter for this woman. Ziegler was a wrong doer. The jury must accept him as a wrong doer—but so was she. She was no unsophisticated virgin. . . . This woman paints herself in robes of white, yet she chose the path of her life. She paints the man who gave her his all as a devil incarnate. As she talks, you can see the horns . . . her silences are broken by the swishing of this tail. But I do not believe the lie she has concocted about this man whose lips are closed in death. . . .

"She knew the game she played was a dangerous one. She played the game until Ziegler began to tire of her. She was getting fat. . . . She was too old. . . . The knowledge that he was growing cold was like wormwood to her. For weeks before the shooting, the knowledge of other women . . . ate at her heart. Then he goes to see a young and pretty blonde. She learns that he is kissing her. It is like a dagger in her heart. The next day, Ziegler is found dead with a shot in his back.

"Take the coat which Ziegler wore when he was shot with you to the jury room when you begin to deliberate, and with it, reenact the tragedy . . . you will see that it was impossible for her to have shot him in the manner she describes in her perjured testimony. . . ."[50]

The jury did as it was told.

It hadn't forgotten that there was no blonde. It hadn't forgotten Miss Dove's testimony. It hadn't forgotten Cora's retelling of the Big Bad Wolf. When it examined Herbert's coat, it saw what Herbert's autopsy report had indicated: Herbert had been shot in the side, from below.

Fifty-five minutes and three ballots later, the jury returned its verdict:

"As the words 'Not Guilty' were read, the spectators who crowded the room, a majority of them being women, clapped their hands, and cheered, and crowded forward. . . . Men shook Mrs. Orthwein's hands; women threw their arms around her neck and kissed her; her attorneys almost had to fight their way out of the courtroom."[51]

The prosecutor sounded resigned:

"You can't convict a woman—a good looking woman—of killing a man."[52]

No one reminded him that he'd called Cora "old" and "fat."

He spoke, thoughtfully:

Mrs. Cora Isabelle Orthwein

"The promiscuous killing of men by women should be stopped—but—it can't be done without the assistance of juries."[53]

The jury's foreman answered him:

"Beauty alone meant nothing to us. We wouldn't have cared if she was very homely or very beautiful."[54]

Cora had the last word:

"I owe the people of Chicago my gratitude. Did you see those women kiss me after the verdict? . . . They know what a woman has to put up with from a man."[55]

Harvey W. Church

3 · Harvey Church

Harvey couldn't stop thinking about Packards. He'd seen them on the avenues, moving through traffic, as stately as carriages. Rickety black Fords, driven by commoners; splendid Packards driven by gentlemen.

Harvey had his heart set on a new one—a twelve-cylinder, bronze-and-nickel-plated beauty, the newest of the new—a Twin Six. Powerful. Commanding. His family could afford one.

His parents lived up in Wisconsin. In Adams, a county seat. Big fish in a little pond. Halfway between Oshkosh and La Crosse. They were country people. Yankee stock. Modest people. Merchant farmers. They were rich. Harvey's father, Edwin, owned land, owned buildings. After the war, when crop prices collapsed, Edwin Church, alone, had money to loan. He bought other people's property, other people's debt. Everyone deferred to him.

"Among critical observers who know . . . the Twin Six stands as representative of the finest. . . . In all the years the Twin Six has been before the public, here and in Europe, its leadership has never been . . . challenged. . . . Wherever the Twin Six owner drives or in whatever company, he travels in the satisfying knowledge that his is the car of cars. . . . To speak of the Twin Six is to speak of something that is singular—something that stands apart and alone . . . the synonym for the ultimate in motoring" (Packard Motorcar Company Twin Six advertising copy).

Harvey was his father's only son, wellborn and able. Four years of high school, one year of college; a lieutenant in the Training Corps. Officer candidate material. Leadership material. Clean-cut; collegiate. His father said Harvey had worked as a clerk and a stenographer and a typist for the Chicago and Northwestern Railroad. Other people said Harvey had been a brakeman. Hired during one of the strikes after the war. A scab. He'd had some close calls with people who didn't like him taking other men's jobs.

Harvey's parents sent him to Chicago to buy a house. He bought one: a handsome, two-story, gray stone, with bay windows, on a good street. The house was in his mother's name, in Eva's name. He and Eva lived there.

Eva had had seven children, but five had died young, swept away by accident and disease. Only Harvey and his older sister, Isabel, remained. Harvey was his mother's precious son. In his youth, he had had an awful accident, a terrible, terrible fall that had frightened everyone. He was never the same after that, Eva said. "Bashful and sullen," Eva said. Isabel noticed something else, something odd. "He had a strange desire to butcher chickens," she said. Maybe she was just being squeamish, but the neighbors noticed, too. They talked about Harvey, but never in public, out of respect for Edwin and out of kindness to Eva. "No one ever liked him," they said. "A crybaby"; "full of wild stories," they said.

All this was in the past, now.

Eva took care of Harvey. In the house he'd bought, their handsome house with its bay windows. Harvey was his family's heir and its emissary, sent to make his mark in the city. Every day, he would go out and return and Eva would be there with his supper.

It was only proper that a family like the Churches, a family so eminent, should own a Packard. A Packard bespoke; a Packard embodied. A Packard attested.

Harvey was resolved.

He would buy one. His parents were too modest—too old-fashioned—to buy "such an extravagance" for themselves. He would buy a tonneau—devil take the expense—and drive, in dignity, where he wished. He would sit in the open, dressed in his cap and tweeds, upright, behind the wheel; his mother (or his sister or even his father) would sit in comfort in the compartment behind him—and he, their fine young man, would deliver them to their destinations.

Unfortunately: At the moment, Harvey drove a six-year-old Harroun. A four-cylinder little roadster. (Made by a company run by the fellow who'd won the first Indianapolis 500 back in 1911. Henry Ford had made a name for himself, racing cars on cinders strewn across the ice of Lake Michigan. Roy Harroun had tried the same thing: designed a single-seat, stream-lined Marmon "Wasp" and then driven it, blazed it, across the finish line at Indianapolis. On the strength of that, Harroun had raised some money and started building cars in an old factory outside of Detroit. You'd think that a mechanic and inventor like Roy Harroun would have been ashamed to put his name on such a piece of junk.) Harvey had bought his because Harrouns were innovative—and rare. They were also unreliable and hard to repair.

Just last week, Harvey had gotten into a smashup while he was out for a drive. He'd had to take his car into a garage, down the street from where he and Eva lived. The place was run by a fellow named Gus—Gus Benario. Three of Harvey's buddies worked there. One, a tightly wound guy named Leon Parks, was Gus's night manager. The place was OK—Gus had even posted bail for another one of Harvey's buddies, a guy named Walker, after Walker had done something stupid and robbed a grocery store. The point is: when the guys at Benario's told Harvey it would cost $150 to fix his piece of junk, he believed them. Fixing that old Harroun would cost more than it was worth. The guys got it running—but in his mind, Harvey was already driving a Packard.

Isabel came for a visit. She was living in St. Paul. She and Harvey went for a drive. As Isabel recalled, Harvey had been very clear about his plans: A Twin Six Packard tonneau, equipped just the way he wanted, would cost $5,400. He'd trade in his Harroun, then cash some Liberty Bonds to make up the difference. The Liberty Bonds (issued by the federal government during World War I) had been presents to Harvey and Isabel from their father: Edwin had bought them, at a discount, from farmers in Adams and Marquette who were desperate for cash.

Isabel listened to Harvey's plans. She laughed in surprise. What an idea! (What a silly idea), she said. Their folks didn't need a fancy Packard. Harvey had his mind made up, though.

Packard's Chicago showroom was located on the city's downtown "Motor Row." Big cars behind big plate glass windows. Packard's Chicago sales staff and service staff were like all other Packard staffs in the United States: all men; well educated, well spoken, well groomed, highly trained, highly attentive. (One particular Packard Motorcar Company advertisement was illustrated with a painting of a king, dressed in ermine, knighting a handsome young man who knelt before him, armored and helmeted, surrounded by his fellows. The ad read, "Packard men bear the imprint of the organization. They are selected and schooled for but one quality of work and service . . . From skilled management to designing engineer, Packard cars are produced by men who know and love fine things. . . . From suburban dealer to manager of sales, Packard's clientele are served by men who uphold the Packard principles: men who know that the patronage of the distinguished brooks no compromise with quality. . . .")

The salesman who dealt with Harvey was a Harvard-educated, former U.S. Army tank corps captain named D. J. Daugherty. Daugherty had been a football star in his youth; he'd coached football at a private school before he'd enlisted. He'd been a member of the White Bear Yacht Club, where he'd raced in weekly regattas. Harvey looked like a callow youth (Harvey was small but he was strong; he'd held his own against some tough railroad men) compared to Daugherty. Harvey tried to keep a poker face when Daugherty strode over and asked if he could help. Harvey told Daugherty that he wanted to buy a car for his father. He said his father lived way up north, in Eagle River, Wisconsin, but he owned a lot of valuable real estate in Chicago—and needed a Twin Six. A tonneau. Daugherty showed him one. Harvey said it would do, but he'd have to ask his father. If his father approved, asked Harvey, could Mr. Daugherty have it ready for him by Thursday? Certainly, said Daugherty. And how, he asked, would Harvey prefer to pay for it? Packard does a strictly cash business. The only credit we extend is based on approved collateral. Daugherty quoted the price that Harvey already knew. Would Liberty Bonds in $500 denominations be satisfactory? Harvey asked. Certainly, answered Daugherty. We'll need your name and address and so on—just for the paperwork. Daugherty filled out the forms.

As soon as Harvey left, Daugherty's sales manager checked Harvey's credit: the house he said was his belonged to his mother; his bank account had a balance of $500 in it; there'd been no checks written and no withdrawals made in some time. Still—Liberty Bonds were as good as cash. And—sales had been a bit off lately. Daugherty filled out some more paperwork—and waited.

While Daugherty's boss was vetting Harvey, Harvey went shopping. Shopping for—of all things—a pair of handcuffs. He walked into a jewelry store; the jeweler referred him to a friend of his at an Army surplus store. The clerk there sold Harvey a pair of cuffs for $2.95.

Harvey waited a few days, then called Daugherty. His father had given him the go-ahead. He would pay with Liberty Bonds. Daugherty said he'd have the car ready for him. Harvey said the Liberty Bonds were at his bank. He'd feel more comfortable if Daugherty would meet him there to complete the transaction. Daugherty said he'd be pleased to do that. Harvey gave him the bank's name and address. They set a time.

Harvey was disappointed when Daugherty pulled up: he wasn't driving, and he wasn't alone. Packard policy required that a licensed and insured mechanic drive any vehicle that was to be delivered. Daugherty introduced his driver: Carl Ausmus, a good-looking, able-bodied, ex-Army enlisted man, about the same age as Harvey.

Daugherty was a bit surprised when Harvey told him the Liberty Bonds were at his house. Harvey turned to Ausmus: "Mr. Daugherty and I can take care of things from here," he said. Harvey peeled off a ten and some ones from a roll in his pocket and handed them to Ausmus. "For your trouble," he said. Harvey knew about the art of tipping. Gentlemen knew such things. "Mr. Daugherty and I will finish up. He'll meet you back at the office," Harvey said. Ausmus looked at the money, then looked at Harvey. *Packard*, he said, paid him to deliver vehicles. That was his job. Harvey put the money back in his pocket. "Suit yourself," he said. The three men drove to Harvey's house.

Later, a neighbor said she remembered noticing the Packard drive up, with three men in it. She remembered seeing Harvey and another man get out and go into the house. The next time she looked, she said, the car was still parked outside, but no one was in it.

Harvey's mother came home in the middle of the afternoon. "What's this, Harvey?" she said. "It's our new car, Mother." He showed her the bill of sale. A blue bill of sale. "How on earth did you ever afford it?" Eva asked. "Isabel and I decided to surprise you and Father," Harvey said. "We paid for it with those Liberty Bonds."

Eva said exactly what Isabel thought she would: "It's such an extravagance! Your father and I don't *need* such a thing. We're not that sort."

Harvey folded the bill of sale and put it in his breast pocket. Eva clucked. Harvey opened the passenger compartment, held the door for her. She settled herself. "The seats are comfortable," she said. "Soft," she said.

By the end of the afternoon, Harvey had shown the bill of sale to several neighbors. He'd convinced Eva—and two of her lady friends—to go for a drive. The ladies chirped and changed their clothes. Harvey drove them to a scenic view called Indiana Point. "Lovely," they all said.

By the time they got home, it was nearly suppertime.

Harvey went out back, to the garage, to tinker with his Harroun. Eva started cooking. Harvey was sweaty and dirty when Eva called him in to eat. "Are you all right, son?" Eva asked. "What were you doing back there?" "I had to move that old Harroun around," he said. Then he had an idea (Harvey was always full of ideas). "Let's drive up to Adams tomorrow, and surprise Father," he said.

The next morning, that's exactly what they did.

Harvey and Eva hadn't been gone long when a boy, walking across a bridge ten miles west of the Loop (the bridge crossed the Des Plaines River), noticed a body floating, snagged, mid-river in the shallows. A man called the police. Police threw a net over the body and dragged it ashore with grappling hooks.

It was the body of a man. He hadn't been dead or in the river for long. He was big, so the police had trouble getting him out of the water. He'd been beaten so badly that the police couldn't tell, by looking, which of his wounds had killed him: He'd been strangled with a rope—still tied around his neck. His throat had been slashed—twice. His head had been beaten in, maybe with a blackjack, maybe with a club. Worse yet: "The man had gone to his death in handcuffs. The manacles were still locked around one wrist. . . ."[1] Police found a gold watch, a fountain pen, and $27 in the dead man's pockets. "Certainly not a robbery," they said.

Daugherty and Ausmus hadn't returned to the office after they'd delivered Harvey's car. Police got a call from Daugherty's boss about the time they hauled the corpse out of the river. They asked Daugherty's sales manager to come to the station. He identified Daugherty, then told the police about Harvey and the tonneau. Within a day, detectives had traced the handcuffs on Daugherty to the store that had sold them to Harvey. The clerk—and the jeweler—both remembered him.

Ausmus was still missing. Police dragged the river upstream and downstream. Detective John Norton (Carl Wanderer's nemesis) had risen to the rank of "acting lieutenant." The papers called him "Chief of the Homicide Bureau." Norton sent telegrams to every Wisconsin town on the road, north to Adams. "Arrest and hold Harvey W. Church, wanted for murder in Chicago." The telegrams described Harvey's Packard and gave its license plate. "Wisconsin police were [asked] to be on the look out for [the car] and for Ausmus, who, police believe, may have been kidnapped and forced to drive the car."[2]

Harvey was driving the Packard—with Eva in it—when he stopped at a drugstore on Main Street in Adams. The town's marshal had received one of Norton's telegrams. Harvey had switched plates—changed the

Packard's for the Harroun's—but Packard tonneaus were less common than Model Ts in Adams; the marshal took note. He arrested Harvey, then telegraphed Chicago. Norton sent two detectives in a car to bring Harvey back. Then he headed straight for Harvey's house.

What Norton and his men found in Harvey's basement made them reconsider their kidnapping theory.

Harvey's bedroom was down a flight of stairs. There were two bloody hats under his bed: a felt hat with Daugherty's initials in it; a straw hat with Ausmus's. Someone had left a bloody hatchet on a tool chest next to Harvey's bed. Someone had also thrown documents—with Daugherty's and Ausmus's names on them—into the furnace, next door to Harvey's bedroom. The furnace hadn't been lit. The papers were intact.

The little room across from the furnace—the coal bin—looked like someone had slaughtered a young heifer in it. There was a pool of blood on the floor, smears and splatters of blood on the walls and the ceiling. Old newspapers, splotched and splattered with blood, lay piled on the floor.

Someone had left an old baseball bat leaning against the wall of the laundry room. The bat was sticky with blood. Someone had also left a bloody ax there, too.

Norton's men cordoned off the house. A crowd gathered. A crew of detectives began digging up the backyard. Neighbors watched. The crowd grew. Police brought in electric searchlights; the men kept digging through the night. The crowd held steady. At dawn, a commissary crew carried pails of coffee through the crowd, to the men in the yard. The men dipped their cups, drank, and went back to work. By now, they'd dug up the whole backyard and the ground on both sides of the house. The crowd grew larger.

Norton told his men to start on the garage. It had a dirt and cinder floor. Harvey's old car was parked next to one wall. A detective sergeant noticed something peculiar about the wheels on one side of the car. "Look," he said, "the wheels . . . have sunk into the ground. The wheels on the other side are alright."

Norton ordered his crew to move the car and start digging. Eight inches down, they hit a layer of bricks. "We've struck the foundation floor." Norton knelt down to look. The bricks had been laid snug, but they hadn't been plastered. "Pry 'em up," he said. As soon as they did, they saw a man's shoe. Neighbors, reporters, cops, and Packard men pressed against the windows and crowded the doors of the garage.

After a few minutes of digging, detectives uncovered a man's legs. The man had been bound with four coils of rope; his legs had been drawn up to his chest; he'd been buried on his side, his face to the wall. One of Ausmus's friends leaned through a window. "That's Carl," he cried. "He was wearing the blue serge [suit] and shoes like that when he left the office."

The detectives stopped digging and waited for the coroner, Peter Hoffman, to arrive. Hoffman shoved his way through the crowd, accompanied by a medical examiner named Reinhart. Hoffman had Ausmus's friends brought in; he ordered the detectives to uncover the man's face. Ausmus's friends identified him, but it wasn't easy: Ausmus had been beaten so savagely that his face had been almost obliterated. A huge discolored bruise—"caused by a terrific blow," Reinhart said—extended from Ausmus's left shoulder to the bottom of his rib cage. Ausmus's Army watch was still on his wrist. Reinhart found a gold pencil and two five-dollar bills in his pocket.

Hoffman noticed a thread protruding from Ausmus's mouth. He told Reinhart to pull it; it broke. Reinhart pried open Ausmus's jaws. A heavy piece of cotton, a foot square, had been shoved down his throat. Whoever had done it may have meant to suffocate him. It hadn't worked. Ausmus had been buried alive. Even after his legs had been drawn up to his chest, Ausmus was too big to fit in the hole that had been dug for him. Someone had stomped on his neck and broken it to get him down into the ground.

Reinhart spread out the wad of cloth he'd pulled out of Ausmus's mouth. It wasn't just a rag. "It was the front part of a woman's brassiere." The brassiere belonged to Eva.

Norton spoke to reporters:

"In all my years of police experience, I have never seen anything like this. This is an atrocity that is doubly brutal because it seems to have been so . . . needless. Two men murdered for an automobile! Only a fool could have cooked up such a plan. Only a fiend could have executed it. . . . What makes it appear . . . like a one man job is that it might have been hard to find more than one with the turn of mind necessary to its accomplishment."[3]

Harvey and his Packard drove back to Chicago—followed by a car of Chicago police detectives and several cars of reporters. Harvey's mother, his father, and two lawyers, hired by Harvey's father, sat behind him as he drove. The convoy reached Chicago at three o'clock in the morning. Harvey's parents were escorted to a hotel. Harvey was taken to be interrogated.

Neither Hoffman nor Norton was permitted to question him. Robert E.

Crowe—the new state's attorney for Cook County—had pulled rank and intervened. The case of Harvey Church, "the handcuff slayer," belonged to him.

(Three years later, in 1924, Crowe would make a national name for himself, when he investigated *and* prosecuted Leopold and Loeb. Crowe had gotten his first, local headlines in 1919 when, as a Circuit Court judge, he'd presided over the trial—and ordered the execution—of a janitor named Fitzgerald who'd assaulted, then strangled, a five-year-old girl. The Fitzgerald case led to Crowe's being appointed state's attorney—just in time for Harvey.)

Crowe carried himself like a prosecutor who lived and breathed the Old Testament. Scowls, frowns, and suspicious looks marked his public face. He relished guilt and punishment more than he understood innocence or reasonable doubt. Public amputations, impalements, and burnings might have pleased him. His political ambitions were as fierce as his belief in retribution. His goal was to become the Republican boss of Cook County. (To accomplish this, Crowe would ally himself with "Big Bill" Thompson, one of the most venal mayors in the besotted history of Chicago municipal government. Thompson certainly wasn't the Devil himself, but he did collect regular paychecks that smelled of fire and brimstone.)

Crowe was sufficiently cautious to use an investigator named Newmark to do the dirty work of forcing Harvey to confess. Newmark was a big, powerfully built man who wore a derby to make himself look even more imposing. As a courtesy to Coroner Hoffman—and to Chicago Police Chief Charles Fitzmorris—Crowe permitted a detective captain named Mullen to assist Newmark in his interrogation.

A police detail escorted Harvey to Newmark's office; reporters settled themselves outside the door to eavesdrop. Newmark and Mullen took turns shouting at Harvey, then asking him questions. Harvey either didn't answer them or denied everything. Once, he shouted so loudly that reporters outside on the sidewalk heard him: "I'm telling you the truth," he yelled. "I didn't kill them!"

Newmark and Mullen were waiting for the sun to rise. They planned to take Harvey on a tour. After a few more hours of shouting, they dragged Harvey downstairs and shoved him into a car. Reporters followed.

"At high speed, the cars swept through the city to . . . Fulton Street, Church's home. It was 9:31 when they arrived there; a crowd of several hundred murder fans were already at the house.

"Church's arrival caused a distinct stir among the crowd. Hisses, pointed fingers, loud remarks of 'There's the murderer!' [greeted him]. Then came more somber whispers—talks of lynching bees—of justice by the rope.

"Investigators . . . rushed Church inside . . . police cleared the yard of spectators. . . . Then, from the rear door of the house, the lad was taken through the yard to the garage. . . . Church staggered slightly as he walked through the garage door. In an apparently desperate effort to control himself, he straightened [his stance].

"The Harroun car . . . had been returned by the police to the spot [where] it was found on the first day of the search. The grave of Ausmus below its wheels had [not] been filled in. . . . To this spot, Church was led. 'Kneel down there,' Newmark said. Church sank slowly.

" 'That's where you buried him, isn't it?' Newmark shouted. Church leaned forward, peering beneath the car, his eyes half closed.

" 'You killed him, didn't you—and dragged his body here and buried him. We've got the body! Confess! You'll feel better if you do! . . .' Question after question was volleyed at him.

"Church, like a trapped man, swung his head from side to side. Tears came to his eyes and rolled slowly down his cheek.

" 'I—I—didn't do it! I didn't do it!' he gasped. He turned his head away as if in fear of the spot.

" 'Look at it! Look at it! What are you afraid of?' Newmark snapped. 'You killed him, didn't you? You put him in there alive—you stomped his shoulders and head down and broke his neck, didn't you? Why are you afraid to look there now?'

"Church gasped again and crumpled. Flat on the ground, he lay for a minute, apparently in great distress. The officers picked him up and rushed him down the steps into the basement.

"They stopped just inside the door. . . . 'How do you account for this?' . . . A few steps further and there was a post on which were splatters of dried blood. . . . 'Whose blood is that?' was shouted at him. Church wavered for a moment, then shook his head. They pushed him to the coal bin.

"In one corner was a pool of slowly drying blood. Newmark bent over it and with a sharp gesture of his hand towards it, looked full into Church's face.

" 'Whose blood is that?' he volleyed. Church shook his head.

" 'You killed them there! You killed them both there! You know you did! Don't you?' Church turned his head; his face grew pale; he didn't say a word.

" 'Don't be a coward!' Newmark shot at him. 'Fess up! You killed them there—you know it and we know it. Don't be a coward!' But the youth, his head still shaking . . . turned away. . . .

". . . 'No! No!' Church gasped. . . . 'I don't know anything about this!'

" 'You've seen the dope we've got on you!' Newmark shot back. 'You thought we were kidding you when we said we had the goods!' "[4]

From the coal bin, Newmark dragged Harvey to the furnace; from the furnace, Newmark dragged him up the stairs, out of the house, past the crowd, back into the car. Next stop was the Lake Street bridge. Reporters watched and listened to everything; photographers made pictures of Newmark's gestures and Harvey's stumbles.

"The party drove to the undertaking rooms of William Dietzel. The place was locked. An officer kicked in the door and Church was hustled . . . [into] the room where, on a slab, [lay] Daugherty's body. . . . They stripped the sheet from it and pushed Church up in front of it. . . . 'You killed him, didn't you?' . . . Church broke. A gasp like that of a dying man came from his lips. He straightened up [then] began to fall. 'Grab him! Get him out of here!' Newmark snapped." It was noon by then. Church hadn't slept in more than a day.

They drove back to Newmark's office. "Church . . . slumped down in his chair. 'Can I see my mother for a moment?' he asked.

" 'Confess and you can . . .' said Mullen. He asked Church, 'Do you mean to tell us that you didn't see Daugherty and Ausmus in your home when you were there?' "

Church looked around the room. He said nothing, then he broke. "Yes, they were there!" "You killed them, didn't you?" Church looked at Mullen and Newmark again. Then in a quiet voice: "Yes. I killed them."

Newmark rushed out of his office. "Church has come through!" he shouted to the reporters. "He killed both men. He's confessed!"[5]

Newmark wouldn't have been so relieved if he'd known how many confessions Harvey had in him. Newmark's methods—his use of fatigue, fear, and humiliation—didn't include the beatings that Hoffman and Norton had—probably—used to break Carl Wanderer. There was no need: Newmark's psychological "third degree" broke Harvey as thoroughly as if he'd strapped Harvey to a rack. Emotional suffering produced the same sort of confession as acute physical pain.

Harvey told Newmark whatever Newmark wanted to hear. "I did it all myself," Harvey said. ". . . If you check up on the way things were left in the house, you can see that I'm telling the truth."[6]

The truth Harvey offered to Newmark (and to Mullen, and to two other people in the room: Assistant State's Attorney Charles Wharton, whom Crowe had entrusted with prosecuting Church once the case went to trial, and Acting Lieutenant Norton) was this:

Ausmus drove Harvey and Daugherty to Harvey's house. He offered Daugherty a drink. "I never say no to a drink," Daugherty said. Harvey headed for the basement. Daugherty followed. Harvey picked up a handgun. (Police said they'd found the gun in a drawer in Harvey's bedroom.) "Is this the gun?" Newmark asked Harvey. Harvey said it was. The weapon was a cheap .32 caliber, "dresser drawer"/"pocket revolver" called a "bulldog." ("British bulldogs," made by reputable British and Belgian firms, were used as personal, defensive sidearms by military officers and policemen. George Armstrong Custer had fired a few rounds from his "bulldog" before Sioux warriors hacked him to death. Cheaply made "bulldogs" were manufactured and sold by so many firms in the United States and Europe that, as a class, "bulldogs" came to mean what police, during the late twentieth century, called "Saturday night specials.") Harvey said he'd found the gun in one of the houses his father had bought in Adams. He'd brought it with him to Chicago for the same reason, he said, he'd bought the handcuffs: He'd been involved in "labor troubles" up in Wisconsin and needed to protect himself.

Daugherty was expecting a drink, not a stickup, when he went downstairs. Harvey told him to turn around, then put his hands behind him. Daugherty did as he was told. Harvey handcuffed him.

Then—the exact order of events varied as Harvey confessed different truths to different people—Harvey either slit Daugherty's throat, then strangled him, then beat him to death with his baseball bat. Or: Harvey didn't slit Daugherty's throat; didn't strangle him; didn't beat him to death. Didn't. Didn't. Didn't.

Whatever and whoever killed Daugherty had killed him by the time Ausmus came looking for his partner. Harvey pointed his gun at Ausmus and told him to kneel. Ausmus knelt. "I know what Chicago holdups are like," Ausmus said. "He was yellow," Harvey told Newmark. Harvey tied up Ausmus. In fact, Harvey hog-tied him. Then Harvey beat him to death. Or, at least, he tried to beat him to death. Or, maybe, he didn't point his gun at Ausmus. Maybe he just smashed him up as he came down the stairs. Whatever happened, Ausmus was still making noise. Which is why Harvey stuffed that piece of cloth—Harvey called it a "light colored piece of goods"—into Ausmus's mouth. Harvey said he'd never noticed that the cloth was a piece of his mother's brassiere. How would he know whose brassiere it was? Harvey also said that *he'd* never stomped on Ausmus's neck to get him to fit in the hole he'd dug for him.

In the typescript of the confession Harvey made to Newmark, Harvey had—for some reason—used the word "we" when he'd talked about burying Ausmus. Harvey's "we" upset Newmark—and Crowe—when they read the typescript. Harvey had immediately corrected himself after he'd said it. Later in his confession, Harvey had used the word "we" again—but not corrected himself.

No one noticed these slips until later. Harvey's misuse of the personal pronoun was less worrisome than the brutal how and why of what he'd done. Since Assistant State's Attorney Wharton had the job of convincing a jury of Harvey's guilt, he took over the interrogation. Harvey had used a gun on Daugherty; he'd ambushed Ausmus; brutal surprise had enabled him to overcome, then kill the two. But: How in the world had Harvey managed to single-handedly lift Daugherty's body over the parapets of the Lake Street bridge? And why—why?—did he really do what he'd done? Wharton needed to hear a plausible, believable explanation for the "how" of Harvey's crime. He also needed to hear a relatively plausible reason for it to have happened. If a jury believed Harvey had killed two innocent men for the sake of a car they might send him to an asylum instead of the gallows.

Harvey said he'd waited until three-thirty in the morning to shove Daugherty's body into a gunnysack, then drag it out to his car. (His *new* car.) Wharton was willing to accept this—but the bridge's parapets were as high as Harvey's chest. Harvey weighed 135 pounds. Daugherty weighed 220. "Show us how you did it," Wharton said.

Lieutenant Norton volunteered to be Daugherty. The lieutenant weighed 210 pounds. He lay down on his back on the floor. "Show us," said Wharton. Harvey did. He knelt down, and then, as Wharton and Mullen and Newmark watched, he lifted Norton onto a table. He didn't do it all at once—he held Norton, propped him up, balanced him in stages. Harvey was no little Goliath, but he used his strength well. He proved he could do what he said he'd done.

But why?

Harvey explained: A few days before he'd killed the men, he'd received an anonymous phone call. A man had threatened to kill him and his mother and his father unless, said Harvey, "I obtained a car worth more than $5,400 by September 10th. . . . The caller hung up immediately. That was all he said. . . . He threatened the life of my father, mother, and myself."

That was enough to satisfy Wharton. No ghosts, no voices, no spirits. Someone had forced Harvey to do it. Extortion, pure and simple. Who wouldn't butcher two men to save his own family?

Mr. Crowe seemed very pleased. "Church's statement is airtight and can not be broken-down," Crowe declared. "Mr. Wharton deserves the greatest possible praise for the manner in which he conducted the examination of Church and his skill in arranging the confession." Mr. Crowe announced that he himself would be "personally supervising the preparation of the case." He promised "a new record for speed in prosecution."[7]

Coroner Hoffman had a somewhat different reaction to Harvey's confession. "A tissue of lies" was the way he described it. He prepared to convene a coroner's inquest. No matter what Crowe believed or intended, there would be no criminal trial unless there was an inquest. Crowe could pull rank—but Hoffman controlled the beginning of the legal process.

Hoffman asked Crowe to release Harvey so he could testify at the inquest. Crowe agreed, but demanded Harvey be returned as soon as possible. Crowe had good reason to be suspicious.

Harvey's police escort didn't take him directly to the inquest. Instead they stopped and waited while Harvey had a quiet little conversation with their chief, Charles Fitzmorris. Fitzmorris was a big, smart, good-looking man who was used to speaking his mind and used to being right.

Fitzmorris agreed with Hoffman about the confession Harvey had made to Crowe's people. A single, threatening, anonymous phone call, the ambush and brutal killing of two able-bodied men, the single-handed disposal of Daugherty's body—there were too many implausible parts to Harvey's story. Church must have had accomplices.

While Fitzmorris chatted with Harvey ("We've arrested your friends," Fitzmorris said) a crowd of five thousand people gathered outside the funeral home where the inquest was to be held. "Thousands of persons lined both sides of the street for more than a block in both directions . . . several women were knocked down. There were a few, isolated cries of 'Lynch him,' but for the most part, the motive of the crowd seemed mostly curiosity."[8]

Harvey was led past the bodies of Ausmus and Daugherty, laid out on marble slabs in a room next to the chapel where Hoffman had assembled his jury. Police led Harvey to the front; reporters sat behind him. Harvey turned around. "This is something of an experience," he whispered to a reporter. "I wouldn't mind it so much if you fellows weren't always shooting off flashlights. The smoke gets in my eyes and makes me sick."

The reporter smiled. Harvey smiled. "I never smoked or chewed or anything," he said to the reporter. "My only bad habit was cleaning my finger nails."

Harvey laughed politely so the reporter knew he was joking. He looked up, then he gasped. A detective sergeant was standing across the room, absentmindedly swinging the baseball bat police had found in Harvey's basement.

"On the table beside the detective were the bloodstained [hats] of the victims and other gory bits of clothing. . . . [Church] blanched, turned away, and lapsed into silence. . . .

"[Church] arose nonchalantly in answer to the coroner's call, 'Harvey Church, will you stand up!' "

Hoffman read a statement: "Any information you give during this inquest will be used against you at trial."

That's when Harvey did something that no one—at least no one who worked for Mr. Crowe—had anticipated.

"I think I'll testify at the court hearing," Harvey said. "That would be better, I guess."

Hoffman looked surprised. He may have been. He may also have sensed that something might be changing in Harvey. Something like his confession.

"Does that mean that you don't want to testify here?" Hoffman asked. Newmark and Mullen thought they'd broken him. They had. Fitzmorris had patched him up.

"I'll wait until I get a chance to be heard in Criminal Court," Harvey answered.

Hoffman began to call witnesses: two medical examiners, Lieutenant Norton, Assistant State's Attorney Wharton, the stenographer who'd written down Harvey's confession.

Hoffman asked Norton to read the confession aloud. Harvey's "I-did-it-all-by-myself" confession.

In a somber voice, Hoffman asked Harvey if the statement, just read, was correct.

That's when Harvey said something that Hoffman—and Fitzmorris—had hoped he'd say.

"No," Harvey answered. "That's not the whole truth."

The reporters were surprised. Mr. Crowe's people began to listen very attentively.

"What do you mean by that?" asked Hoffman. "How can your words, written exactly as you spoke them, not be 'the whole truth'?"

"I would make the statement," Church answered, "that that is the essence of the truth of what I said, but not the truth."[9]

Harvey's fear and anger (combined with Fitzmorris's persuasiveness) had given him just enough strength to dodge his own guilt. Newmark had hurt him. Crowe wanted to hang him. Harvey wasn't going to make it easy for them.

2 AIDED CHURCH IN MURDERS

Pal Confesses Handcuff Slaying Plot

TWO VICTIMS LURED TO DEATH IN BASEMENT

Three Men Were to Share in Auto Sale[10]

"Harvey W. Church had two accomplices in the handcuff murder by which two automobile salesmen . . . met a brutal death last Thursday night.

"Early last evening [following the coroner's inquest], Church admitted that his confession, made on Sunday, was, in detail, untrue; that his horrifying crime was a plot in which he and two others had equal share.

"A few hours later, Leon Parks, 24 years old . . . confessed to State's Attorney Crowe, Chief of Police Fitzmorris, and Chief Investigator Newmark that he—and one other man—were the accomplices of Church in the commission of the double crime.

"The third man, he said, was Clarence Wilder. . . . Parks is the night manager of the Benario garage on West Lake Street. Wilder was an accomplice and former roommate of Church, who had been connected with the garage as an accessory salesman. . . .

"For the first time, Parks's confession bared the real motive of the crime. It wasn't just the love of a fine car that inspired the killings, he said. The three had planned to steal the car from Daugherty and Ausmus, sell it, and split the $5000 they expected to receive for it. . . .

"The breakdown of the garage mechanic followed his being brought face to face with Church. Church repeated the story he'd told Newmark a few hours earlier, implicating Parks. . . .

" 'Well,' said Parks, 'if you've squawked, I'm going to squawk.' "

Harvey W. Church, Clarence Wilder, and Leon Parks

Everyone—Fitzmorris, Hoffman, Norton, Crowe, Newmark, Wharton—was eager to know who did what to whom. But: In the same way that Norton had been delighted when he'd learned about Carl Wanderer's seventeen-year-old girlfriend—At last! A familiar, carnal, *sane* motive!—so everyone was relieved to learn that Harvey wasn't a crazy loner. Harvey was just greedy. He was nothing but a common car thief. An ordinary—normal—car thief.

Harvey himself had called Norton to tell him he'd lied. "Norton," he said, "I'm as happy as I can be. I'm going to open up and tell the truth."

"The truth" was that it was all Parks's idea.

A few nights after Harvey brought in his old Harroun, Harvey said, "Parks . . . he says to me, 'Wouldn't you like to make some easy money?' I says, 'How?' He says, 'By stealing a car and selling it.' I says, 'Could you get away with it?' He says, 'Don't worry about that. . . .'

"I thought it over in my mind. On Wednesday, September 7, I met him in the garage and told him I was going down to the Packard Company and get a Twin Six car the next day—and he said he would be over at my house with a man when I got there . . .

"I asked him what he was going to do. He said he was going to bind the gentleman that brought the car—and also my hands, leaving my feet free so that [later] . . . I might get up and make an alarm . . . I told him I could do that. . . ."[11]

Wilder was the man Parks brought along to help him. They both had guns. They stuck up Daugherty. They told Harvey to handcuff him. They were the ones who killed Daugherty. They did the same thing to Ausmus. The only difference was that, instead of handcuffs, they told Harvey to tie up Ausmus with some rope. Then they killed Ausmus. The two of them—not Harvey—were the ones who buried Ausmus. The next morning, it was Wilder who helped Harvey throw Daugherty over the bridge.

Attorney Wharton was thrilled when he heard all this.

"Church is not a man with a disordered mind," Wharton told the press. "The fact that he evinces interest in greater and lesser degrees shows that his mind functions normally. . . . Throughout the questioning, Church carried an air of conviction. He impressed me with his desire to be truthful. He manifested a strong desire to purge his conscience and soul of consequences of his crime. Throughout the inquisition, he . . . seemed to want to describe the killing as accurately as possible and without omitting any essential fact."

In fact, Wharton told reporters, Church's new confession was the "most wonderful demonstration of memory and concentration I have ever seen in an untrained mind. When one reads [Church's new] statement, one marvels that such a person could remember the details of so atrocious a crime in as perfect a sequence as his recital shows.

"Church has great resistant power, both physical and mental. He shows . . . the strength of a country boy who had not yet been weakened with the diseases of city life."[12]

Unfortunately:

Parks's version of events didn't match Church's. When police leaned on Parks, he repudiated everything he'd just said. Police sat him down at a table across from Church. For three hours, Church read, reread, and initialed each typed page of his new, one-hundred-page confession. Parks watched him and trembled. Church taunted him: "Watcha waiting for? Are you yellow? You know it's true—if you say it isn't, you're a liar." Parks sank down in his chair. Then he grabbed a pen.[13] "It's no use," Parks said. "I thought if I could get my confession thrown out, I might have a chance to keep from hanging. But—they'll hang me anyway. I might as well sign up."

Too bad.

"The puzzling features of the murder were not cleared up with the revision of Church's confession and the supplementary statement of Parks. Some investigators were inclined to discredit the story that the principals in the murder had hoped for no reward other than a share of the $5000 to be obtained from the sale of the car. . . ."[14]

Police arrested Clarence Wilder—the third man implicated in the "handcuff murders." They arrested him the same day Parks wilted and "signed up."

Wilder produced an alibi: "He said he was at work, all day Thursday, the day of the murder, in the Levi Shoe Factory at West Van Buren and South Loop Streets. His employers deny this."[15]

While police checked Wilder's alibi, Harvey changed his *new* confession—the one he'd just spent three hours initialing; the one that Attorney Wharton had hailed as proof of Harvey's prodigious memory and his rock-solid sanity. Parks was still part of "Confession #3," but the identity of the third man changed.

It wasn't (said Harvey) *Clarence Wilder* who'd helped Parks kill the two. It wasn't *Clarence Wilder* who'd helped Harvey throw Daugherty over the bridge. No, no. It was *Milton Walker*.

Harvey had changed his mind after police presented Walker to him in a lineup. "Which one of these guys was with you and Parks?" Church picked Walker. "It was *him*," Church said, "not the gentleman I referred to."

"What made you think that the man's name was *Walker* instead of *Wilder*?" Mr. Crowe asked Church. "Just what Parks told me," said Church. "When we were disposing of Daugherty's body . . . Parks said to me that his name was Walker."

Crowe winced when he heard this:

"In his second confession, Church had declared emphatically that Parks was not present when the body of Daugherty was taken [to the bridge]."[16]

More problems ensued. Denials, corrections, and befuddlements unfolded like a vaudeville routine:

"Walker asserted that he had never seen Church.

"Parks declared that he knew Walker as Walker but had had no dealings with him.

"The identification of Wilder was similarly muddled.

"When Wilder was arrested, he admitted that he knew Church and had roomed with him [at a place on West Monroe Street] a year ago. Church in his [first] confession had referred to his acquaintanceship with Wilder. Today, however, he repudiated all that with the flat declaration that he does not know Wilder and never was acquainted with him.

"Mr. Crowe ordered Walker and Wilder to be kept in custody until their alibis could be further investigated."[17] (Walker's alibi was unassailable: he was still in jail—for robbing a grocer—on the day Daugherty and Ausmus were killed.)

"I am convinced," declared Mr. Crowe, "that both Parks and Church are trying to shield Walker, whether in this case or some other. I believe [Church] may be induced to tell a straight story, yet."[18]

Fitzmorris and Hoffman had been sure they were right (about Harvey having accomplices) and that Crowe and Newmark were wrong (about Harvey being a loner). They'd used Harvey against Crowe, but they hadn't anticipated that Harvey would use the four of them against each other. Crowe had deferred to the coroner and the chief; Crowe had taken credit for their ideas. Now Harvey's newest "tissue of lies" was falling apart in Mr. Crowe's hands—while everyone was watching.

"All our men are working steadily, harmoniously, and in coordination in this case," Crowe told the press. "There is no friction—and there isn't going to be any. We are working for purposes of prosecution—not for purposes of publicity. We are examining all witnesses to determine the value of their stories in a trial court. . . ."[19]

As a result:

Wilder was released. His alibi held. Parks was released because Crowe, Newmark, and Fitzmorris all knew that they'd threatened Parks, then put words in his mouth.

Crowe was back to where he'd started. Or, as Norton first said: "Only a fool could have cooked up this plan. Only a fiend could have carried it out." Harvey had told people what they wanted to hear—what he kept calling "the truth"—once, twice, three times. Crowe asked Harvey to tell him the truth, once again.

"Parks told me Wilder was in Philadelphia," Harvey explained. "I thought if I named him—or any one—the detectives would let my father and mother go." (Harvey's parents were still in a Chicago hotel. Not under arrest, but not free to go.) "That was the reason I gave *Wilder's* name. He really didn't have anything to do with it."

Crowe replaced State's Attorney Wharton with another assistant state's attorney named Edgar Jones. Jones was prepared to believe that Harvey did it all himself. Ben Newmark, chief investigator, "still clings to the theory that the murderer had accomplices."[20] "Parks and Church are both guilty," Newmark said. "There is a third man. . . . We are after him now. . . . We do not know who he is."

Crowe was tired of other people's theories. Late one night, he ordered police to pull Harvey out of his cell in the county jail and take him to an outlying police station.

Norton, Newmark, Wharton, an investigator named Smith, and Crowe himself took turns questioning Harvey. They let one reporter—a reporter from the *Chicago Tribune*—watch and listen. Hours passed.

"Church was obdurate and sullen. Then . . . shortly after dawn, he calmly said, 'I killed him. . . . The police wanted an accomplice, so I gave them one. They insisted I couldn't do it alone, but I did.' "[21]

Harvey's interrogators asked him the same questions Wharton had first asked: How could a little guy like Harvey have overwhelmed a big guy like Daugherty? How could he, all alone, have lifted Daugherty's dead-weight up and over the parapets of the Lake Street bridge?

"Give me a chance and I'll show you . . ." Harvey said. "Give me a man as big as Daugherty and I'll pick him up and show you."

"Detective Sergeant 'Billy' McCarthy stepped forward. McCarthy weighed 190 pounds." (The coroner had changed Daugherty's weight from 220 to 188.) "It was just after 7:00 AM when handcuffs were handed to Church. In the winkling of an eye, he had snapped the cuffs on McCarthy and laid him on the floor. The detective let his body go limp . . . Church wrapped his arms around him and began to lift.

"In amazement, the watchers saw him slowly lift McCarthy from the floor. The only sound was the labored breathing of the murderer. . . . Before [anyone] realized it, Church had raised . . . McCarthy to the level of his waist and placed him on the table.

"Church stepped back. 'See,' he jerked out, 'I did it.' "[22]

"I did it myself," Harvey said. "I didn't intend to kill him at first. Things just moved too fast for me. . . .

"I wanted the car. . . .

"Daugherty came to the house. I didn't have the money. I invited him to the cellar. I covered him with the revolver and snapped the cuffs on him.

"Then something came over me. I don't know what. . . . I hit him with a ball bat. Then I just went 'nutty' I guess. I grabbed up an axe and I cut his throat. I pounded him, again and again.

"Then Ausmus came. I hit him and he died. I left the bodies and took Mother for a ride.

"Later, I returned and buried Ausmus. I was all heated up and perspiring. Mother noticed it. . . .

"I went to bed, but I couldn't sleep. At 3 o'clock, I got up and took Daugherty's body to the river and threw it in. . . .

"I told the truth when I first made a confession. No one would believe me. The police seemed to think that someone else was in on it. The more I thought about it, the more I thought that if I dragged another one in, I'd go free. . . .

"Leon Parks never had anything to do with it. Neither did Milton Walker . . . Police said Parks had confessed. I decided to change my story. That's all there is to it."[23]

There was more to it, though. Much more.

Harvey had killed two Packard salesmen for the sake of a tonneau. Carl Wanderer had killed his pretty, young, pregnant wife *and* a perfect stranger because he wanted to reenlist in the Army.

Wanderer hadn't been immediately arrested after he'd done what he'd done (and once Wanderer had been arrested, he was labeled as crazy), for the same reason that experienced men like Chief Fitzmorris and Coroner Hoffman had refused to believe Harvey after he'd confessed (the first time). Harvey told his interrogators what he'd done and why he'd done it, but the most experienced police professionals in the city thought he was lying. Harvey might as well have been trying to convince sixteenth-century churchmen about the solar system or fourteenth-century physicians about microbes.

Harvey inhabited a state of mind—an early-twentieth-century state of mind—in which advertising had begun to turn water into wine. Anyone with common sense would think that a man who butchered two other men because he wanted a Packard—or a man who would kill his wife and a stranger because he loved the Army—anyone would think that people like that *had to be crazy*. Because if they weren't crazy, if they were normal, then they presaged a state of existence in which water ran uphill and darkness shone like the sun.

Harvey was more than a little crazy. His craziness made him receptive. His receptiveness made him ahead of his time.

State's Attorney Crowe understood. He decided Harvey was sane.

Sane enough to be punished. Sane enough to be hung.

Harvey's trial began on the last day of November 1921.

The weeks in jail had changed him.

" '*The People of the State of Illinois versus Harvey W. Church . . .*'

"The bailiff droned on, but the people in the crowded courtroom of Judge John Caverly had eyes and ears only for the figure of the youth, slumped down in [a] cane-bottomed chair, his coat and trousers ragged, dirty, misshapen; long, dirty locks of his black hair, uncut for weeks, partly concealed his eyes, set and glassy, as he stared . . . at something that [seemed to have] hypnotized him. . . . A short, black beard could not hide the deep lines in his face. . . . The boy who had entered the prison debonairly, a few weeks ago, boasting that he would soon be free, is 'paying the penalty.' . . . His eyes with their haggard, mesmerized stare, never left the floor. . . . He was led away, stumbling, shuffling. . . . An attorney for the defense indicated that the plea will be that [Church's] confession was obtained . . . through beatings and coercion. The defense also asked prospective jury men about dementia praecox, katatonia, and hebrephrenia, indicating the possibility of a plea of insanity."[24]

(Three years after Judge John Caverly presided over Harvey's trial, he presided over the trial of Leopold and Loeb. Caverly was a British immigrant who'd paid for his legal education by working as a water carrier in the steel mills outside of Chicago. Early in his legal career, he'd devoted himself to building a juvenile court system for Cook County. He had a reputation for showing sympathy for "youthful offenders." He would show none for Harvey, but his decision *not* to execute Leopold and Loeb was based largely on their age. Their youth.)

As the prosecution began to present its evidence—crime scene evidence, forensic medical evidence, the testimony of such witnesses as the jeweler and the surplus store clerk—Harvey began to sink deeper into his chair, and deeper into himself. From the day he'd been arrested (September 11) to the day (September 18) he'd confessed, the second time, to killing both men himself, Harvey had dressed and acted like a wisecracking college

Harvey W. Church, sitting, head down, in a courtroom

boy—articulate, ironic, and argumentative. Then, at his arraignment on October 6, he'd simply stopped talking. On December 1, he refused to leave his bed. On December 2, he began what soon became a hunger strike. Guards carried him, upright, into court; there he sat, hunched, mute, and filthy. On Christmas Eve, the day he was convicted, Harvey no longer stood or walked on his own, no longer responded to language, gesture, sudden movement, or sudden sound. The press—and the public—attributed Harvey's physical collapse to guilt, remorse, and fear. Fear of death, they said, had sucked the life out of him. The prosecution—Mr. Crowe in particular—thought Harvey was faking.

Harvey must have known there was no escape. Except one. He knew he was locked in jail, but he also knew he didn't have to be present when they hung him. Harvey withdrew and withdrew and withdrew. Slowly, incrementally, in plain sight, Harvey left.

Since the prosecution knew that every one of Harvey's confessions, true and false, had been forced out of him, the state based its case, entirely, on circumstantial evidence.

Harvey's defense called his mother and his sister. They recited the long list of his accidents, head injuries, horrific falls, and strange behaviors.

Next came the defense's mental health experts—three "alienists" who each testified that Harvey was insane. One of them was Dr. William Hickson, chief of the city's Psychopathic Laboratory—the same man who had quickly diagnosed Carl Wanderer as a latent homosexual who suffered from dementia praecox.

The jury could see there was something wrong with Harvey, but they thought it was guilt. The jury spent five hours reviewing the evidence. One ballot was all that was needed.

Two bailiffs carried Harvey into court. Two bailiffs held him upright as the verdict was read. Harvey was out of range. He'd pushed off from shore the day his trial had begun. He was out of sight of land when the jury sentenced him to death.

Mr. Crowe was gratified.

He made a short speech, appropriate to the holiday season.

"Cook County is extremely fortunate in having twelve men who, despite the sentiment of Christmas, had the courage to find Harvey W. Church guilty of murder and fix his penalty at death. The courtroom was filled with the spirit of Christmas during the trial. During its entire three weeks, the 'Peace on Earth, Good Will to Men' sentiment grew and reached a climax. . . ."[25]

A date was set for Harvey's execution. His defense had learned a lesson from Carl Wanderer's defense: It filed a motion for a sanity trial.

Harvey no longer left his bed. His jailers had begun to force-feed him. He seemed so profoundly withdrawn—so obviously catatonic—that his defense wanted him carried into court each day and deposited there, so he might serve as his own "Exhibit A." The prosecution objected. The press couldn't resist the chance to take a look.

"A reporter accompanied a physician and a psychiatrist to [Church's] death cell . . . 'Exhibit A' lay on a hospital bed . . . on his back. The examining physician applied a ['deep pain,' sterile needle, puncture] test. Such a test, the physician said, 'would revive a patient from the deepest state of normal coma.' There was no reaction.

" 'There has been a complete mental, moral, and physical degenera-tion,' said the physician. 'One cannot think of him in terms of human kind. What lies here is merely a lump of flesh.' "26

"Church is dead, mentally," a psychiatrist said. "I don't think he would live were he turned loose. I think he's past the stage of consciousness. Hang-ing him will extinguish the spark of life—the other side is gone, now."27

Harvey's sanity trial lasted two days. He wasn't in court. His defense called three of the same alienists who'd testified on behalf of Carl Wan-derer at *his* sanity trial. The prosecution called three others. One of them had also testified (on behalf of the prosecution) during the Wanderer trial. (Three of these six "expert medical witnesses" would testify, three years later, during the trial of Leopold and Loeb.)

The jury deliberated for two hours. Its second ballot was unanimous: Harvey was sane. "Stupefied by fear" said one juror—but sane enough to die.

A pair of physicians examined Harvey in his cell one last time. They took his pulse, tapped his elbows and knees with rubber mallets, checked his pupils. His eyes had rolled over, backwards, in their sockets. They applied what they said was an "infallible test to determine whether or not one is feigning a state of coma." Ether-soaked cotton was held under Harvey's nose, like smelling salts. "It would, as one physician put it, 'awaken the seven sleepers of Ephesus.' It did not awaken Church."28

On the wall above Harvey's bed, someone had hung a framed page of verses:

> The bounty of the house is order
> The beauty of the house is contentment
> The glory of the house is hospitality
> The crown of the house is godliness.

At three-thirty the next afternoon, two guards tied Harvey to a kitchen chair. They handcuffed his hands behind him, then strapped his arms to his body.

Carpenters had built gallows in a courtyard. Cells facing the courtyard had been evacuated. Seventy-five witnesses sat on pine benches.

Guards carried Harvey, backwards, in the chair, up the steps to the scaffold.

Harvey's heart beat for fifteen minutes after the trap was sprung. The witnesses waited.

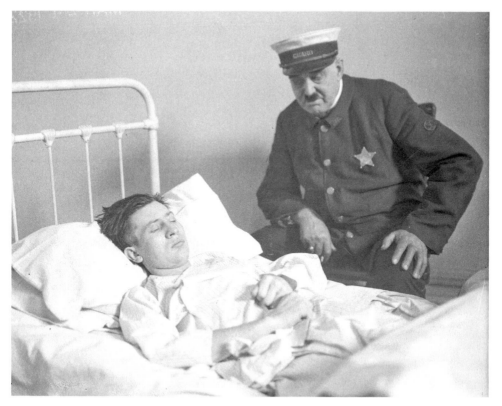

Harvey W. Church, in bed; police officer beside him

Coroner Hoffman tried to convince Harvey's parents to have him autopsied.

"I wish to determine," Hoffman said, "whether Church was really in a comatose condition through willpower.

"I still believe," he said, "that Harvey Church did not commit the two murders, unaided. I suspect that there was at least one more person implicated in the double crime . . . Church's lips were sealed for weeks and he went to the gallows mentally dead.

"I believe that there is but one way to explain this and that is that Church had been drugged while in his cell to keep him from talking."[29]

Harvey's parents refused Hoffman's request.

They shipped Harvey back home by train. They unloaded his coffin a few stops before Adams to avoid the crowd that had gathered there. They buried him in a cemetery twelve miles out of town.

Eva died, five years later, in December.

A car hit her. While she was crossing a street in the town of Friendship.

Thomas Catherwood

4 · Catherwood

It was the twenty-second of November, two days before Thanksgiving.
Thomas lied to his wife—told her he'd gotten a job with a freight company,
downtown. "I'd been walking the streets . . . until my feet were sore."[1] No
one was hiring. Lean times. People with plenty of money sent their cooks
to buy fresh, young turkeys and veal roasts and smoked hams and chickens for fricassee. People like Thomas and his wife—they couldn't afford
a handful of walnuts or a couple of oranges. Maybe—if they were careful—they could make their money last another two weeks. Then—nothing.
The streets for Christmas.

Thomas had been in the Navy. That's when he met his wife. He'd joined
up in 1917; came out in 1920. A mechanic: a fellow with a future. He proposed. They were both in their twenties. They married just as the bottom
dropped out of everything.

They lived in Springfield for a while. Thomas's hometown. His old man
had died when he was just a kid. Thomas had eight brothers and sisters.
He and his brother watched out for each other. It didn't matter: there was
no work.

Thomas's brother-in-law (his wife's brother), Clarence, told them that
things were a little better up in Chicago. Clarence had a job in an REO truck
plant. Clarence's wife, Betty, had just had a baby. "You can live with us,"
they said. "You can stay with us until you find something, here." So they
did. Thomas found work with Western Electric. They got an apartment
of their own. Six months passed. In August, Western Electric let Thomas
go. Now it was nearly Thanksgiving, and all Thomas could do was lie
to his wife.

Ten o'clock in the morning. It was cold. Thomas walked over to Clarence's place to get warm. Betty was there, tending the baby. She asked

Western Electric plant building

Thomas if he was hungry. He said he was. She made him some coffee and sent out for some cake. They sat and talked. Time passed.

Betty wrapped presents. She was pregnant again. Eight months pregnant. She'd bought little gifts for her new baby, her Christmas baby.

She knew Thomas had been looking for work. Thomas told her, "If things don't happen pretty soon . . . my wife and I'll be destitute . . . we'll have no place to live." "Well," said Betty, "don't worry about that, Tom. You folks are welcome to come and live with us anytime that you want to and we will get along all right."[2] Thomas said he didn't want to do that, "but she insisted. . . . I finally agreed I would talk it over with my wife. . . ."

Someone knocked at the door. It was Betty's neighbor Mrs. McClune, from across the hall. Thomas excused himself to go to the bathroom.

Mrs. McClune said she was going downtown. Did Betty need anything?

"I wish you would get me four yards of corduroy to fix the baby buggy," Betty said. "Use your judgment about the color, but I want to get it ready for Christmas."[3]

Thomas came back and sat down at the table. Mrs. McClune nodded hello. Betty opened her purse and took out a bankbook. There was cash between the pages. Fresh, flat, green bills. "Here's $10," Betty said to Mrs. McClune. "I don't know what the stuff will cost." Mrs. McClune left.

"The sight of the money seemed to craze me," Thomas said. "I'd been walking the streets. . . . I asked her for the money. She told me she was going to use it for Christmas presents—but she might spare part of it for me.

"I said, 'No. I want it all or nothing. . . .' I got up and walked toward her. She turned pale. She said, 'Why, Tom . . . you wouldn't hurt me, would you?'"[4] She dropped the bankbook and backed away. She kept looking at him. She didn't cry out; she didn't want to wake the baby. She didn't struggle; she was so pregnant.

"I grabbed her by the throat and pushed her into the bedroom, on the bed. Her face turned white. . . . I believe that I had killed her. . . . I thought I might as well do a good job.

"I laid her across the bed and pulled a rope out of my pocket. I wrapped it around her neck four or five times and pulled it tight. Her face turned black. . . . Why I did it, I do not know."[5]

Thomas took the money out of the bankbook, threw the bankbook in the stove. The baby was still asleep in his crib. Thomas walked out of the apartment; the door latched and locked behind him. He headed home.

He took a streetcar, then another. He peeked at the money: a twenty and three tens. He was disappointed. Very disappointed. He wadded up the bills and pushed them under his pipe tobacco, deep down in his pocket tin.

When the streetcar reached Thomas's stop, he felt so restless he didn't know what to do. He walked into a barbershop and got a haircut, then he went home. His wife thought he'd come back early from his new job.

Clarence came home from work at six. The baby was crying. He found Betty. There was a thimble on her finger. He ran next door. Mrs. McClune told him about Thomas.

"The rest was simple. . . . Within an hour, police had Catherwood under arrest. . . . The slayer was grilled all night. . . . At 3:00 AM, he broke down and confessed. From the bottom of a can, beneath a layer of pipe tobacco, he brought forth the spoils of his crime."[6] "I had to get money, some way," he said. He handed over the cash. Fifty dollars. *Fifty dollars.* "That's all," he said. "I didn't spend a cent."[7]

When Thomas's wife heard he'd confessed, she became hysterical. His jailers put him under a suicide watch. The State's Attorney's office declared Thomas's crime to be "the most cold blooded murder case ever committed in Chicago."

Thomas pleaded guilty at his arraignment. He threw himself on the mercy of the court. The judge acknowledged his plea. He sentenced Thomas to life.

More than twenty years passed.

More than three hundred convicts (a record number, the papers said) applied for parole in 1943. One was an automobile thief who'd killed a federal agent; one was a bank robber; one was a cat burglar who liked to terrify women. One was a bomb maker; another was a hit man. A fellow named Frank Kohler had been sentenced to fourteen years for killing his own baby boy. Frank claimed the kid's crying drove him crazy. Frank applied for parole. Thomas did, too.

There's no record of what the Parole Board decided about Frank or the cat burglar, or even the man the papers called the "Hoosier Romeo"—a man who'd specialized in marrying, then swindling women.

The mass killings and collective insanities of the Second World War may have affected the board's attitude toward the individuals who petitioned them. Perhaps the hit man was released and the cat burglar wasn't. One thing is clear: the board turned Thomas down.

Thomas applied again in April 1945. In Italy, Mussolini had just been captured, shot, and strung up, next to his mistress. In Berlin, Hitler and Eva Braun had just killed themselves.

Back in Springfield, the board denied Thomas's petition.

Every year after that, in May, Thomas asked to be paroled. Every year, the board said no. Truman defeated Dewey; North Korea invaded South Korea; Senator McCarthy investigated Communists in the Army and the State Department; the United States tested its first hydrogen bomb. Years passed. Sunrise; sunset.

In May 1954, Thomas made his eleventh application for parole. He'd broken the rules only four times since he'd been in jail: he'd talked during

Illinois State Penitentiary, Joliet, Illinois

chapel; stolen some soup; taken food with him from the mess hall; been caught while engaging in what was called "self abuse."

The board voted to let Thomas go. He was fifty-nine years old. A heating company in Springfield agreed to give him a job. He reported to his parole officer for the next five years. Then he vanished.

Thomas Roach

5 · Roach and Mosby

"Two colored boys" found her at nine o'clock in the morning.[1] A naked, bloody, dead, white woman, thrown in the back of an old moving van, parked in an alley, behind some flats on Cottage Grove. The neighborhood around Cottage Grove was changing from white middle class to black working class. Changing fast. The alley where the woman was found ran behind a block that was still white. That she'd been found in a moving van was an irony that few newspaper readers would have missed.[2]

Police followed a trail of the woman's blood, through a yard, up a flight of stairs. Russell Mosby was washing blood out of the dead woman's clothes—worth some money, why throw them away?—when the police walked in. Mosby confessed immediately. That is, he blamed Tom Roach. It was Roach's place. All Mosby did was rent a room. Sure, he knew Roach—but that lady was dead, on the floor, and Roach was standing there, having a drink, when Mosby came home. Mosby didn't know who the lady was. Tom told him he didn't know either. Tom said they'd had a few drinks. That was all Mosby knew. Nothing.

About the still on the stove? Sure, said Mosby. He and Tom cooked some, sold some. Moonshine. Yes it was. But he didn't know anything about the woman. They better ask Tom.

And where was Tom?

Tom was working. At the streetcar barn. He was a conductor. The papers said he'd been wounded in France—"a wounded veteran of the American Expeditionary Force." Tom's mother said he'd been "a good boy until he began to run with gangs."

Roach confessed as fast as Mosby did. He said he'd taken his wife to the hospital Tuesday night, "so I was free to do as I chose. . . . I took the woman to my flat. . . . We had some drinks. . . . We danced. . . . She got rough and hit me. I got my revolver and struck her over the head. . . . It was a playful tap. . . . She didn't laugh, then. She fell on the floor. . . . God knows why I did it."

And Mosby?

Roach said Mosby walked in later. Fifteen minutes later. Or—was it?— Mosby came home, *then* fifteen minutes *after* Mosby walked in, the woman died. One thing certain: He and Mosby didn't leave their place until the next night. They stored the woman in the bathroom; then, the next night, they stripped her and hauled her outside.

And the woman? Where'd Roach meet her?

Roach began a new story: "I met this woman Wednesday night, as I was on my way home. I was going to visit a friend of mine, Mrs. Blair. . . . The woman asked if she could go along. . . . I agreed. She said that she knew Mrs. Blair, but I didn't find out her name. We stayed up at Mrs. Blair's place for twenty minutes. Then I started home. At my door, I started to leave her, but she asked to come in and I invited her.

"She was hysterical. She told about having trouble with her husband on account of his having wrongfully accused her of going around with other men.

"She threatened to kill herself. She was very quarrelsome.

"Mosby was in the flat and said something to her and she answered back. We had been drinking moonshine. There was a general fight. . . .

"I hit her once with the pistol, but she only laughed at that. . . .

"She resented the attentions of Mosby. . . . He started getting rough with her . . . he beat her up with his gun. Then she took something out of a little bottle she carried on her waist and she died.

"We undressed her to wash the blood out of her clothes. Then we took the body out to the moving van. That's all I know about her. . . .

"I'm sorry I hit her. After all, she was my guest. She was very abusive."[3]

The *Chicago Tribune* described the woman's murder as the "sequel of a moonshine orgy."[4] The *Tribune* also reported a different sort of sequel to a different sort of drunken murder:

"CORONER'S JURY EXCUSES MAN'S CRIME . . . Fritz Meinhausen, who, on April 4, shot and killed Mrs. Anna Peters and also his wife, was not held criminally responsible by the coroner's jury because, quoting a portion of the verdict: 'We find from the evidence that . . . the fatal shooting was the direct result of . . . Fritz Meinhausen's intoxicated condition. We, there-

Russell Mosby

fore, do not find him criminally responsible for the death of the deceased and recommend his discharge from police custody.' "[5]

Anna Peters was a dressmaker who'd been fitting Mrs. Meinhausen for a dress. Mr. Meinhausen came home drunk. He'd mistaken the fitting for something else. That's why he shot both women.

"Police," wrote the *Tribune*, "were amazed at the verdict. . . . 'The law makes no allowance for intoxication in killings,' said Coroner Hoffman. . . . 'This verdict easily becomes the most astonishing verdict any coroner's jury has ever brought . . . during any time in office.' "[6]

Tom Roach pleaded guilty at his arraignment. Russell Mosby refused to admit anything—except helping Roach drag the woman out of their apartment. The State's Attorney's office charged Mosby with murder. Roach agreed to testify against him.

Police began searching for the dead woman's identity. The only clues they had were a postcard the woman had dropped in Roach's apartment, and Roach's story about visiting his friend, "Mrs. Blair," whom the dead woman said she knew.

The only useful information the postcard had on it was its postmark: New Haven, Connecticut. Nothing came of that. As to "Mrs. Blair": The dead woman may have known a lady with that name, but it wasn't Mrs. Blair whom Roach had visited.

Maude Correll was the woman Roach had stopped to see. Mrs. Correll told the police that she, in fact, knew the dead woman. Her name was Anna Corliss. Or was it "Corlitt"? Anyway: Anna had just been divorced. Her husband had deserted her. Mrs. Correll said Anna had rented a room from a woman named Mary Davis.

Mary Davis's neighbors said they hadn't seen Mrs. Davis for quite some time. Disappeared, they said. Gone missing. Police spent two days looking for her. When they found her, they took Mrs. Davis to the morgue and showed her the body. Mrs. Davis said she didn't know who the woman was. She sure wasn't someone named "Anna Corlitt." Mrs. Davis didn't know any "Anna Corlitt." "Annie Colwell" was the name of *her* roomer. Mrs. Davis said she hadn't seen Annie for a while. Of course, she hadn't been home too often herself. Still—she'd met Annie's mother and sister.

Police found Annie's mother and sister and took them to the morgue. Both women collapsed when they saw her body.

Three days later, Mosby confessed. One newspaper described him as a cook; one newspaper described him as a janitor; one described him as "the colored handyman of Thomas Roche."

A month passed.

Mosby and Roach repudiated their confessions. Prosecutors said they would charge both men with murder and ask that both men be executed. Since both men had confessed, there'd be no jury trial. A judge would hear their cases.

Two months passed.

Mosby went before Judge John Sullivan. "In return for pleading guilty and turning in state's evidence, Roach is expected to receive a life sentence."[7] "In a description of one of the most revolting scenes ever heard in the Criminal Court building, Roach placed the blame on Mosby, telling how the latter had beaten the woman over the head with a gun, choked her, and stamped on her prostrate body."[8]

Four days later, Judge Sullivan sentenced both men to life. They rode the "Murder Special" train, straight to Joliet that night. Manacled, under guard, at opposite ends of the same car.

Arthur Foster

6 · Arthur, Eleanor, and Kate

Eleanor. Lovely Eleanor. Blonde, dimpled, dark-eyed, and heavy-lidded, her hair in loose tresses. A prepubescent Gibson girl. Sometimes she looked her age—an eleven-year-old schoolkid, dressed in a shirtwaist, hands in her lap, hair in ringlets, topped with a big white bow. Other times, she looked as pensive, as chaste as a saint, a girl with a Botticelli face.

Otto Trostell, Eleanor's father, had died when she was five. Her mother, Kate, still wore her wedding ring. Kate worked as a night manager for Western Union; she tucked the company's little yellow pencils into every pocket and fold of her clothing; she lost or left or forgot so many of the little things that they became markers, signs of where she'd been or where she'd gone.

Kate and Eleanor now lived with Kate's sister Margaret and Margaret's husband. Kate's other married sister, Ruby, lived nearby. Their brothers, John and Fred, had families of their own, but kept watch over their sisters and their niece. Kate could leave her office at midnight, catch the late trolley, and know that Eleanor was snug in a nest of family. That's why—recently—when Kate felt "too blue" she'd stay away for a few days, even for a week, until she felt better. Her family worried—but they understood: Kate was "nervous." Nervous people had "sinking spells." They knew Kate's spells would pass. They always did.

Two months ago, in September, Kate had collapsed—fainted, faded away—while she was on a walk with Eleanor. A year before, she'd had some sort of a blackout while she was by herself, on Halstead at Sixty-ninth. Police had helped her. During the worst of her spells, Kate would talk about "ending it all." That frightened Margaret and Ruby, but they knew Kate was only talking. Kate would never leave Eleanor.

There was a man in Kate's life. A man who'd been there since they were both kids. A man Kate didn't want, had never wanted. Arthur Foster was his name.

Arthur was a strong, solid guy. One hundred and seventy-five pounds, thick as a side of beef. Not very quick, not very talkative. Smart enough, though. He chewed tobacco; smoked it when he couldn't chew. His clothes stank of it. He worked for a trucking company. Hauled ashes. The kind of man who wouldn't and couldn't be moved. A rock.

He'd loved Kate since she was sixteen. Kate was Eleanor's age when they'd met. She may not have been as beautiful back then as Eleanor was now—but there was enough of Kate, flesh, bone, and eyes, mother in daughter, for anyone to understand why Arthur had fallen in love with her. Why he was still in love with her.

Kate had said, "No," long ago. When she was eighteen, Arthur had introduced her to his friend Otto. When Kate and Otto married, Arthur had acted like a gentleman. Wished them well, kept his distance, behaved himself. Then, in 1916, Otto died.

Arthur had been in love for eight years. Holding his heart, taking shallow breaths, hoping. He began to court the widow Trostell. He became a family friend. Took Kate and little Eleanor out for drives. Bought little presents; let himself be invited for Sunday dinner, for Thanksgiving, for Christmas. In 1920, he took a deep breath and proposed. He and Kate had their picture taken; he sat, bathed and shaved, his hair just cut, dressed in a blue suit, a clean white shirt, and a nice tie, handsome, anxious, respectable. Kate stood next to him, one hand on his shoulder, her other arm, relaxed, by her side, not smiling, not frowning, calm.

Then she had a nervous breakdown. Margaret and Ruby had never liked Arthur. None of Kate's friends had ever liked him. Kate tried to keep living on her own. When that didn't work, she asked Ruby and Ruby's husband to board with her. When that didn't work, Kate moved in with Margaret.

And Arthur?

Arthur's chest exploded. He couldn't, wouldn't, didn't leave Kate alone. Once, he drove up to her house while she and Eleanor were out in the yard. He pulled a gun and chased Kate inside. Eleanor never forgot that. Once, he broke into Kate's house and shot up the place. Kate's neighbors called the police. The police arrested him. Kate didn't press charges. Once, when Kate and one of her friends from the office were standing outside, taking a break, Arthur drove up, leaned over, and asked Kate to "go riding" with him. When Kate said, "No," he walked up to her and hit her in the face. Kate's friend "asked her why she didn't tell her brother . . . Kate said she was afraid of a scandal." "Foster threatened her more than once," the woman said. ". . . Kate was afraid he would kill her."

Eighteen months of this. Then, in July 1922, Arthur began showing up at the Western Union office on Saturday nights. He'd wait outside in his car. Kate would come out at midnight, headed for the streetcar, headed home. She'd walk outside—he'd ask her if she needed a ride. She's say, "No." He'd threaten her. That went on, every Saturday night, for six months.

Then, one Saturday night, the night of December 2, Kate left work, carrying a sack of groceries for Sunday dinner. She didn't come home. The streetcar conductor on the trolley she always took remembered how odd it was, not seeing her that night.

Margaret worried; Ruby worried. Eleanor was frightened. They waited a day; they waited another. This wasn't the first time Kate hadn't come home when they'd expected her. They waited one more day, then they called the police. They were frantic. They knew. It was Arthur.

The newspapers found out. Eleanor told a *Chicago Tribune* reporter that she was offering a reward. The *Chicago Tribune* ran a photograph of Eleanor, dead center, on its back picture page. "SEEKS MOTHER Elois Mitchell offers $100 reward for return of her parent."[1] The *Tribune* printed a picture of Kate and Arthur next to the one of Eleanor. "WOMAN AND REJECTED SUITOR SOUGHT."

The story of the orphan girl searching for her widowed mother caught everyone's attention. "Everyone" included Charles Fitzmorris, the city's chief of police, John Hughes, Fitzmorris's chief of detectives, and Detective Lieutenant John Farrell, Hughes's senior investigator. These men may or may not have had sisters; they may or may not have had daughters. But a widow, an orphan, and two sisters—frightened, angry, resolute—and the loss they'd suffered stirred them. Fitzmorris, Hughes, and Farrell, and all the men they commanded, began the hunt.

Detectives detained Arthur. They didn't arrest him. They just turned him upside down and started shaking him. They discovered how heavy and thick he was. "The granite man," they called him. Arthur's indifference made Farrell very, very suspicious. Margaret and Ruby were agitated: anger and grief tormented them. Arthur just sat where they put him. He knew Kate had disappeared, he said. But he hadn't seen her since Thanksgiving. Thanksgiving? Farrell said. Yes, Thanksgiving night, Arthur answered. You ever take Kate driving? Sure, Arthur said. Kate and Eleanor. We used to go driving. Where's your car, then? asked Farrell. At my father's place. Parked in the garage behind the house. Down on South Leavitt. Parked it there—and left it; haven't driven it for days. And your truck? asked Farrell. Not my truck. I drive for Ripley Teaming. It's their truck. What do you do for Ripley? asked Farrell. Haul ashes, said Arthur. That's what I do. Haul ashes.

Farrell led two squads of detectives to the house on South Leavitt. One group examined the car; one group began to dig up the backyard. Farrell sent another squad to dig through the dump where Arthur took his loads. Ripley's records showed Arthur had dumped six loads of ashes there one day after Kate had disappeared.

Arthur's car was littered, smeared, and splattered. There were dark stains on an old lap robe in the backseat. There were more stains—splatters—on the car's running board. On the floor, Farrell's men found a brown button from a lady's coat; on the front seat, they found a little yellow Western Union pencil. Farrell sent two men to search Arthur's rented room. They found a new blue suit with stains on its right sleeve—the same sort of stains they'd found on the lap robe.

Suit and lap robe were sent to the coroner's chemist. Farrell asked Margaret and Ruby to describe the clothes Kate wore to work the night she didn't come home. Then he showed them the brown button from Arthur's car. Margaret screamed; both women fainted.

Arthur said nothing when Farrell showed him the button. Farrell had him brought to see his car. Farrell pointed at the stains and splatters. "Is that Kate Trostell's blood?" Arthur said nothing. Two weeks later—and still detained—Arthur gave an interview to a reporter from the *Chicago Daily News*. He talked about the mess in his car. "I chew tobacco when I'm driving," he said. "Sometimes I shoot wild and hit the fender."

Arthur was right about that. But the stains on the lap robe proved to be blood. Whose blood? The coroner's chemist had no way of knowing. The button and the pencil were Kate's. But they proved only that Kate had ridden with Arthur.

Farrell's second squad found nothing in the dump; the backyard at South Leavitt yielded nothing, either. Arthur's father's house was a block and a half—a long, empty block and a half—from the Ashland Avenue bridge over the Chicago Sanitary and Ship Canal. Farrell began to think that Arthur might have dumped Kate's body there. The canal flowed south from the lake. It had a current; barges and scows used it. It was as much a swamp and a sewer as a stream.

Police had held Arthur—without charging him—for three days. Arthur had just hired a lawyer. The judge, an old dog named Oscar Hebel, was more than sympathetic to the police. Hebel warned Hughes and Farrell: they had two more days; then he'd issue a writ of habeas corpus. Charge Arthur or release him.

Arthur hadn't been fed for two days; he hadn't been allowed to do more than shut his eyes before a police sergeant kicked him awake. On his first day, Arthur had answered—or at least replied to—the questions Farrell had asked him. By the second day, Arthur had stopped talking. One of Kate's friends, Dr. Edna Shaefer, was convinced that Arthur had killed Kate for her jewelry—$1,000 worth of rings, lockets, and brooches that Otto had given her. Farrell had Arthur pulled from his cell and shoved into a chair in an empty office. Dr. Shaefer walked in, carrying a Bible. She took off her coat, rolled up her sleeves, and started reading from the Book of Psalms. Arthur's lips moved silently as he repeated the words he heard, but once Shaefer finished, Arthur still had nothing to say.

No sleep, no food, threats, appeals to love, appeals to conscience, recitations of incriminating evidence—nothing cracked him. Farrell had only one tool left. A wedge that could split stone. Farrell talked to Hughes. It was midnight, verging on the third day of Arthur's detention, when Hughes sent a car to bring Eleanor to the station.

" 'You must talk to Mr. Foster,' Hughes said. 'It will be for your mother's sake. This man knows where she is. We know he knows, but we can't make him tell us. You see if you can get it out of him. . . .'

"The child trembled with fright at the thought of facing Foster, but agreed, at last, to try. She was taken into the cell where Foster sat, haggard and weary but . . . stubbornly silent . . . Foster didn't look up as Eleanor entered. He slouched in his chair, his head lowered, awaiting a new attack by detectives. Then he heard, instead of threats, the little girl's frightened appeal: 'Mr. Foster, I want my Mama. You tell me where she is. Please give me back my Mama.' "[2]

Arthur just shook his head. "I don't know where she is, honey."

"Eleanor went closer until she could look up at his face. Tears streamed down her cheeks and dropped onto Foster's clenched fists."[3] "Her long tresses tumbling about Foster's face, her arms twined tightly around his neck, and her body shaken in a paroxysm of sobs, the child begged him:

Eleanor Trostell

'Tell me,' she cried. 'You were with her that last night. You know where she is. I want my Mama. Give her back to me!' "⁴

"Foster drew back from her as if afraid. For the first time, his voice rose above the dull tones of . . . denial. 'I don't know,' he exclaimed. 'They're lying to you, Eleanor. I wasn't with your mother that night.' 'You were!' the little girl screamed. 'You killed her. You know you did!' She broke down, sobbing bitterly, and Chief Hughes led her away.

"Foster, shaken by the girl's grief, was left alone for awhile. Then, detectives led him silently to Chief Hughes's office and had him look inside. Eleanor lay asleep on a couch. Her face was swollen from crying. Dark circles showed under her eyes. Her hands and lips twitched nervously.

" 'You're killing this little girl,' they said. 'Her heart is broken. Worry over her mother is making her sick. She'll die unless you tell the truth.'

"Half an hour later, Foster confessed. 'She's in the Canal,' he said. 'She jumped in.' 'Where?' demanded Farrell. 'Where the bridge is, on Ashland.' "[5]

"Show me," Farrell said. Detectives took Arthur to the bridge. " 'This is the spot,' Foster said. 'She jumped out . . . while we were driving.' "[6]

Wooden stairs, thick with ice, led down from the street to an old shack. Bill Scott, a former county commissioner, ran the place as a saloon. A wharf led to the canal. High weeds bordered it on both sides. Four old scows sat anchored, under the bridge. There were a few old shacks, here and there, in the distance, but no one lived in them.

Detectives followed Arthur down the stairs, then through the weeds to the bank of the canal. "That's where she jumped in," Arthur said. "I couldn't help her. That's the last I saw of her."[7]

Fitzmorris ordered a harbormaster's tug to take him and Hughes to the spot at dawn. Squads of police and detectives began the search as their commanders watched and issued orders.

The temperature was close to zero. Ice bobbed in the yellow water. The sky was lit by bursts of flaming methane, vented from refinery chimneys. Huge gas storage tanks stood, far off, in clusters.

Hours passed. Arthur had been taken back to his cell and allowed to sleep. More men—city workers and policemen—joined the search. Tugboats, flat boats, men with pikes and poles and draglines—all searched for Kate's body. They found nothing. Someone reported finding a yellow pencil stub; someone reported seeing the imprint of a shoe—all wishful thinking.

Shortly after noon, a police sergeant kicked Arthur awake and brought him to Hughes. "Are you sure the body is in the Canal where you said it was?" Hughes asked.

Fred Mitchell, Kate's older brother, joined the search. He stood watch on the wharf near Scott's saloon; sometimes he joined a crew, probing the muck with a pike. "I don't know where Kate's body is," he said, "but there is no doubt in my mind that she is dead and that Foster killed her. He threatened her time after time . . . when he was drunk; he said that he would kill her and throw her body in the Canal."[8]

Two night watchmen for the Santa Fe railroad told police they'd heard a woman screaming, before dawn, on December 3. They said the screams had lasted on and off for four minutes. "We didn't get there in time to see what caused the screams, but we did hear an automobile speeding away."[9]

The problem was that the men had stood watch along the tracks at Thirty-fifth and Kedzie—more than a mile south of the Ashland bridge, where Arthur had led Farrell and his men.

"Are you sure the body is in the Canal where you said?" Chief Hughes asked Arthur.

Arthur reconsidered.

He changed his story.

Kate was sick and depressed—"despondent and in ill health," he said. "Because of a recent operation," he said.[10] That's why she killed herself, he said. Arthur gave Hughes the name of the doctor and the midwife who'd performed the abortion. "Squads of police were sent to find those named by Foster."[11]

"As God is my judge," Arthur said, "Kate jumped into the river. . . . She jumped in after a quarrel. . . . I couldn't save her. I didn't kill her. . . . I'm not afraid to die. Give me some wire and I'll hang myself."[12] Arthur said he'd spend his last paycheck—$28—all the money he had—to buy flowers for Kate's funeral. If and when anyone ever found her.

A day passed.

No one—no reporter, no detective, no coroner, no lawyer—not even Arthur—mentioned Kate's abortion again. Kate's fainting in September, while she'd been out on a walk with Eleanor—had that been a sign of anything other than her frailty? No one asked, no one speculated, no one answered the question: "If Kate had had an abortion, who was the father of the child?" No one asked how or why Arthur knew the names—never published—of the doctor and midwife who may (or may not) have performed the abortion. No police detective and no reporter asked if the abortion that Kate (may have) had led to the quarrel that—Arthur said—caused Kate's suicide.

Instead, one day after Arthur said he wanted to hang himself, he gave an interview to the *Chicago Daily News.* Two police detectives sat in the room while he spoke.

Arthur denied he'd ever confessed. He'd never said anything about anything to Hughes. "The bunk," he said. It was all nonsense.

Kate throwing herself in the canal?

"I don't know where she is," Arthur said. "I'm not even sure she's dead. About two months ago, while we were crossing the Ashland Avenue bridge, she told me she had half a mind to drown herself there. That's all I know about it."

What about all those stories—all those reports—about him threatening Kate? Pulling a gun? Chasing her into her house? Firing shots?

"That's all bunk," Arthur said. "I never fired shots at her in my life."

Didn't they have their "ups and downs," though?

Sure, Arthur said. But he'd seen Kate Thanksgiving Day. He'd taken Kate and Eleanor out for a ride. "She was in good spirits," Arthur said. "As friendly as ever. We didn't have a single unpleasant word. . . .

"Other times, though, she acted blue. Ever since her breakdown, she was despondent. She talked about killing herself—but I didn't pay much attention. I thought she was just 'down in the mouth.' . . .

"That's how I got the idea she might have drowned herself in the Canal. She told me she had half a mind to jump over the . . . bridge. So I told the cops to look there. I didn't confess anything because I don't have anything to confess. See?"[13]

Two days later, searchers pulled a woman's coat and hat from the canal. Hughes rushed to the spot. Judge Hebel put Fitzmorris on notice: Police had one more day to find evidence of murder. A police explosives expert briefed Hughes about the use of dynamite to bring bodies to the surface. Searchers found Kate's pocketbook the following day. Her Western Union ID card and her bankbook were in it. Margaret burst into tears when Hughes showed her the pocketbook. Judge Hebel extended his deadline: one more day.

It was December 18. Arthur had been held since December 6. Fitzmorris asked the sheriff of Cook County to take custody of his prisoner. Fitzmorris and the sheriff planned a legal shell game: they'd shift Arthur from one jurisdiction to another; each shift would reset Hebel's clock. Hebel found out and stopped their game. It didn't matter whose jail cell Arthur occupied: December 19 was the date of Arthur's habeas corpus hearing.

"If Judge Hebel will not help us," Fitzmorris told a reporter, "I'll call State's Attorney Crowe . . . to determine what steps we can take. . . ." Crowe had been waiting for the call. A dead widow, a pretty little orphan, two grieving sisters, a foul-smelling brute—Crowe was pleased to be seen helping Fitzmorris do his job.

City workers began carting dynamite to the canal. Hughes said he'd dynamite all thirty-five miles of it, down to Lockport, if he had to. Crews set off their first charges at dawn on the day Hebel convened Arthur's hearing.

Arthur's attorney began by asking Arthur to take off his jacket, pull up his shirt, and turn around. "That lump you see on Mr. Foster's back, Your Honor, is the result of police beating my client while in custody." Hughes and Farrell testified next. They said that the blood in Arthur's car, the recovery of Kate's pocketbook from the canal, and Arthur's statement that he'd been present at the time of Kate's alleged suicide—all argued against Hebel issuing a writ. Hebel acknowledged the strong "circumstance of the evidence." No matter: he ordered the county to release Arthur in four days. Police had permission to continue to question Arthur. Hebel's deadline was real.

December 20, December 21, December 22, December 23. Laborers, tugboats, and dynamite: they found nothing but an old whiskey barrel. Hughes decided to use Eleanor again. He brought her to Arthur's cell. She rushed to him. "Please, Mr. Foster, bring me back my Mama. Bring her back for Christmas." Arthur picked up Eleanor and kissed her. She let him. "I'd like to, honey," he said, "but I don't know anything about her." Hughes showed Kate's pocketbook to him; Arthur looked at it as if it were a tin plate or a stool. Eleanor wept. "I don't know anything," Arthur said. He thought for a minute. "Maybe she ran off to be married to someone else."

State's Attorney Crowe offered Fitzmorris some legal advice. The result:

On the day of Arthur's release, Kate's sister Ruby swore out a murder warrant against him. Guards escorted Arthur from his cell. He stood before Judge Hebel. Hebel ordered his release, then immediately accepted Ruby's warrant for his arrest. Guards marched Arthur back to his cell. Arthur's attorney made a motion to dismiss Ruby's warrant. He told reporters he hoped Arthur would "eat Christmas dinner at home."[14]

Christmas Eve.

Hughes had Arthur driven to Ruby's house. Detectives walked Arthur up the steps and into the living room. Christmas at home. A fire, crackling in the grate; the smell of baking in the air; a tree, strung with garlands, hung with ornaments. Presents. And—little Eleanor. Tearful, lovely little Eleanor. She wept and pleaded. "Tell me where my Mama is," she cried. "I wish I did know," Arthur said. He took Eleanor in his arms. She let him. "Maybe she's run away with some fellow," he said. Detectives drove him back to jail.

While this was going on, a young man whom no one knew walked into an ice cream parlor in Oak Park. People looked up as the little bells on the door jingled. The young man stood still and then, as everyone was returning to their sodas and ice creams, he said, in a calm, clear voice just loud enough for everyone to hear, "I've just swallowed four grams of strychnine. I'm going to kill myself. Good-bye."

He collapsed. Someone called the police. An ambulance took him to the hospital. Doctors pumped his stomach. They thought he might live.

Christmas came.

Eleanor spent the day on the banks of the canal, shivering and flinching as crews exploded their charges.

Late in the afternoon, the young man who'd swallowed the strychnine regained consciousness. A police officer from Oak Park leaned over and asked him his name. "John Shippie," the young man whispered. He motioned the officer to come closer. He could barely speak. The officer thought he was about to hear some sort of deathbed confession. He was right. Almost.

"Arthur Foster . . ." whispered the young man, ". . . told me . . . he killed Mrs. Trostell. I saw her body . . . in his car. He said he'd kill me if I talked. I was afraid. That's why . . . I tried to kill myself."

Hughes didn't know any of this until the next day. That's why he had Eleanor picked up from Ruby's house, late on the night of Christmas Day. Eleanor was still all Hughes had. He asked her help. She didn't refuse.

Arthur's attorney had bought him a Christmas dinner and had it delivered to him in his cell. Arthur was feeling better than he'd felt in weeks. That may be why he didn't crack when Eleanor walked in again. She pleaded with him until daybreak. Sometimes he'd shrug; sometimes he'd answer her. She'd fling herself at him, snuggle into his lap, twine her arms around his neck, plead and pull at him and cry. Arthur kept chewing his tobacco. Sometimes he'd chew a little faster. Sometimes he'd turn his head away and squirt some juice on the floor. Hughes had Eleanor bundled up and taken home.

Oak Park police called Hughes with John Shippie's story. Judge John Haas had just ordered Arthur to be evaluated by the city's Psychopathic Laboratory. Dr. William Hickson—the same man who'd evaluated Carl Wanderer and Harvey Church—was asked to test Arthur's sanity and IQ. The call from Oak Park came in soon after that. Hughes immediately sent a message to Judge Haas. "John Shippie's amazing confession has caused Judge Haas to override the protest of Arthur Foster's attorney and order the suspect held until January 11."[15]

This was Shippie's story:

"I've known Foster for about two months," Shippie said. His voice was weak. Doctors had cautioned police not to press him. Shippie would pause, close his eyes, take a few breaths, then resume his story. "That Sunday

night," he said, "we arranged a party. My girl—I'll never tell her name—
Foster and Mrs. Trostell. . . . We met Mrs. Trostell and Foster . . . he was
driving his car. . . . We drove to Scott's saloon. . . . We stayed there a short
time. . . . Then Foster drove us to North Clark and Superior. . . . I dropped
my girl off. . . . The three of us continued driving around. . . . I got out
and bought a pint of whiskey in a Greek saloon. I gave Foster a drink and
arranged to meet him at 10:30. . . . Foster arrived on time—I climbed into
his car. . . . I saw Mrs. Trostell huddled in the rear seat and . . . I thought
she was asleep. Foster startled me. . . . 'Kate is dead and I've got to put
away the body'. . . . I was terror stricken. . . . Foster saw me shudder . . . he
became hard. 'You've got to help me and you've got to keep your mouth
shut or I'll fix you so you'll never talk again.'

"I kept thinking about how I could get away. . . . I figured that if I could
get out of the car and go into some store, I could sneak out the back. . . .
I told Foster I wanted cigarettes . . . he let me out . . . I ran up an alley. I
never saw Foster again."[16]

The next day, Shippie said, a man he knew only by the name of Howard
sent him a message. Foster was prepared to pay him hush money. Howard
would deliver it. Shippie agreed to a meeting, but he knew it was a trap.
"I knew Howard would lead me to some secluded spot where he would
shoot me."[17]

Police brought Arthur to see Shippie. The Psychopathic Lab's Dr. Hickson had finished his tests and was writing his report. Oak Park doctors
had sedated Shippie with ether. Arthur was told to stand by Shippie's door
and wait for him to open his eyes. Nurses, doctors, police officers, detectives—Arthur was the only one in the crowd wearing handcuffs. Shippie
opened his eyes, propped himself up on his elbows, and looked at Arthur.
"That's Foster," he cried. "I saw Kate's body on the rear seat of his car at
Thirty-first and State on the night of December 2."

Sniffing ether usually didn't clarify a patient's memory the way it had
Shippie's.

"That man is raving," Arthur said. "I've never seen him in my life."

Farrell talked to reporters in the hall outside Shippie's room. He was as
unimpressed with the young man as Arthur. First of all: Kate hadn't left
work until midnight. Second: Shippie wasn't who he said he was. Shippie
had told reporters that he was the nephew of Chicago's recently deceased,
former police chief, George Shippy. He also said he was the nephew of the
mayor of Cambridge, Massachusetts, where he'd attended two elite private

day schools—the Roberts School and the English High School. Police knew otherwise: Shippie had been a clerk in a steel mill in Leaf River. Three months ago, he'd stood up during a stage show at a theater in the Loop and announced that he was about to kill himself. He'd swallowed something, then collapsed. Police came; an ambulance was called. Doctors examined him. He hadn't taken poison. They asked him a few questions, then transferred him to the city's Psychopathic Hospital. A staff psychiatrist evaluated him. "He was suffering from a mental ailment which made him think he was the key figure in every big murder mystery."[18]

The police's first—and only—eyewitness was insane. According to Dr. Hickson, so was Arthur. Hickson's report was very brief. Perhaps because he remembered the effect his evaluation of Carl Wanderer and Harvey Church had had on their cases.

"In reference to the case of Arthur Foster, 33 years old: Our examination shows that his case, on the intelligence side, is one of a high grade moron, and, on the affective side, to be afflicted with dementia praecox katatonia."[19]

Kate's body surfaced at the Lockport, Illinois, dam, on the Sanitary and Ship Canal, on January 23. Men who worked at the dam's power plant

Three men at Lockport dam, Sanitary and Ship Canal

spotted it in an eddy and brought it ashore with poles and hooks. There was a Western Union pay envelope with Kate's name on it in her pocket. Diamond rings on her left hand and a locket confirmed her identity.

Eleanor had been living with her uncle John and his family since Kate disappeared. Two nights before Kate's body surfaced, she'd appeared to Eleanor in a dream. "Where are you, mother?" Eleanor asked. "I don't know," Kate said. "Ask Foster."

Hughes sent Farrell to John Mitchell's house. "Oh, where is she?" Eleanor cried. "I want to see her. Why doesn't she come?" Her uncle John said it was a very good thing Foster hadn't been set loose—otherwise something bad might have happened to him. "There might have been another murder soon," John said. "I'll get him if police don't," Eleanor cried. "I want him to hang."

Hughes sent a police car to bring Kate's sisters and one of her neighbors to Lockport to identify the body. "It's Kate," Margaret said. "Her face is not changed except for the marks on her forehead. I'll see that Foster hangs for this if I have to spend the rest of my life doing it. . . ."

The bruises on Kate's forehead had hemorrhaged. There were marks on the back of Kate's right hand, caused, said Hughes, by "her attempt to shield her face." The marks on Kate's forehead, above her right eye, had been the result of a "terrific blow," said coroner's physician Dr. Joseph Springer. "The wound above the eye was distinctly discolored," said Springer. "That proves, conclusively, that it was inflicted before death." The blow had been powerful but not fatal. Kate went into the water, bloody, but alive. Her body had water in its lungs. Kate had drowned. "Foster can explain those bruises," Margaret said. "I am certain they were made when he took her into his automobile on the night she disappeared. She wouldn't have gone with him otherwise."

Fitzmorris and Hughes knew they now had enough evidence to convene a coroner's jury. From coroner's jury to grand jury—Arthur was headed to trial.

Crowe sent Edgar A. Jones, his "First Assistant State's Attorney," to present the case against Foster. Before the hearing, Hughes had Arthur, handcuffed to a deputy sheriff, led to the bier where Kate's body lay. Arthur flinched and pulled away. "Whose body is it?" asked coroner's physician Springer. "I can't tell," Arthur said.

Farrell was the state's first witness. He described the seven-week search he'd led. Kate's friend from work Katherine Whallon took the stand next.

Jones asked her to describe Kate's relationship with Arthur. "She lived in mortal dread of him," Whallon said. "She once spoke of leaving Chicago to escape Foster. She said she disliked openly fighting him for fear her brothers would make trouble and she would lose her job." Whallon described how Arthur would pull up next to them while they were walking. How he once threatened Kate's life unless she got in his car. How Kate would come to work with welts and bruises on her face. Once, Kate told her, Arthur had beaten her with a gun butt; once he'd punched her and "cracked her jaw open."

Eleanor testified next. She talked about the time Arthur pulled a gun and chased Kate into the house. She described all the times Arthur had frightened, and threatened, and hurt her mother. Eleanor shook her fist at Arthur. "You know you killed my mother, Art. You know you did." Eleanor walked over and glared at him. Arthur flinched and turned pale.

Ruby and Margaret followed Eleanor to the stand. "I just ask that this dog of a murderer be given justice," Ruby cried.

Arthur's attorney, John Byrne (the man who'd sent Arthur that Christmas dinner), "made such strenuous objection"—insisted so vehemently that he be allowed to cross-examine witnesses—"that Deputy Coroner Kennedy finally ordered him" to leave the hearing room. Byrne refused. Police officers threw him out.

The coroner's jury took five minutes to reach a verdict. "From the evidence heard, we conclude that the violence was committed and the body was thrown into the canal by one Arthur Foster. We, the jury, recommend that Foster be held to the grand jury on the charge of murder."

Arthur had refused to testify during the hearing. Now, he sat silently and puffed on his cigar. "His hand trembled; but he gave no other sign."[20]

"It is clear to my mind," Hughes told reporters, "that Foster met Mrs. Trostell the night she disappeared; the two quarreled, he knocked her senseless, and then flung her body into the Canal. We have a hanging case against him, despite his denials."

Arthur pleaded not guilty. Byrne had advised him to do that. "They've got nothing on me," Arthur said. He spoke to reporters. It was Kate's family, he said, its constant bickering and backbiting, that had driven Kate crazy. "I don't know anything about what happened to Kate. I was at home on the night she disappeared and I have three witnesses to prove it. I told the police she was in the river because I'd heard her say, repeatedly, that she was going to kill herself that way. . . . Kate was a nervous wreck. It wasn't today or yesterday that she started to talk about killing herself.

She had trouble with her two sisters most of the time since I've known her—and that was most of her life. . . . The bickering had been going on, continuously. . . . The burden of that family was always on Kate's shoulders. It was that that killed her—not any act of mine. Little Eleanor knows how unhappy her mother was. She'd admit it if her mind hadn't been poisoned against me."[21]

The grand jury indicted Arthur two weeks later.

"Eleanor Trostell, the fourteen-year-old daughter of the dead woman," was the principal witness against Arthur.[22]

Eleanor—the avenger. From orphan child to vengeful adolescent in only two months. By the time Arthur's trial began in May 1923, the *Chicago Daily News* decided Eleanor was really thirteen. Did the papers have such bad reporters and such inattentive editors that they'd consistently misrepresented Eleanor's age?

Maybe Eleanor—and Margaret and Ruby and Fred and John—had decided not to tell people how old Eleanor really was. Maybe the papers just made a mistake—the way they'd first called Eleanor "Elois." They'd quickly corrected her name, though.

For weeks, as police searched the canal and the papers reported every visit Eleanor made to Arthur in his cell—all the tears, the tresses, the hugs, the cuddling, and the pleading—Eleanor remained an eleven-year-old orphan child. The effect Eleanor sensed—and the police knew—she had on Arthur involved more than guilt. When the police began using Eleanor to crack Arthur, she was almost the same age Kate had been when Arthur had first met her. Chief of Detectives Hughes convinced Eleanor to talk to Arthur, but Eleanor did more than talk to him. Sitting on his lap, wrapping her arms around his neck, letting him kiss her—that went beyond the call of duty.

Arthur was whipsawed between guilt, fear, tenderness, and longing. Why didn't he incriminate himself? Why didn't he break?

Perhaps because anger and fear were stronger than guilt and remorse. Perhaps because Kate had actually jumped into the canal. Pursued by him, beaten by him, stalked by him—but not thrown into the water by him. Arthur's aggression, combined with the emotional and physical damage caused by a (possible) abortion, had broken Kate. She jumped because she'd been pushed.

The other possibility was the one described by Hughes: Arthur had beaten Kate unconscious then thrown her off the bridge. Struck her so hard because the child she (may have) aborted was (or even worse: wasn't) his. Thrown her into the canal to deceive police. Kate was suicidal, wasn't she?

Arthur was culpable and he was guilty. Guilty of what, though?

Crowe's office decided Arthur was guilty of murder. Not manslaughter. Murder.

None of the state's witnesses had seen Arthur kill Kate.

Worse yet: When Arthur went to trial in May 1923, Judge Jacob Hopkins quickly ruled that the bloodstains, the button, and the pencil that Farrell's men found when they'd searched Arthur's car and room were not admissible.

The state did have the evidence of Kate's body—its bloody marks and bruises and the water in its lungs. It also had the two watchmen who'd heard a woman's screams the night Kate died.

Margaret and Ruby, Kate's coworker, and Kate's neighbor—all testified about Arthur's abuse of Kate. Eleanor was the state's star witness. She wept; she accused. The jury melted.

Arthur's lead attorney, Everett Jennings (Byrne stayed on; no reporter ever explained how a man who hauled ashes could afford two attorneys), acknowledged that Arthur had been cruel to Kate. Cruel, relentless, brutal. Arthur was guilty of assaulting Kate, guilty of threatening and harassing her. All true. But all in the past. No one had seen Arthur murder Kate. In fact: Kate had talked openly about killing herself. Talked about it for some time. No one could deny that Kate was suicidal. As to Kate's bruises: the canal was full of chunks of ice the night she'd died. If she'd jumped from the Ashland bridge—as she'd often talked of doing—she'd probably been injured when she hit the ice as she hit the water.

Assistant State's Attorney Sam Hamilton brushed aside Jennings's arguments like a man sweeping crumbs off a table.

"Just put yourself in the place of that poor woman," he said. "See in your mind the way she tried to save herself by hanging to the side of the automobile from which Foster was trying to push her into the muddy water of the Canal. Foster asked her to go for an auto ride and, when he got in the vicinity of the Canal, he picked her up in his arms and shoved her through the door of the car.

"She clung to the side of the car. He hammered her fingers to make her lose her grasp; when she could hang on no longer, he gave her a mighty push and she fell. A loud splash resounded in the night as the body hit the dirty water and went under. Foster waited for a moment or so and then drove back to his home.

"What should be the penalty of the crime? Hanging by the neck until dead."[23]

The jury took ninety minutes to decide that Arthur had murdered Kate and should hang for it.

"The verdict was a surprise even to the state as rulings made by the court had barred from the record much of the evidence upon which it had hoped a conviction would be obtained."[24]

Arthur didn't move or blink or sigh when he heard the verdict. Everett Jennings immediately entered a motion for a new trial. Arthur looked bored.

Crowe called a press conference. "Two months ago," he said, "I ordered my Assistants to strike with all their might at murderers." Eight men had been brought to justice since then: a thief who'd killed a policeman; two crooks who'd murdered another crook; a robber who'd shot a cigar store clerk; a man who'd shot and killed a cabdriver; a man who'd murdered the wife of a traveling salesman. And now, Arthur Foster. "It is a record," Crowe proclaimed, "an achievement that will call a halt to killing in this city."

Two months passed.

Judge Hopkins agreed to hear arguments on Jennings's motion for a new trial. At issue: Was Arthur a murderer or just "the innocent victim of an insidious net of circumstances"? Was the state's circumstantial evidence sufficient to hang him?

The papers reported the hearing as if it were only a bit less consequential than the Lincoln-Douglas debates.

"There is not the slightest evidence to prove that Arthur Foster threw Mrs. Trostell into the Canal," Jennings argued as Hopkins listened. "You cannot substitute the ingenuity and genius of the State's Attorney for evidence." Sam Hamilton countered with a list of legal precedents—convictions based on circumstantial evidence that had been appealed, then upheld by the State Supreme Court. Hamilton was as circumspect as he'd once been impassioned. Jennings was as emotional as he'd once been restrained. The *Chicago Tribune* reported that the hearing was attracting an unusual amount of legal attention: "It may prove a precedent, many attorneys say, for many another [case] to follow."[25]

Judge Hopkins announced his decision three days later: "I cannot send a man to the gallows on mere suspicion. I believe Foster might have thrown Mrs. Trostell into the canal. I suspect he might have killed her. But

Arthur Foster

there is no one to say that the scream that came from the canal was uttered by Mrs. Trostell. There was nobody who saw Foster with her.

"The [State] Supreme Court undoubtedly would reverse the case on some pretext or other. The Supreme Court does not send men to the gallows when there is doubt as to their guilt. Therefore I sustain the motion for a new trial."[26]

Arthur smiled when he heard that. Guards took him back to his cell.

He was released on $15,000 bail eight months later. (Equivalent to $150,000 today.) The papers didn't report who put up the money.

In October 1926, the State's Attorney's office filed a motion to strike Arthur's case from the trial docket. Judge Hopkins accepted the motion.

Arthur walked.

Logan Square Trust and Savings Bank

7 · The Banker

A mailman found Fred Popp, late in the afternoon, slumped over the wheel of his car. Mr. Popp's custom was to go to the bank, his bank, the Logan Square Trust and Savings Bank, first thing in the morning. He'd review accounts, conduct business, then leave to keep appointments. The day he died, he came to the bank as he usually did—but instead of driving to the Loop for a meeting, he drove to a little park, so far south and so far west of the city it was almost in Cicero. He turned onto a stretch of dirt road, found a nice quiet place, and pulled over. Then he blew his brains out.

He didn't leave a note. The only thing the coroner found in Mr. Popp's pockets was a checkbook—$61,000[1] worth of canceled checks, ranging from $5,000 to $20,000, had been carefully pasted back onto their stubs. The checks had been drawn on an account that Mr. Popp's oldest son, Paul, the cashier[2] of Logan Trust, had opened in his own name at a bank in St. Louis. Nearly every check had been filled out by Paul; every one of them had been payable to him; every one of them had been endorsed by him.

The coroner was certain Mr. Popp's death was a suicide, but the checkbook with its pasted stubs made him wonder.

Mr. Popp had lived a rags-to-riches, Horatio Alger kind of life. He'd begun as a mailman, working a route so sparsely settled that he needed a horse and a cart to get around. Needed a horse and a cart—but couldn't afford them. The route he trudged, from house to distant house, slowly became more settled, and as it became more settled, Mr. Popp bought land. He bought it and sold it; bought more and built houses on it; sold and bought and built and sold. The neighborhood became the Logan Square neighborhood, and Mr. Popp grew rich. Thirty years after Mr. Popp delivered his first letter, thirty-two years after he'd met and married his sweetheart, Mary Wheeler, Logan Square Trust and Savings Bank was about to open

Henry S. Savage

the doors of its new $300,000 headquarters—an iron-gated, four-columned, white marble monument to prosperity, and to the hard work and good sense that had produced it.

A day after Mr. Popp's body was identified, the state's bank examiner, Henry Savage, a plump, balding, middle-aged man with French cuffs and manicured hands, closed Logan Trust to examine its books. The audit report that Logan had sent to the state auditor in 1922 showed everything to be in order: deposits of $2.4 million; total number of individual savings and checking accounts: 15,000. Logan reported it held bonds and securities valued at almost $700,000; it had outstanding loans totaling $1.6 million.

Late in 1922, soon after the bank had made its report, a gang of five well-dressed thieves robbed the bank of $19,000. Mr. Savage quickly discovered that the bank had so many nonperforming loans on its books, and so many worthless stocks and bonds in its safe, that it was a wonder the thieves had found any cash to steal. Worse yet, Logan's officers were stockholders in the same deadbeat companies that had received loans from the bank; the stock certificates and bonds in Logan's safe were issued by the same fly-by-night corporations in which Logan's officers had invested. "Unlisted stocks and bonds of undetermined value" was the way Mr. Savage described the mess he found. "Bad paper" were the words State's Attorney Crowe used when he read Mr. Savage's report.

Mr. Popp's body was still aboveground when Crowe's assistant state's attorneys began questioning the bank's vice president, David Wiederman. Wiederman was a big, bluff, hail-fellow-well-met, ex–football star, a former Army captain who'd been Mr. Popp's second in command—his executive officer in charge of all operations. Paul Popp also had some explaining to do: he was the one responsible for the 1922 fairy tale the bank had sent to the state auditor. He was also the one whose name appeared on the front and back of the checks his father had carried to his death.

David Wiederman hid behind his lawyer. Paul talked to Crowe's assistant state's attorneys.

His father, said Paul, had been an investor in Logan for many years. In 1920, Logan found itself "overextended": the depression that followed World War I affected the bank—its loans and investments—as it had affected everyone. Fred Popp had money when no one else did. He bought more and more shares of Logan's capital stock, and along with Paul, and Paul's new brother-in-law, Albert, the Popp family became Logan Trust's majority shareholders. Fred Popp became Logan's president; Paul became the bank's cashier and one of its directors; Albert became a "bank executive." David Wiederman traded stock he owned in other companies to buy a big block of Logan Trust's capital stock. Stock trading made Wiederman Logan's vice president.

The trouble began.

Mr. Popp had made his money in real estate. He admitted he didn't know much about stocks—but, fortunately, his new vice president did. (Wiederman had been the director of another bank—Stoney Island Trust. Stoney

David Wiederman, Jr., vice president, Logan Square Trust and Savings Bank

Island's president, William Scott, was also the director of a brokerage firm. Scott's firm had a reputation for selling nothing but "bad paper." Scott himself was forced to resign from Stoney Island because of his personal use of bank funds.) Popp relied on Wiederman for stock advice. Wiederman recommended nothing but dogs and deadbeats.

One of Wiederman's favorites was a company called Lower California Fisheries. Fred Popp, Paul Popp, and Logan Trust bought into it. Since the company was based in Los Angeles, Mr. Popp began to travel there. He

June Bacon and her lawyer, Charles Erbstein

took the train—a "fine, fast, super fine, highclass train," the Golden State, run by the Rock Island Line/Southern Pacific Railroad. "Half the train is devoted to the comfort of the business traveler." "Two days, three nights." "Saves a whole Business Day."

Which is how, on board that train, Mr. Popp met June Bacon. Bright, beautiful, blonde June. Born in South Bend, Indiana—but born for finer things. June sang. Sang in big hotels in Chicago. Was on her way to sing in big hotels in L.A. Two days, three nights. On board the Golden State.

Mr. Popp made several more trips to L.A. during the next year. He became a member of Lower California Fisheries' board of directors. June began to call him "daddy." He bought her "the biggest diamond in Chicago." June came back to the city to try it on—and stayed. She had a "wonderfully rich soprano voice." She also had "artistic ambitions." Grand opera was her destiny. An artist like June needed a patron. In fact, as one of June's friends later said, "June was genuinely fond of Mr. Popp." That's why she didn't say no when Mr. Popp offered to build her a house. "A regular palace,"[3] according to one of June's other friends. "Just a comfortable place for an artistic working girl to live" was how the mother of another acquaintance described it. In fact, it was more than comfortable. Visitors might enter through its arched and columned front door, but June came and went through a tunnel that Mr. Popp had thoughtfully built between the house and its two-car garage.[4] June said that Mr. Popp had dug the tunnel so she could run errands without "soiling her satin pumps." Mr. Popp used the tunnel whenever he visited her. June began to talk about her "millionaire daddy," but not one of her neighbors recalled ever seeing Mr. Popp as he came and went.

Mr. Popp paid for everything: the house and the car, the Persian rugs and the velvet drapes; the library with its grand piano and all its books; the wicker furniture for the sun parlor; the damask chairs, mirrors, and chaises for the boudoir; the maids (first a Swedish one, then a French one, then an African-American one); the voice lessons; the fur coats; the dresses and the gowns.

The money traveled underground: from Mr. Popp to the bank in St. Louis, from the bank in St. Louis to Paul, from Paul back to his father. Paul was forced to explain this to one of Mr. Crowe's investigators, but when a newspaper reporter asked Paul, he said, "I don't wish to talk about that. I wish that could be kept out of the papers."[5] Ten thousand dollars was the last sum that Paul passed to his father, but Mr. Popp had begun to bestow more than gifts on June: several months before he died, Mr. Popp gave June a piece of real estate worth $100,000. The land was a dowry present. Mr. Popp was fifty-three, and June—June might have been thirty.[6] Mr. Popp wanted to marry her.

There were two, unexpected problems: the more time Mr. Popp spent with June, the less time and attention he devoted to Logan Trust. David Wiederman began to loot the place. By the time Mr. Popp was dead and

State's Attorney Crowe had begun asking questions, Wiederman had embezzled $56,000. On several occasions, he forged the names of depositors,[7] then signed the notes over to himself. He used the money to pay off stocks he'd bought on margin. On another occasion, he simply walked out of the bank with $20,000 worth of securities in his briefcase. He used the stock as collateral for a personal loan.

Mr. Popp found out about all this a few days before he shot himself. He'd also found out something else: three months before he died, Mr. Popp discovered that June had a boyfriend. A boyfriend who was with June whenever Mr. Popp wasn't. The last of June's succession of maids tattled on her.

The boyfriend's name was Frank Wolzny. He also went by the name of Ross Miller. Frank/Ross listed the Sher-Lak Hotel as his residence. When Mr. Crowe's investigators questioned him, Frank said he'd once met a man named Ross Miller—but he didn't know him very well. Frank said he'd met Ross at June Bacon's house. Frank admitted he visited June often. There was nothing wrong with that, was there? After all, he and June were engaged. As for Mr. Popp, the dead banker, Frank said he didn't know him, had never met him. He said he was surprised to learn that Mr. Popp had given June everything she owned.

June's maid told a different story:

"Mr. Frank Wolzny . . . was Miss Bacon's 'sweetie.' He was there every evening when Mr. Popp was not. . . . He would call me up to find out if 'the coast was clear'. . . . Mr. Popp told me that those two, Miss Bacon and Wolzny, were trying to get money out of him. I overheard Miss Bacon say to Frank to let her handle it. . . .

"One time, Frank and Miss Bacon were talking and Frank said he needed money. Fred Popp said he would not give up any money . . . he paid all the bills. He kicked about the fine rugs and the draperies, but after he got a cussing from Miss Bacon he paid. . . .

"Frank and Miss Bacon were constantly after Mr. Popp for money. . . . Mr. Popp told me that they were after large sums from him, but that he would confess to his wife and quit them. I believe Mr. Popp tried to make a settlement with them.

"I was between two fires. Mr. Popp insisted I tell him everything that took place when he was not there, and Frank insisted I tell on Mr. Popp. . . .

"Frank and Miss Bacon used to fight and quarrel about Mr. Popp . . . Mr. Popp told me he was so worried about the fix he was in, he wished to tell his wife all—even if it broke him up—and go to California.

"That Bacon woman bled Mr. Popp constantly for money until he could stand it no longer. . . ."[8]

Instead of confessing to his wife and going to California, Mr. Popp decided to stay in town—and to start going out with one of June's friends, a "piquant brunette" named Clair Heilman.

Depending on who was asked and when they answered, Clair's relationship with June was either close or distant. "I was one of June's best friends," Clair said. They'd met in South Bend; they'd known each other since they were teenagers. "My daughter was never a good friend of June's," Clair's mother said. Clair's mother spoke to reporters a few days after Mr. Popp died. Clair herself had left town, as fast as she could. Headed to California. Maybe. "Clair hardly knew June in South Bend. Not that I ever saw or heard anything, but, well, you know how a mother feels. . . . I was never anxious for Clair to run around with her."[9]

Everyone agreed that June had introduced Clair to Mr. Popp back in 1921. Times were tough in South Bend. June invited Clair to visit her in Chicago. A year later, Clair and her mother and her sister moved to Chicago. Mr. Popp found them a nice apartment near Logan Square.

No one could agree about what Clair did before she came to Chicago, or what she did once she moved to town. Some people said she'd been a manicurist; some people said she'd been a masseuse. Clair's neighbors in Chicago said she used to give massages to "masculine patients in her own home, and occasionally was importuned to give a treatment at a patient's home."[10] None of the neighbors approved of all the men who came and went, or all the fancy cars that pulled in and pulled out in front of the building. The neighbors complained. The landlord said there was nothing he could do: Mr. Popp had vouched for Clair and her family.

Clair's mother said that Clair was "just a home girl . . . who had even given up the idea of becoming a manicurist because it wasn't up to her class."[11] It was true, Clair's mother said, that Clair had, occasionally, gone out with June and Mr. Popp when they visited clubs at night. They'd all been friends; Mr. Popp had been a good friend. He'd taken an interest in Clair. He'd advised her about real estate. But—Clair's relationship with Mr. Popp was no different than June's relationship with him. "Platonic," Clair's mother said.

Clair Heilman

As to all those stories about Mr. Popp lavishing gifts on people: "Gifts!" Clair said. "Why Mr. Popp never gave me so much as a flower. . . . It is absolutely untrue that I have any knowledge of Mr. Popp ever giving June one cent. I never saw him give her anything, and I never heard anything about it, although I was often a guest in June's home for a week at a time."[12]

No matter.

Three months after Mr. Popp began to pay more attention to Clair than to June, June threatened Mr. Popp with a lawsuit. Based on what? "Alienation of affection" was the claim.

Mr. Popp's predicament grew worse:

The directors of Logan Square Trust discovered that the stocks and bonds in the bank's investment portfolio were worthless. David Wiederman had not only given the bank bad advice—he had been stealing from it for months. All because of Mr. Popp. The directors gave Mr. Popp an ultimatum: "Get out, stay out. And make good" on the bank's losses.

The hole Mr. Popp had to fill was $206,000 deep: the funds Wiederman had embezzled, plus $150,000 worth of bad paper. Mr. Popp's personal worth was reported to be $225,000. Most of that was real estate. Its market value would plummet if Mr. Popp sold it all at once. All Mr. Popp really had was $21,000. That plus some life insurance policies worth $160,000.

He was worth more dead than alive. He looked to the left, he looked to the right; he did the math; he made his exit.

Ten days later, 2,500 Logan Square Trust and Savings depositors met at the Logan Square Theater to listen to Henry Savage offer them a deal: If the bank were to be liquidated, everyone would lose 20 percent of his money on deposit. But if enough of the bank's depositors agreed to trade their projected 20 percent losses for shares of Logan Trust's capital stock, the bank—with new directors, under new management—would reopen. One thousand people signed pledges agreeing to Savage's offer. The bank did have $2 million on deposit. The neighborhood was growing. The $300,000 pledged by depositors, plus another $200,000 pledged by the bank's new directors, recapitalized Logan Square Trust and Savings.

Mr. Crowe, with the consent of the bank's new directors, appointed Henry Savage as the bank's new president.

David Wiederman was indicted for forgery, larceny, and violation of state banking regulations.

The Internal Revenue Service announced an investigation of June Bacon. She fainted twice while being questioned by one of Mr. Crowe's investigators.

Clair Heilman returned from California. She gave an interview that began with the words, "I am hunted but I am innocent." She declared her intention to put to rest all rumors, all questions, all gossip, all lies. For example: "My hair's not brunette." And: "As for my job . . . why, I was trained to work. I've had positions in beauty parlors. I've been a milliner. . . . You know, I've had my good times . . . but what I really want is a home. They picture me as a wild girl. I wonder."[13]

Six months later, Clair was in a car that drove off the end of a bridge. She was with two men, on their way to a golf tournament in St Louis. The driver died at the scene. Clair's ribs were crushed; her lungs were punctured. Doctors didn't think she'd live. That was the last anyone heard of her.

Grand jury examining Lake Street Pier, Evanston

8 · Leighton Mount

They called it "class rush." At sunset, the freshmen rallied in one place, the sophomores in another. It happened every September before classes began. Everyone carried ropes, wrapped around their waists, so they could tie their prisoners. Once it was dark, so dark no one could see who did what to whom, they attacked each other; packs of freshmen, gangs of sophomores; a mob of five hundred boys. The girls stayed inside, crowded around the windows of their dorms. The boys chased each other back and forth across the campus, through the streets of Evanston, down to Fountain Square, then back to the lake. Respectable people stayed inside. Local drunks and toughs joined in.

Whoever captured the other would force them to strip, then tie them up and march them off. If they captured their prisoners by the lake, they'd force them to jump in, or they'd throw them in, or they'd row them out, a few at a time, to a raft or a jetty and leave them there—to untie themselves, swim ashore, find clothes before they were caught again. Worse than being dunked or marooned was to be kidnapped—stripped, tied, taken in a car to the forest outside of town, then left there. The next morning, people driving to work would see boys, wearing nothing but leaves and branches, skittering along the side of the road, trying to get back to campus before registration ended.

Within a day, everyone would be back where he or she belonged—the girls in groups, whispering to each other, carrying their books, dressed in their pretty, bright sweaters; the boys, in their tweeds and twills and flannels, strolling with a swagger, telling war stories, wearing their cuts and bruises like show ribbons.

Convocation always began with a prayer; the school's president would give a speech; professors would take their first attendance; football

Arthur Persinger, seated, right.

practice would start. Soon there'd be Homecoming and a Big Ten home game; the marching band would play "Go U Northwestern," the whole crowd would roar, "Rise Northwestern! We'll always stand by you! Rise Northwestern! We'll sing and cheer for you! Varsity! Varsity! Hit 'em hard and low! Varsity! Varsity! Go Northwestern! Varsity! Rah! Rah!"

The university was less than seventy years old when the twenties began. Methodists had founded the place to minister to the territories of the North-west. The school had its traditions, but they were as new and as raw as the region. Football, played hard, played "for keeps," was one of those traditions. So was class rush. Recently, though, rush had begun to change: it had become rougher, rowdier, and tougher—football without pads or helmets.

The rush of 1921 was the wildest anyone could remember: the crowds were smaller, but they were rougher. A sophomore named Persinger showed up at the Evanston police station, escorted by friends. He was dazed and shaken; his friends were angry.

Persinger filed a complaint: four students had kidnapped him from his room at Sigma Nu fraternity. They'd taken him to a cemetery by the lake, tied him to a tombstone, then left him. Hours later, they'd come back, gagged him, blindfolded him, then rowed him out to a breakwater. They'd lashed him to a plank and left him, head down, tipped into the waves. Two fishermen heard his cries, rowed to the rocks, cut him loose, and brought him to shore.

Evanston police contacted the dean of the college. The dean announced a "searching investigation." Walter Dill Scott, Northwestern's new president, placed a personal call to Harry Pearsons, Evanston's mayor. (Scott had just been appointed the year before. Many people had their doubts about him: Scott was a Presbyterian—the first Northwestern president who wasn't a Methodist. He was also a psychologist—indeed, an eminent psychologist—but the discipline itself was too modern and too secular for some people, faculty and trustees alike. In Scott's favor: He'd been a student at Northwestern and had taught there. In fact, he'd even been abducted by sophomores during his own class rush.) Scott reminded Pearsons of facts they both knew: Most of Northwestern's trustees were from Evanston; all of Northwestern's trustees were sober-minded Methodists. What was good for Northwestern was good for Evanston. Young Persinger's unfortunate experience had already been reported in the papers. It reflected badly on the school. Couldn't the police report be modified so that Persinger's treatment be made to seem less harsh? The mayor understood. He called his chief of police, a man named Leggett, and ordered him to change the report. The chief did what the mayor told him to do.

It took two years for all this—the rush of 1921, Persinger's ordeal, Scott's phone call, Pearsons's order, Leggett's revisions—to become kindling for a bonfire. That fire broke out in May 1923. It began smoldering the night Persinger was abducted.

That night, a freshman named Leighton Mount disappeared. Tall, slender, sweet-faced, clean-cut. Vanished.

Leighton had gone off to the rush along with everyone else. He'd gone to the rally at the Star Theater, had tied a rope around his waist, and marched in the crowd, from Patten Gymnasium on to campus. That year, freshmen had painted their faces with iodine so they could tell friend from foe. Leighton had had his face painted—just like everyone else. As late as three o'clock that morning people remembered seeing Leighton, remembered talking with him, out on the Lake Street pier.

The sun came up. People limped back to their rooms. Leighton was a local boy. He lived with his family in town. Leighton didn't come home.

Leighton's father was a well-to-do traveling man. He'd just left for St. Louis. Leighton's older sister, Helen, was a student at the University of

Illinois. She'd left home to start her own semester. Leighton lived with his mother.

"Leighton was always close to me," his mother said. "He was a gentle sort of boy. . . . He and I were companions. That's the main reason he went to Northwestern . . . so we could keep each other company. . . . But Leighton was no sissy . . . he wasn't afraid of a fight. He went to Sunday school, but he was no molly coddle. He loved music . . . he played in orchestras—but he'd get his hands as dirty as anybody."

Leighton's mother remembered the conversation they'd had the afternoon before he disappeared.

"Leighton had been so busy on campus, attending to registration, planning his courses, he wasn't even home for meals, he was being rushed by the fraternities. . . .

"That afternoon, he had a few hours, so he took me out for a drive. . . . He talked to me more as if I were an older brother than a middle-aged mother. . . . We were so close to each other, as we were talking, that I spoke of many things. I said I knew he was at a dangerous time of life for even the best of boys. . . . I told him, frankly, that many boys grow melancholy. I hinted that they sometimes talked of running away from home—or even planned to commit suicide. . . . I warned him, as a son about to enter college life, to play square, not to do foolish things, and—above all—to take his part. . . .

"I remember, as we drove around the campus, I remember one of the boys—he was nice looking and clean cut—jumped up on the running board of the car as we slowed down. 'Hey, Mount,' he shouted. 'Are you coming out with the bunch tonight? It's the big night, you know.'

"Leighton was undecided. He told the fellow he wasn't sure. I told Leighton that I wanted him to get as much as possible out of college life, in friendship and activities as well as studies. I urged him to play the game when the game was worth playing . . . to be a good sport.

"I knew Leighton had been a real boy. I wanted him to be a real man. And so—I urged him to go to the university class rush. And he went."[1]

Leighton's mother went to the police when he didn't come home. She went to the station where Persinger's friends had taken him after he was rescued. The reporters who'd overheard Persinger's story overheard Mrs. Mount's.

The "Mount case" made local and then national news. The *Chicago Tribune*'s headline ran across eight columns of its front page: STUDENT LOST

AFTER HAZING. SEARCH LAKE AND WOODS FOR N.U. YOUTH. National news services carried Leighton's story. Papers, east and west, ran it, half column or full, as a cautionary tale.

Mrs. Mount went to see President Scott. She didn't know that he'd already called Mayor Pearsons about Arthur Persinger. What she did know about President Scott was what everyone who paid close attention to Northwestern's new president—its new psychologist—knew and remembered: in October 1920 Scott had given a memorable—some said a groundbreaking—speech to the university's trustees.

For too long, Scott said, universities had emphasized the teaching of subjects, not students. College men and college women were more than just "candidates for degrees." They were unique individuals with unique capacities. "Grounded in a profound faith in Christian culture, an appreciation of the laws of nature, and an understanding of . . . technological advance," Northwestern was ready to lead the way to the new goal of American higher education—the education of the *individual*, developed to his or her own fullest potential, devoted to a life of service.[2]

"The individual," "the individual," "the individual" were the words everyone remembered. Ninety years ago, those words, spoken with such emphasis, by a college president to his board of trustees, were stirring. Mrs. Mount was sure President Scott would do everything he could to find her boy.

She confided in him.

Leighton had fallen in love, she said. The girl's name was Doris Fuchs. Doris was very pretty, and very nice—but she wasn't right for Leighton. She didn't come from a family like Leighton's—she worked as a nursemaid (a nanny). And—Doris wasn't of their faith.

"My boy," said Mrs. Mount, "told me about Doris. 'Mom,' he said. He always called me 'Mom.' 'I'm in love with Doris.'" Mrs. Mount said she listened. But then: "I talked to Leighton and I talked to her. . . . I had them both over together. They were both young, I explained. My boy had years of study ahead of him. Miss Fuchs was . . . employed. It would have been hard on both of them to wait years before marriage. My son—oh, I tried to be gentle about it. I wanted to do the right thing—but I had to tell them the difference in their viewpoints. Miss Fuchs was a member of the Christian Science faith. She interested Leighton in it. She stimulated his religious thought. . . . But that was the only common meeting ground between the two, besides their youth. I couldn't help but see it. I wanted to be fair to her as well as to my boy. And so—I urged them to just be friends, and nothing more."[3]

Mrs. Mount said that the night Leighton disappeared, Doris had come to her, very upset. Leighton had written Doris a note—a farewell note, a good-bye note that twice mentioned suicide. Doris said it wasn't the first time Leighton had talked to her about "getting out of it all." "Dear Angel," Leighton had written, ". . . I swear I am haunted. 'Mom' remarked tonight it seems that almost every young person wants to run away from home or commit suicide. . . . Perhaps she is right. . . . Goodbye, love . . . I cannot sign my name; somehow it is hard."

Mrs. Mount said she began to weep. She wept all night. She feared the worst: When Leighton was very young, only four years old, he'd fallen out of bed and fractured his skull. He still had a scar from the accident. Doctors had warned Mrs. Mount that such an injury at such a young age would have grave consequences. Before Leighton was twenty years old, the doctors said, "he would probably develop a pronounced melancholy nature . . . which would show in some manner."[4] Leighton was now eighteen. The doctors' predictions were coming true.

Mrs. Mount wept as she confessed all this to President Scott.

Scott recalled the conversation:

"After Mrs. Mount told me this, she asked me to keep it in confidence, which I told her I would do. It seemed to me that Mrs. Mount was very greatly distressed and perturbed—and unclear—in her mind as to what had happened to her son. . . . I felt that Mrs. Mount hoped that Leighton had been carried off by . . . students. She feared he had carried out his threat, but she was doing her best to substantiate her hope that he had been carried off because—if he had been carried off—he would be back. . . ."[5]

Scott tried to calm her. Class rush had started so late and gone on so long, he said, it was likely that Leighton hadn't come home—not because of some mishap but because he didn't want to wake her. "Leighton is probably in class right now," Scott said. "When class is over, he will probably get home, and you—you had better get home so you can meet him, there." Many young men talk about suicide, Scott said. "Lots of boys threaten that and don't do it. I think Leighton will be back."[6]

Mrs. Mount asked the president to search the campus. Search the fraternities, search the forest, search the lakeshore, she begged. Scott promised her: Northwestern would do everything she asked.

A day passed.

Doris Fuchs

Leighton's father returned to Evanston and made an appointment to see Scott. Scott met Mr. Mount in his office—along with the college's dean and someone Scott called the "university's publicity man."

The men talked for an hour. "We made recommendations," Scott recalled. "We recommended that Mr. Mount employ a detective agency, at once, to shadow Doris Fuchs, and particularly, the mail and telephone and telegraph.

I said to Mr. Mount, 'The boy will first get in touch with the girl. Now, watch the girl.' " Scott urged Mr. Mount to tell the detectives to "extend their search to distant cities and particularly the YMCA because Leighton was a YMCA boy."[7]

The Mounts hired the Burns Agency. Agents trailed Doris. They investigated her employment and religious affiliations. They sent inquiries to Burns Agency offices in other cities; they followed up leads as far away as North Dakota.

Another day passed. No Leighton.

Two students came to see Scott. One of them was a handsome young man named J. Allan Mills; the freshmen class had elected Mills as one of its leaders when they'd rallied at the Star Theater before class rush began. Mills told Scott that he and his friends believed Leighton had been kidnapped by Chicago newspaper reporters who wanted to bring dishonor on Northwestern. "I heard rumors everyday," Scott recalled. "I heard rumors that Leighton was seen in St. Louis or in Milwaukee or in Minneapolis or on the South Side, here. . . . I never believed any of the rumors."[8]

Four days after Leighton disappeared, Scott met with Mayor Pearsons and Chief of Police Leggett. Leggett had cleaned up many student messes in his day—the Persinger case included. Pearsons had lived through years of class rushes and fraternity hazings. Scott knew Northwestern better than any president before him. The mayor, the chief, and the president were reasonable and experienced men. Which is why they decided to call off the search for Leighton. The Chicago papers had turned Leighton's "disappearance" into "a tempest in a teapot." The boy was a runaway, pure and simple. He'd used class rush as a way to leave home. He was tired of being told what to do by his mother. She'd ended his romance—so he'd run away to spite her. He'd be back.

A year passed.

No Leighton. No calls, no letters, no telegrams. Silence. No one smelled smoke.

Some people were sure Leighton had run away, that his family knew where he was, that they were too ashamed to admit he was alive—that he was still angry at his mother about Doris. Other people said they were sure Leighton was dead—he was a sissy. He'd committed suicide and his family knew all about it but were too ashamed to tell anyone.

J. Allan Mills, the student leader who'd told President Scott that Leighton had been abducted by reporters, withdrew from school. Some people

J. Allan Mills (left) and Robert E. Crowe

said Mills had withdrawn to avoid being expelled—expelled because of extremely bad behavior while he was a member of a fraternity—the same fraternity to which Arthur Persinger had belonged. Mills's withdrawal spawned rumors. Some people said that he'd carried a gun. Other people said that he'd been arrested for forgery. Some said he'd been arrested in California and was serving time in San Quentin. Others said he'd been arrested in Wyoming and was in the state penitentiary in Rawlins. Truth was: Mills was living in Berkeley under the name Paul Hutton and writing letters to people—especially young women—he barely knew, begging them for money, blaming his bad luck on something that had happened at Northwestern—"that terrible experience" he called it. No one knew what Mills meant by that. No one sent him any money.

Another eight months passed. Spring 1923.

Three carloads of freshmen chased a car full of sophomores through the streets of Evanston. They zigged and zagged and passed each other. They blazed down straightaways at forty-five, even fifty mph. It wasn't class rush and it wasn't a fraternity hazing—it was the end of April; the semester was almost over; freshmen were still chasing sophomores. One of those sophomores was a boy named Roscoe Conkling Fitch—a small, skinny, high-strung young man who happened to have been a friend of Leighton Mount. In fact, Roscoe had been in the crowd with Leighton, back in September 1921, when they'd tied ropes around their waists and had their faces painted with iodine. Roscoe remembered that Leighton had been "depressed . . . tired and worried" that night.[9] He'd never seen Leighton after that.

Now Roscoe was in the backseat of a fast little Ford, being chased by a Haynes—a light, open car—packed with eleven freshmen. Roscoe said a boy named Leahy was driving the Haynes—fast but not very well.

"Leahy's car was right behind us. We turned a corner, and he had to go straight on. He was going so fast, he couldn't turn. We turned on two wheels, but his car couldn't turn so he had to go around the block. . . . The two freshmen cars that were behind him had time to turn and follow us. We were going as fast as we could. . . . Leahy, coming up on us, was going fifty. . . . He came up behind us. . . . Leahy's car was knocked over in a diagonal direction right into the oncoming car of this lady, Mrs. Williston."[10]

Mrs. Williston wasn't hurt. One of the boys in Leahy's car was badly injured. Another boy, a seventeen-year-old freshman named Louis Aubere, died at the scene.

Chicago papers reported Aubere's death as prominently as they'd reported Persinger's ordeal and Leighton Mount's disappearance. Northwestern's dean called a meeting of student class leaders and fraternity presidents. The university's official version—to be disseminated by them to everyone they knew—was that Aubere's death was the result of a tragic automobile accident. An accident that had nothing to do with class feuds or fraternity hazings. Students were not to talk to reporters—the Chicago papers didn't want to report the truth; they only wanted to sully the reputation of the university and the town of Evanston.

Aubere's death came at a rather awkward time for Northwestern.

Walter Scott had accepted the school's presidency knowing that his alma mater was in bad financial health: the school had been running an annual deficit of $100,000[11] for years. The chairman of Northwestern's board of trustees, a man named James Patten, had paid the school's unpaid bills, every year, with his own money. Patten's generosity had kept Northwestern solvent, but the school's faculty were underpaid. Its undergraduates, particularly its women, were badly housed; its library was so small and so out-of-date that its holdings were scattered in a half dozen places around campus. The adjoining buildings that constituted the Chicago campus of Northwestern's medical and law schools were overcrowded and in bad repair.

Bricks-and-mortar and salary money—construction and endowment money—had to be raised. James Patten agreed, but he wanted the money spent in Evanston. Other people on the board—people with less money than Patten—disagreed. Northwestern needed to expand its presence in Chicago. There was a fight. Patten lost. He resigned and took his checkbook with him.

The board took a calculated risk: the board knew that Northwestern's new president was more than an academic. Before, during, and after the First World War, Scott had developed personnel tests that, as a consultant, he'd sold to corporate and military clients. The War Department used Scott's tests to screen and select officers (men like Carl Wanderer); companies used Scott's tests to screen and select salesmen and managers (men like the late D. J. Daugherty).

The U.S. Army made Scott a colonel; the French government made him a chevalier; the American Psychological Association made him its president. The books Scott wrote about the psychology of advertising became fundamental texts. They explained what is now—nearly one hundred years later—obvious: instincts and emotions can be used to sell almost anything to anyone (cigarettes to women; Packards to lunatics). Scott was smart, smooth, and thoroughly "modern." If anyone could raise the new money Northwestern needed, it was Walter Dill Scott.

The board voted to authorize a $25 million capital campaign. It allotted $1.5 million of that to buy land to expand Northwestern's Chicago "campus."

The board turned out to be right:

Chicago, not Evanston, was where the money was. In 1920, just as Scott was coming into office, the McCormick cousins,[12] coeditors of the *Chicago Tribune*, agreed to underwrite a journalism school to be named after their grandfather, Joseph Medill. In 1923, the widow of the retail and catalog magnate Montgomery Ward pledged the first $4 million of an $8 million gift to build a new Northwestern medical, dental, and research center in downtown Chicago. Scott prepared plans for a new football stadium, a new quadrangle of women's dormitories, a new school of education, a new university library, a new. . .

Dead students, injured students, missing students—none of this was helpful. No one noticed the smell of smoke in the air.

One week after Louis Aubere died, a twelve-year-old Evanston boy named Henry Warren got into a fight with his sister and ran off in a huff. Henry had a hideout, a secret place where he went to be alone. Dim, safe, and private—the crawl space under the Lake Street pier.

"Saturday night," Henry said, "I was playing ball with my sister . . . but she wouldn't play fair, so I went down to the pier and crawled into the big hole that was there. I crawled along my stomach toward the shore until I found a piece of clothing and an old shoe. . . ."[13]

The pier where Henry went was the same pier where Leighton was last seen at three o'clock in the morning during class rush, back in September 1921. During the summer, Leighton used to go to that pier to swim—two or three miles every day. "Leighton was an expert swimmer," one of his friends said.[14] "Leighton knew that pier perfectly," Doris Fuchs recalled. "It was on that pier that Leighton, many times, told me abut his theories of life, his philosophy . . ."[15] The two would sit and talk and look out at the horizon. "He'd tell me of his troubles at home, of his desire to 'get away from it all' . . . from the material drawbacks of what . . . was his present form of life."[16]

There were big, flat rocks on the ground where Henry crawled, dumped there to anchor the pier, after it had been built and towed into place, before its decking had been nailed and bolted down.

Henry thought the rags he found were part of an old bathing suit. Then, said Henry, "I saw a leg bone and some other bones. Then I saw a skull . . . I went right home and told my mother."[17]

Henry's mother didn't believe him.

Henry insisted.

Mrs. Warren called the police.

She and Henry met them at the pier. An officer named George Petska crawled through Henry's hole. Planks above, rocks below. A two-foot crawl space, from one end of the pier to the shore. Officer Petska crawled on his belly until Henry, peeking down through the cracks, told him to stop.

Officer Petska found what Henry found. And he found more.

Part of a skeleton with a length of rotted rope looped around its waist. A belt with a silver buckle, engraved with the initials L.M. A right shoe with part of a foot in it. A left shoe—with nothing in it.

The skeleton's bones were scattered, but its skull and rib cage were intact. "There were five large stones," Officer Petska said, "lying on the

Police officer holding belt and rope; belt belonged to Leighton Mount

body, near the waist and ribs." Not one of the stones weighed less than a hundred pounds. "There were three smaller stones," Officer Petska said.[18]

More police came. Officers cut two planks, as thick as railway ties, out of the pier above the skeleton. Since the skeleton lay in Evanston—not Chicago—there was no coroner or coroner's physician to examine the scene and document it before police lifted the rocks off the bones. An Evanston businessman named Harry Rideway watched the police as they did it. Rideway remembered the rocks: two big ones, at least a hundred pounds each, lay on top of the bones before they were disturbed.

LEIGHTON MOUNT FOUND DEAD
Skeleton Was Buried Under Evanston Pier.
Police Believe Him Hazing Victim.

The kindling that President Scott, Mayor Pearsons, and Chief Leggett had thrown into a pile two years before began to burn. Bright enough for everyone to see.

Scott rushed forward to put out the flames.

"Early in the evening, President Walter Dill Scott of Northwestern University issued a statement that Leighton Mount was not a student routinely enrolled in the university at the time of his disappearance."[19]

Someone—perhaps the school's dean, perhaps the university's "publicity man"—noticed that Scott had set his pants on fire.

"Later that night . . . President Scott issued another statement, saying that he had found Mount had been enrolled, but owing to his non payment of tuition, had temporarily lapsed in the relation of 'enrolled student.' "[20] The school's bursar had probably told Scott that premature death was considered a valid excuse for late payment of fees.

Leighton's mother was shown the skeleton's silver belt buckle and its rags. "O, my boy, my boy," she said.[21] Leighton's dentist, Dr. Ivey, was shown the skeleton's teeth. "Yes, I am positive those are the teeth of Leighton Mount," Dr. Ivey said. "Those are the same gold fillings I made. Aside from the record of my work, I have a distinct remembrance of just what work I did for Leighton and of the color and shape of his teeth."[22]

As soon as Dr. Ivey identified Leighton's teeth, President Scott announced he would be making no further comments to the press. "All matters, from now on, have been placed in the hands of the attorney for the University, George P. Merrick." Attorney Merrick issued a statement: "The University is very sorry and deeply regrets the death of Mount and we will do all we can to bring the guilty person to justice. . . . No effort will be made to shield any one, regardless of who is at fault. We have no one to protect."[23]

Cook County Coroner Oscar Wolff didn't believe Merrick. Neither did

Oscar Wolff

State's Attorney Crowe. Evanston was in Cook County, Cook County was in Illinois—Wolff and his investigators, Crowe and his prosecutors had been waiting for a chance to bring their version of the rule of law to Northwestern's company town.

Mr. Crowe had just left for a vacation when Leighton's bones were found. Coroner Wolff asked Edgar Jones, Crowe's first assistant (the same Edgar Jones who'd arranged for Harvey Church to make his final "I did it all by myself" confession), to assign a prosecutor and a police lieutenant to the case. Wolff convened a coroner's jury and announced that he would lead the inquest.

Crowe ended his stay at a health resort "to give his personal attention" to the Mount case. "The attitude that University officials are reported to have taken immediately after Mount's disappearance in September, 1921, and again, immediately after the finding of the skeleton . . . was puzzling, Mr. Crowe declared."[24]

"Mobs are the same, whether composed of university students or underworld toughs," Mr. Crowe said. "Here, where university students are involved . . . justice has been hampered. . . . There is one way to find out how this unfortunate student met his death, and why his body was concealed beneath a pile of rocks under a pier: That is to go through every fraternity and class group of students, and by a process of elimination, find out who has guilty knowledge of the killing.

"I am going to separate the sheep and the goats, the wheat and the chaff, line up the good, honest, upright students . . . on one side. . . . Those on the other can expect little consideration. Every student who has left college since the fatal class rush will be traced and questioned. If the guilty ones are fugitives, we will need to learn it as quickly as possible—we will, too, if Northwestern does its part."[25]

Despite the rocks on Leighton's bones, student leaders—football stars, class presidents, and fraternity presidents, the same leaders who'd been told what to say after Louis Aubere's death—spread the news that Leighton had, indeed, killed himself. He'd drunk iodine, jumped into the lake, and drowned. His body had been washed beneath the pier. "Wave burial" was the phrase well-informed students began to use.

The chief justice of the Cook County Criminal Court, Michael McKinley, gave new directions to a grand jury, already in session: Its new task, McKinley said, was to determine whether Mount had killed himself or been killed. If Mount had been killed, the jury was to determine whether he had died by accident or by intentional act. McKinley briefed the jury about "accessory after the fact." If the jury had reason to believe that Mount had been killed by others—accidentally or intentionally—it also needed to determine whether anyone had helped Mount's killers conceal his body.

Kate Trostell had gone missing in December 1922; Arthur Foster always claimed she'd killed herself. The judge who'd finally blocked Arthur's release, the grand jury that, eventually, brought a murder charge against Arthur—nearly everyone in Chicago had read reports about the Trostell case, day after day, for months before Leighton's bones were found. Less than a week after Henry Warren crawled under the Lake Street pier, Arthur Foster's murder trial began. Stories about watery graves, mysteries of homicide or suicide, the disappearance of the living and the discovery of the dead—all this was in the minds of those who read about and those who investigated Leighton's death.

The grand jury began to issue subpoenas.

Conference rooms, meeting rooms, jury deliberation rooms, empty offices, and antechambers in the Criminal Court building began to fill

Northwestern students, waiting to be questioned

with groups of tweedy students, subpoenaed twenty or thirty at a time, then questioned, one by one. Some students complained they'd be expelled for missing classes, others chanted varsity fight songs as they waited. None of them believed Leighton had been murdered.

J. Allan Mills, "the red haired leader of the freshman class," was traced to Akron, Ohio, where he was found to be working in the rubber shops of the B. F. Goodrich Company. Akron police arrested Mills and held him until two assistant state's attorneys, sent by Crowe, could depose him in jail. Mills's father told him to keep his mouth shut and fight extradition. Mills decided he had nothing to hide: He jumped out a window, climbed into a waiting car, and drove straight to Chicago to tell Mr. Crowe his story.

Mills reached Chicago the same day jury selection began for Arthur Foster's trial.

The grand jury issued subpoenas for Doris Fuchs, Chief of Police Leggett, and Mr. and Mrs. Mount.

Leighton's mother spent two days telling the jury about her boy. Doris Fuchs changed her story about her relationship with Leighton several times: she finally settled on a five-month courtship, no kisses, long conversations about Christian Science—followed by the intervention of Leighton's mother. Doris said she didn't mind: Leighton was only eighteen; she was twenty-five; she was fed up with working as a nanny; she planned to leave town, anyway. In her opinion, Leighton was "a queer, peculiar, shut-in" young man. She'd never loved him.

J. Allan Mills put on a suit and went to see Mr. Crowe. He'd never known Leighton, personally, he said. Yes, he'd helped look for Leighton after he disappeared. Yes, he'd gone to see President Scott to warn him about the Chicago papers. And why was that? Because a reporter had offered him a bribe to stage a dunking for a photographer. Scott had discouraged and dissuaded Mills from doing anything more to find Leighton. As to all those rumors: Mills said he'd never carried a gun, and never served time—in San Quentin or anywhere else. He'd left school of his own volition. The "terrible night"? He was ashamed of how he'd behaved. It was a personal matter that had nothing to do with Leighton Mount.

Crowe told the two assistant state's attorneys he'd sent to Akron to go on to West Virginia to depose other students. Arthur Persinger was one of them. Back in Chicago, Chief Leggett took the stand and confessed to falsifying police records. He said Mayor Pearsons and President Scott forced him to do it. Mr. Crowe announced he was prepared to subpoena Northwestern's board of trustees.

Evanston's commissioner of public works, a man named William Blanchard, was subpoenaed. Blanchard had supervised the construction of the Lake Street pier.

"Mount's body could not have been washed under that pier; it is physically impossible," Blanchard said. "The pier is what we call a breakwater. It was built in the summer of 1921 and floated to its present position. Rocks were then dropped into it until it was full and thus permanently anchored in place.

"The pier was completed on August 29, 1921, four weeks before Mount's death. In early September—two weeks before Mount disappeared—I inspected it. It was solid and there was no hole in the planking. There was no room for a body to wash in."[26]

Two local boys—the Cook brothers—were subpoenaed. They'd known Leighton, and had spoken to him at three o'clock in the morning, at the

Honey Sullivan (right) and State's Attorney McLaughlin

end of the class rush. They'd joined the search for him the next day. "We went up and down the shore," said Thomas Cook, the older of the two. "I remember we went out to the Lake Street pier where the skeleton was found a few days ago. I remember there was a hole in it—a hole that was just about where [the police] chopped the hole, now . . . It was as if some loose or rotted boards had been pulled away."[27]

President Scott's son, John, was subpoenaed. Elizabeth "Honey" Sullivan, the leader of an Evanston gang of "sheik bandits," was subpoenaed. John Scott said his father had ordered him not to participate in class rush. Honey Sullivan denied that any of her gang had used freshmen as "punching bags" during the melee.

Three other Evanston boys came forward, on their own, to say that before Leighton disappeared, they'd chopped their own hole in the Lake Street pier. Not the hole the Cook brothers noticed—but another one, farther from shore. They'd wedged a board in it, for diving. "We had to move our board several times . . . we chopped around [our hole] because [our board] kept pulling up [planks]."[28] Nine months later—in the spring of 1922—other boys widened the hole so they could duck under the pier to change into bathing suits.[29] *That* was the hole that Henry used when he ran off, after his sister had cheated at baseball.

Two holes. Much confusion.

"Surely this calls for an explanation from men experienced in murder mysteries," declared Mr. Crowe.

He summoned his experts:

Chief of detectives, Michael Hughes, and homicide detective—now Lieutenant—John Norton (the same John Norton who'd traced the serial number of Carl Wanderer's Colt .45).

Crowe sent Hughes and Norton to Evanston to examine the Lake Street pier.

They measured the holes. "Hole No. 1"—the hole made to wedge a diving board, then enlarged so boys could wriggle under the pier to change clothes—was 20 inches wide. The other hole—"Hole No. 2"—the one the Cook brothers noticed—was a jagged diamond shape, no more than six inches wide.

"All other possibilities being eliminated, we must conclude," reported Hughes, "that it was Hole No. 1 that Leighton Mount was lowered through to his sand and stone grave. Other conditions being taken into consideration, it is logical to assume that this was done on the night of his death, which, I take it, was the night of Northwestern's class rush."

Hughes chose Hole No. 1, not because he was sure it was 20 inches wide back in September 1921, but because Hole No. 2 was too small for anything but a cat or a rat to scamper through.

"There is barely room," continued Hughes, "between the rocks and the underside of the pier planks to permit a person, wriggling on his stomach, [to reach] Hole No. 2 [adjacent to where Henry Warren found Leighton's skeleton, and where Evanston police cut their own hole to extract Leighton's bones]. If removal of [Leighton Mount's] body was accomplished before rigor mortis set in, one or two slender persons could probably have disposed of the corpse in ten minutes.

"That settles that. It could have been done; it was done, precisely in the manner I have outlined and in no other.

"Now we take up: 'Who did it?'

"Lieutenant Norton and I agree that the stones said to have been piled on top of the skeleton render any suicide theory absurd. The first mistake was made in permitting the Evanston police to remove the skeleton. . . . A photograph should have been taken . . . before anything was done. . . . A coroner's physician should have been the first to touch the bones. . . . The Evanston police made a mess of it by taking the [skeleton] out in pieces."

Lieutenant Norton added:

"I am sure it was a body that was put there, not a skeleton. . . . I am also of the theory that it was the work of frightened students."

Hughes recommended: "Every student then in both freshman and sophomore classes [should] be closely questioned, no exception made."[30]

President Scott testified before the grand jury the same day Hughes and Norton reported to Mr. Crowe.

Mr. Scott made it plain that Northwestern was blameless—and so was he. He and the university were bystanders to the Mount family's misfortune. He knew only what Mrs. Mount, in her agitated state, had told him. And what, asked Judge McKinley, had Mrs. Mount said? Mrs. Mount, said Scott, had told him that she feared her son had taken his own life. She'd hoped he'd been abducted—but she feared he'd killed himself. President Scott said he'd tried to calm Mrs. Mount—but after listening to her he'd also come to fear the worst.

"Campus lies! Campus lies!" said Mrs. Mount, when Scott's testimony was read to her. "I did everything President Scott told me—but now, I'm going to fight to the finish. I kept quiet for they kept telling me my son would come back. But now I know Leighton was murdered. Now that I've learned the things Mr. Scott told the grand jury. . . . I'm through with protecting him and the university. . . . The men responsible for Leighton's death and for the failure to solve his disappearance are going to have to take the blame."[31]

The members of the grand jury went to Evanston to examine the pier for themselves. The jury saw that the pier had been built with heavy timbers; it had been closed on all sides, bolted together, then ballasted with rocks. There was no way anything but sand, pebbles, and refuse could have washed into it.

Crowe asked that subpoenas be issued for forty-one students who'd left Northwestern within four months of Leighton's disappearance. Mrs. Mount told Mr. Crowe that President Scott had called her, less than a week after Leighton disappeared, to tell her, in confidence, that he had expelled sixteen students who'd been unusually rough and rowdy during class rush. Scott had asked Mrs. Mount to keep the expulsions secret. He said that any publicity might jeopardize the students' chances of being admitted to other colleges, elsewhere. Crowe ordered his investigators to follow up on what Mrs. Mount told him. Northwestern's registrar said he had no record of the expulsion of any group of sixteen students. When Crowe's men asked to see the records, the registrar refused.

Crowe's investigators had questioned more than a hundred students by the time they brought in Roscoe Conkling Fitch. Fitch was one of the sophomores involved in the auto accident that had killed Louis Aubere. Fitch seems to have been waiting like an actor, listening for his cue. Back in Michigan, Roscoe's father had been a county prosecutor—a big fish in a small pond. Everyone back in Ludington was proud of Roscoe—knew him and admired him. "He was one of the smartest boys we've ever had," one of Roscoe's teachers said. Everyone in town thought Roscoe would follow in his father's footsteps. Follow—and then surpass him. "Everyone expects Roscoe to be a great corporation lawyer some day."[32]

The discovery of Leighton's bones only a week after Louis Aubere's death—the two deaths had sounded like drum rolls and trumpet flourishes to Roscoe—portents of a brilliant and dramatic legal career. Roscoe had stood beside Leighton, been chased by Aubere: Roscoe was ready. Nervous but ready.

"In a story full of twists and quirks, tears and laugher, [Roscoe Conkling Fitch] last night confessed to State Assistant Attorneys that he knew all the details of the disappearance and killing of Leighton Mount."[33] Secret conferences between student leaders and President Walter Scott, carefully prepared press releases that were meant to serve as secret scripts—Roscoe told investigators "an amazing story" of cover-ups that began with Leighton's disappearance and continued with Aubere's death. "Fitch did not vary through long hours of grilling. He spoke frankly about these hush-up policies without hesitation . . . every effort to twist him failed."[34]

Eight times over the course of twelve hours, Fitch seemed on the verge of "telling all" about Leighton's death; eight times, Roscoe drew back like a hero in a melodrama. "I dare not talk," Fitch said, "for I have been warned by the men at the top to keep quiet and I must do it. . . ."[35]

"Fitch's story kept a full force working at the State's Attorney's office until after midnight. . . . Robert E. Crowe himself was called into a telephone conference by his assistants. . . ."[36]

"I know all about the Mount case," Fitch kept saying. "I could tell you

Police officer William Lanning (left) identifying evidence during grand jury investigation

everything, but I am pledged not to . . . you'll never find out . . . the other students who know are pledged to silence and they'll never break their pledge."

"Who pledged you?" one of Crowe's men asked.

"One of the most prominent students in school."

"Who was he? . . . Was he John Scott [President Scott's son]?"

"I cannot answer," Fitch said. "I dare not. . . . He told me never to mention his name. . . . He said to follow President Scott's testimony before the grand jury; that the University would come out on top and that I'd be protected in everything. . . . I must keep quiet about the Mount case. . . . If I don't, I'll lose my credits and be kicked out of school."[37]

Halfway through the questioning, Crowe's men gave Roscoe his dinner. The food changed him. Tears and tremors changed to embarrassed smiles.

"I don't know anything about the Mount case," Roscoe now said. "It was the Aubere case I was telling you about. . . . I'll tell you the truth about Aubere if you'll protect me."

Crowe's office issued subpoenas for the freshmen who were in the car with Aubere. Fitch's histrionics—his accusations and retractions—seemed to have embarrassed Mr. Crowe.

"Reports that this office is about to drop the investigation and that no progress has been made are false," said Mr. Crowe. "Reports given to me by my assistants show that someone is covering up and that some persons are protected. We are going to the bottom and we will find out who is doing the covering and why. . . . The investigation is far from over. The investigation . . . will go through to the finish. . . . If persons who have been withholding information think they are fooling anyone, they are wrong."[38]

A day after Roscoe ended his fan dance, the jury in the Kate Trostell/Arthur Foster case reached a verdict: Arthur was a brute and a murderer. He deserved to die.

Mr. Crowe began to quietly and privately question people about Leighton's life and death. Wholesale subpoenas and witnesses who played to an audience had been of no help. Crowe became more selective and more circumspect.

Crowe discovered that before Leighton disappeared, he'd sought the advice and counsel of a Christian Science practitioner named Herman Steinborn. Crowe asked Steinborn about those counseling sessions. Crowe also asked Dr. Clarence Neymann, former director of Chicago Psychopathic Hospital, to give his professional opinion about Leighton's mental and emotional state before he disappeared—and about the character and veracity of such witnesses as Roscoe Fitch and Henry Warren. In addition, Crowe interviewed Doris Fuchs in private. And he carefully questioned Henry Warren, out of public view.

Dr. Neymann interviewed Roscoe Fitch for two hours, then made an evaluation: "A sphinx without a secret," was the way Neymann described Roscoe. "A publicity seeker, puerile, a boy . . . enchanted with the . . . limelight, who now sees that the limelight has its disagreeable sides."[39]

Herman Steinborn, the Christian Science practitioner, told Crowe about the conversation he'd had with Leighton on September 5, 1921.

"He came professionally," said Steinborn, "my name having been given to him by a friend. He complained of a severe headache in the front of his forehead and asked my assistance in obtaining relief. . . . I let him do most of the talking.

"Leighton said he was madly, insanely in love with Doris Fuchs, but she looked on him only as a friend. . . . He said he was in constant trouble at home. . . . He was tired of school . . . and wanted to give up his college work. . . .

"Leighton said his mother had interfered in his friendship with Doris . . . I remember one phrase he used: 'The only bright spot in my life is Doris.' "[40]

When Crowe spoke with Doris herself, she told him what she'd already told the grand jury: Leighton was a friend; they talked about philosophy and religion; he often talked about how unhappy he was at home; he talked about suicide on at least two occasions. "When Leighton disappeared, I was certain he had carried out his threats."

Crowe asked Doris, Steinborn, and Neymann two questions:

Was Leighton the type of young man who'd run away—and stay away—from home? Was Leighton the type of person who might kill himself? Doris and Neymann thought Leighton was so unhappy that he was as likely to have killed himself as to have run away. Steinborn disagreed: Leighton was deeply discontented, but not suicidal.

Finally, Crowe spoke with Henry Warren.

Henry surprised him. There were no stones, Henry said. No stones—and not much that looked like a skeleton. Leighton's bones were scattered; his belt and its initialed buckle were off to one side. There were rocks, everywhere, said Henry. But Leighton's bones were on them, not under them.

Henry told this to Mr. Crowe, in private, then he told it to the grand jury, in public.

SECRET MOUNT QUIZ IS BARRED. NEW EVIDENCE
Suicide Clews Are Brought Forward.[41]

Crowe asked Dr. Neymann to interview and evaluate Henry, to examine him as he'd examined Roscoe Fitch. "A lad of unusual brightness," said the doctor. Henry's "memory could be depended upon to report detail with accuracy."[42]

Chief Hughes and Lieutenant Norton were right about only one thing: The Evanston police had "made a mess of it." Fabricated police reports followed by fabricated evidence.

Only this was certain: Leighton's skull, his teeth, and his belt buckle had been discovered under the pier. Coroner's physicians had been able to make a skeleton from the bones that had been collected. There had been a body under the pier; it was likely to have been Leighton Mount's.

After a four-week investigation, Crowe and Wolff knew no more (but no less) than they had before they'd begun issuing subpoenas: Northwestern was a very private school; the police in Evanston were not to be trusted.

The coroner's jury heard much the same evidence as the grand jury. Coroner Wolff led his jury to a verdict. To do that, Wolff found it necessary to replace one of his jury's five members. The man Wolff fired had been foolish enough to post a $10,000 reward, payable to anyone who found Leighton Mount alive. The man had done this despite new evidence presented by Evanston police officer George Petska. "There were seven or eight rocks on top of the bones," Petska told Wolff's jury. Seven or eight rocks "weighing from fifty to a hundred pounds each. . . . It would have been impossible for the water to wash the rocks in that position."[43] No one doubted Officer Petska. Stones were stones; a policeman was more trustworthy than a twelve-year-old boy.

"We the jury find that Leighton Mount came to his death on or about the 22nd of September, 1921, and that his body was found under the pier at the foot of Lake Street on April 30, 1923 at about 6:00 pm.

"We are unable to determine how or in what manner he met his death, but we are of the opinion that he came to his death at the hands of some unknown person or persons. . . . We recommend that . . . if possible such person or persons be apprehended and held on the charge of murder to the grand jury. . . ."

Three days passed.

The grand jury milled around like infantry at a crossroads. Murder or suicide? Suicide or murder? No one had a map.

Three days passed.

Mr. Crowe got a telegram.

It came from Clifton, Arizona. From a Mr. D. H. Rouw. Mr. Rouw described himself as "a traveling representative of a San Francisco collection house." A traveling bill collector?

". . . did not know I was sought as witness in Mount case until informed by local sheriff . . .

"I witnessed affair in Evanston in 1921," wrote Mr. Rouw. "Have good

J. L. Mount (left), father of Leighton Mount

information and will assist all I can. If my presence is desired, wire transportation and expense funds at once by Western Union."

Crowe ordered his assistant prosecutor Charles Wharton (the same Charles Wharton who, as an assistant state's attorney, had praised Harvey Church's fine mind, unspoiled, rustic health, and splendid memory) to go to Arizona to depose Rouw.

Rouw was so eager to talk that, after he telegrammed Crowe, he told his story to two Arizona newspapers. Rouw said that, back in September 1921, he and another traveling man were driving along the lake, up in Evanston, when they noticed students lowering a body into a hole in a swimming pier. It happened "just as the sun was setting."

Rouw corrected himself: Come to think of it, he hadn't been with anyone when he saw what he saw. He'd been alone, walking along the pier, enjoying the breeze, "late in the evening."

"I noticed a queer-looking party ahead of me. I watched them idly for a while. . . . I was struck by the fact that they seemed to be carrying something heavy. . . .

"I drew a little closer and saw it was a man's body. At first, I paid little attention . . . believing it was probably . . . a party of celebrants, carrying a drunken companion. . . . But soon I saw them stop. This interested me. I did not want to seem to interfere. . . . I stopped at a discreet distance.

"I saw them lower the body through a hole in the pier. . . . Four of them lowered the body while perhaps fifteen others stood around. They all looked and acted very scared. . . . All of them wore funny looking college caps. . . ."

Rouw said the students noticed him. They approached him. Surrounded him. Told him to keep his mouth shut.

Rouw said he went to the police. They told him not to worry.

" 'If we investigated every time the boys up at the University played a prank we'd have no time to protect the citizens and keep law and order in Evanston.' " Rouw said the police officer had smiled as he said this.

"I didn't know, of course, that a man had been killed there. If I had, I certainly would have protested more strongly. But I had read of college pranks and blindfolding and all that sort of thing, and I dismissed it from my mind."

Rouw said he'd stood so close to the students on the pier—and they'd stood so close to him when they'd threatened him—that he was sure he could identify them. "One of them had bright red hair," Rouw said. "One of them was fat."[44]

When Prosecutor Wharton arrived in Clifton, he hired a court stenographer to come with him when he went to see Mr. Rouw.

The stenographer wrote down Rouw's story as he told it. Wharton read the transcript, then asked Rouw to sign it. He warned Mr. Rouw: Once you sign it, you signify it's true. If it's not true—you'll be guilty of perjury.

"Well men," said Rouw, "I don't believe I will sign."

Wharton was surprised. "But you said it's true," he said to Rouw. "You'll go with me to Chicago and tell the grand jury what you've told me here."

"Well," said Rouw, "I guess I might as well admit that I was lying. I framed the story to get a free ride back to Chicago. It's all a hoax."[45]

Wharton returned to Chicago.

Judge Michael McKinley dismissed his grand jury.

Mr. and Mrs. Mount buried their son's skull and bones.

No new witnesses came forward. No suspects were ever identified. Leighton's case went cold.

Years passed.

Walter Dill Scott retired in 1940. He'd raised more than $40 million (equivalent to ten times that amount today) for his alma mater. A grateful university named its new student center—its student union—after him. Scott Hall. It was the right thing to do. The man who talked to millionaires was known for his common touch. Students loved Mr. Scott's openness, his tolerance, the interest he took in each and every one of them. As individuals.

Walter Dill Scott

Fred Thompson (right), seated with his lawyer, Frank McDonnell

9 · Fred-Frances

Fred never said much about his folks or about the people who adopted him. Born in Ohio, in Youngstown; raised outside of Columbus, on a farm. Everyone knew Fred wasn't put together right. "Tits on a bull," country people would have said. "Dr. Jekyll and Mrs. Hyde" was how Fred explained it to the jury, once his lawyer put him on the stand in his own defense. That young lawyer of his was bright—he had X-rays and two sex experts ready to go if anyone challenged Fred. No one did, though.

Fred said he stayed on the farm until he was thirteen. Miserable, scared, ashamed, confused. He never exactly explained to the jury what parts of him were girl parts and what parts of him were boy parts, but puberty made everything stand out. That's why he ran away. To Chicago. Lived on the streets, got high, turned tricks. In the same part of town where Carl Wanderer went shopping for his "ragged stranger."

For every week Fred lived as a boy, six months he lived as a girl. The trade liked girls, so Fred did what came naturally: he turned into Frances. Fred was cute; Frances was a little angel.

The police arrested Frances as often as they noticed her—hauled her into Morals Court, charged her as a "delinquent juvenile," then charged her for "operating a transient boardinghouse."

That boardinghouse of hers was a sign of success. By 1915 Frances, age twenty-five, was working out of two adjoining apartments in a building at Erie and La Salle. At six o'clock every evening, she'd change into a low-cut gown and entertain clients. No more cheap tricks off the street. "Prominent guys, right in this city," Frances said. None of them had any idea that Fred was inside the corsets Frances wore. A coquette, she was, with a pretty face, tiny hands, and a sweet little mouth.

By then, she was married. Legally married, by a justice of the peace in Indiana. To an out-of-work, junkie mechanic named Frank Carrick. A frail, consumptive, twitchy little guy who said he didn't know anything about Fred until he had been married to Frances for several months. It didn't make any difference to Frank, though.

Frances cooked, and shopped, and sewed. The double apartment at Erie and La Salle didn't last long; the tricks got cheaper, but Frank was never jealous. Work was work. It paid the rent, bought the dope. Heroin, passed around and snorted. A nice, quick, dreamy high. Frances liked it, but Frank needed it. Frank started using needles. Life went on.

Frances kept a parrot and a cat. She had a nice contralto voice. She bought a player piano, and music for it. She loved to sing. She could put a song across—nothing special, but good enough to substitute at clubs like the Erie and the Athena on North Clark.

She loved hats—"lids" she called them. "A girl's got to have a new lid," she'd say. She owned dozens of hats. And wigs. Many wigs. And shoes. Size fives. For her little feet. The apartment was strewn with her things—frocks, shoes, silk undies, stockings. Bills, letters, recipes, cookbooks, official notices, whiskey bottles, cure-all pamphlets—Frank didn't care. The next fix, the monkey on his back—that's what Frank cared about. Frank became a problem.

In 1920, a whore named Helen introduced Frances to a sweet girl named Marie Clark. Marie and Frances looked so much alike that, later, in Municipal Court, the judge mistook them for sisters. Marie was a Polish girl, from Michigan, a farmer's daughter who'd run away from home just like Frances. She loved heroin more than Frances did; she was more of a user, on her way to needing it like Frank.

Marie said she fell for Frances the moment they met. "She was a wonderful girl," Marie said. It didn't matter when Helen told Marie about Fred. "I fell in love with him," Marie said. "We went together for a couple of months. Fred wore girl's clothes. Swell ones, too, most of the time."[1]

They got married in 1921. A minister at the Moody Bible Institute performed the ceremony. Fred wore a suit for the occasion. Frances lived like that—like Fred—for the next five months. He and Marie bought five acres of land in Elmhurst and left Frank and his needles—and Frances and her corsets—behind. Country life didn't suit them, though. They moved back to Chicago; Frank moved in with them; Fred went back to being Frances.

Marie hated the arrangement. She was jealous of Frank. She was jealous of "the gents" Frances "dated." Frank hated Marie as much as she hated him. They'd fight—the four of them. Frances would turn into Fred and side with Marie, then after dark he'd become Frances again, and "step out" on dates. In the mornings, Frank and Frances would go shopping at the local delicatessen. The lady who owned it remembered them well: "Frank Carrick would come in here with his wife, Mrs. Carrick, such a sweet lady. She always did the shopping and knew just what she wanted. . . . Then sometimes, in the early afternoons, Marie Clark, who lived with the Carricks, would drive up in a Chevrolet car. She would look as if she had just come from a party. And with her would be her husband—'Mr. Thompson,' she called him. He'd help his wife pick out stuff. . . . I knew Mr. Thompson well, but not so well as 'Mrs. Carrick' . . . I never suspected."[2]

Marie cracked. She started using needles. She moved back to Michigan to try to kick the habit, cold turkey. Her parents took her to a hospital in Detroit. She got blood poisoning and nearly died. She called out for Frances. Marie's parents reached her. Frances rushed to Detroit and nursed Marie back to life. Marie survived. No one meant more to Marie, no one loved Marie, as much as Frances did. Marie moved back to Chicago to live with Frances and Fred and Frank. Life went on. Until the first week of June 1923.

Richard Tesmer and his wife, Anna, came home late in the evening. They'd been visiting Mr. Tesmer's sister. They'd had dinner, talked about work and the weather, played some cards, stayed a bit longer, then said good night. They were respectable people: their daughter was a senior at Northwestern; they drove a nice, sensible car; they owned their own apartment. They'd been married for twenty-five years; Mr. Tesmer had a good job with a big insurance company. He had to be up early the next morning.

Mr. Tesmer drove down the alley behind their building, parked, climbed out, swung back the garage doors. A man and a woman walked up to him. They both had guns.

"Hands up," said the woman. She was a slim, young blonde, a flapper. She wore a modish hat with a floppy brim. She spoke to Mr. Tesmer as calmly as if she were asking him for directions or the time of day. "Hands up and be quick about it," she said. Mrs. Tesmer remembered her voice, how soft and relaxed it was.

The man went through Mr. Tesmer's pockets: $10 in cash; a check for another $9. The girl snatched Mrs. Tesmer's purse: $5 and change.

"Give me your rings," said the girl.

"But I only have my wedding ring," said Mrs. Tesmer. Mrs. Tesmer looked the girl in the eyes. She remembered "those blue eyes . . . I'll never forget those blue eyes. . . . She wasn't nervous. . . . She was smiling."

"Off with it then," said the girl; she took Mrs. Tesmer's hand. "I remember her eyes and a very protruding nose," said Mrs. Tesmer. "She had a brown dress . . . I remember how she flourished her skirt."

"Please don't take my wedding ring," said Mrs. Tesmer. "I haven't had it off since I've been married." She pulled her hand away.

Mr. Tesmer reached out to his wife.

"You will, will you?" said the girl. She was smiling when she shot him. He died in the alley. "The smile," said Mrs. Tesmer. "I'll never forget that smile."[3]

Mrs. Tesmer screamed; the man jumped behind the wheel of the Tesmers' car; the girl hopped in next to him. The Tesmers' daughter, Clara, was at home that night; she opened her window and yelled as the car pulled away. Neighbors rushed into the alley.

Police found the Tesmers' car, abandoned so far north on Broadway it looked as if the thieves had been heading for Evanston. Police found fingerprints on the steering wheel and the doors. They made photographs and filed them. Their first arrest came before noon the next day: Honey Sullivan, Evanston's "flapper bandit." They hadn't been able to connect Honey to Leighton Mount's murder, so they tried again with the Tesmer shooting. Mrs. Tesmer looked at Honey, but shook her head. No luck.

Detective Lieutenant Hugh McCarthy issued a statement: "The girl who pulled the gun in the alley Tuesday night was evidently a novice at it and must have been full of drugs."[4] A woman named Ethel Brown had recently been arrested in the company of a gang of thieves; the thieves had just been sent to Joliet; Ethel hadn't been charged with anything. Police released her but, before they did, they'd caught a man trying to smuggle drugs to her in jail. McCarthy ordered his men to find Ethel and her connection.

State's Attorney Crowe issued his own statement: The flapper with the blue eyes, the brown dress, and the floppy hat may have had the sweetest smile in all the world—"but she can't beat the rope, this time. . . . This murder is one of the most cold blooded ever staged in Chicago."[5] Crowe ordered his senior assistant state's attorney Edgar Jones and Special Investigator Scott Stewart to lead the hunt for the "smiling flapper bandit." Attorney Jones made a public promise: "The list of women murderers who have been freed in Cook County is going to stop at 29. This girl will get the death penalty."[6] Crowe assigned Assistant State's Attorney Samuel Hamilton and Assistant State's Attorney William McLaughlin to prosecute the case against the girl once she was caught. Crowe chose McLaughlin because he'd just won murder convictions against two other women. Crowe chose Hamilton because he'd just convinced a jury to hang Arthur Foster. Whoever had killed Richard Tesmer, Crowe and his men wanted her hung: there would be no more Cora Isabelle Orthweins while Mr. Crowe held office.

Lieutenant McCarthy's men couldn't find Ethel Brown.

Mrs. Tesmer insisted they show her everyone they arrested, as soon as they arrested them.

"June . . . a little country girl from Michigan" became Tesmer suspect No. 3. June was known to sing in roadhouses. A sharpie named Irving Schlig had a snapshot of June in his pocket when police arrested him on Wednesday night. Police showed June's photograph to Mrs. Tesmer. The widow shuddered when she saw it. "I'm sure that's the woman . . . those eyes!" Police couldn't find June.

Mrs. Tesmer said the same thing she'd said about June when police showed her a photograph of suspect No. 4: Jessie Marie Morelock. Jessie Marie was a waitress; her sister told police that a chauffeur named "Boston Red" Harlem had "virtually kidnapped" Jessie Marie from her bedroom the night Mrs. Tesmer was shot. Police couldn't find Jessie.

Suspect No. 5: Mrs. Goldie Madsen. Mrs. Madsen had quit her job waiting on tables at the Devon restaurant the night Mr. Tesmer died. Goldie's husband, Mars, had filed a complaint against her, charging her with abandoning him and their two children. Police couldn't find Goldie, but they did find the man she went with on Tuesday: Thomas Boyd, a cook at an all-night lunchroom on the South Side. Boyd said he'd noticed Goldie standing in front of the Atlas lunchroom on Bryn Mawr. They'd struck up a conversation, then gone to Lincoln Park and had a few beers. After that, they'd gone to the Limits Hotel. The next morning, Goldie asked Boyd to walk her to the El stop at Fullerton. The last he'd seen, she'd gotten on the nine o'clock train. She said she was going home to Indiana to see her folks.

Suspect No. 6: Mrs. Margaret Dear, widow of Earl Dear. Earl was hanged in 1919 for killing a chauffeur named Richard Wolfe. The widow Dear began to keep company with William "Chubby" Ladner, a junkie and thief who had a record, dating back to 1914, for stealing everything and anything he could sell to buy drugs. Over the course of nine years, Ladner had been charged with—but never convicted of—stealing furs, Liberty Bonds, frocks, even money from a telephone coin box. Since he and Mrs. Dear were both addicts and had begun working as a team, police went looking for them. They never found Mrs. Dear. (As to Chubby: the FBI arrested him in 1934. They convicted him of passing counterfeit money in Boston. He spent three years in Leavenworth.)

Suspect No. 7: Mrs. Gertrude Getson, "a gunwoman of record." When police showed Mrs. Getson's photograph to Mrs. Tesmer, she said, "If she has blue eyes, she's the fiend who killed Richard." Unfortunately, Mrs. Getson didn't have blue eyes—and was in jail in Michigan.

Suspect No. 8: "Miss Billie Conn, aged 21." After Miss Conn was arrested, her father, Abraham Cohn of Hammond, Indiana, came forward to identify his daughter. Miss Conn's real name was Edna Belle Cohn. She was seventeen.

Suspect No. 9: Anna Senback. Arrested, then released.

Suspect No. 10: Marge Bennet. Mrs. Bennet was shown to Mrs. Tesmer, but Mrs. Tesmer couldn't identify her.

Morgan Collins, Chicago's new police chief,[7] announced that he was taking personal charge of the Tesmer investigation. "A chief of police should be the commander in the field as well as at headquarters. This is one of the most important cases the Chicago police have ever handled. When women . . . rob with revolvers and kill wantonly, no effort should be spared in the interest of justice."[8] Chief Collins had himself driven to the alley behind the Tesmers' apartment. He watched as four policemen reenacted the holdup. He then returned to headquarters where, it was reported, he made preparations to issue new orders.

Suspect No. 11: Thelma Shoma. Thelma and her sister, Mildred, had been arrested, questioned, then released in 1921, after a man named James McDonough had been shot through the heart on Shields Avenue. Thelma's family were ne'er-do-wells from Pittsburgh. Pittsburgh police had learned of the Tesmer murder and suggested Chicago police talk to Thelma. Nothing came of it.

Suspect No. 12: Lillian Erickson Page. Arrested, released, then remanded to the Sarah K. Hackett Home for Girls.

Suspects No. 13 and No. 14: Peggy Le Bean and Mrs. Bertha Schillo. Both Miss Le Bean and Mrs. Schillo had blue eyes. Miss Le Bean was said to be an actress "accustomed to registering smiles, tears, fear, and hopes on the silver screen in Los Angeles."[9]

Mrs. Tesmer and her daughter

Police ordered Miss Le Bean and Mrs. Schillo to wash the lipstick and rouge off their faces, and wipe the mascara from their eyes. They were then told to walk into a darkened room where Mrs. Tesmer sat waiting. Detectives handed each woman a .38 revolver; detectives told them to smile while they aimed their weapons at Mrs. Tesmer. "In a volley of underworld jargon, Mrs. Schillo expressed her contempt for police."[10] Miss Le Bean was more cooperative: she "found it easy to curve her mouth in a beguiling smile."[11] Neither woman got the part. "No," said Mrs. Tesmer, "they're not the girl. That girl smiled like a fiend."[12]

Then—at last—police got lucky. The papers called it "a hot tip."

"A man whose name police would not disclose, said to have been masquerading as a woman the night Mr. Tesmer was killed, was taken into custody last night by Lieutenant Hugh McCarthy."[13]

MASQUERADER IDENTIFIED BY TESMER WIDOW
Posed 13 Years as Wife
Pleads Alibi.

"Fred G. Thompson, identified positively by Mrs. Richard Tesmer as 'the terrible woman who killed my husband,' smoothed 'her' henna bob, deepened the masquerole under 'her' gimlet eyes of blue-grey, and traced a crimson cupid's bow about 'her' wide spread mouth, as police locked him up last night in the men's quarters of the Hyde Park station.

"The thirty-three-year-old man, known for thirteen years as Mrs. Frances Carrick ... rubbed stubby fingers over a chin smeared with rouge and whiskers. Then he grunted, 'Hell, I wish they'd give me a safety razor and a shot of gin.' "[14]

A squad of detectives led by a sergeant named Cusack had raided the Thompson/Carrick/Clark apartment in the middle of the night. Frances met them at the door, dressed in a kimono. Sergeant Cusack told her to get dressed. She changed into a blue silk skirt, matching blouse, and green straw hat. Cusack's men dragged her out, "kicking, screaming oaths, and shouting boasts." They drove her to Mrs. Tesmer's apartment.

Cusack warned Mrs. Tesmer: She had to be certain, this time. Cusack handed Frances a .38 and told her to smile and point it at Mrs. Tesmer. "I ain't ever held a gun in my hand," Frances said. The gun wobbled. Mrs. Tesmer didn't hesitate, though. "It was the coldest rap I ever saw," said Cusack, "and I've seen many identifications. Mrs. Tesmer was positive. Absolutely positive."[15]

"That woman's crazy," Frances said. "She already identified four or five girls. ... She said she was waiting for blue eyes. Mine are grey."[16] No matter.

Cusack arrested Frances. Police at the station didn't know whether to put her in the Women's House of Detention or the men's jail. David Jones, a city physician, and Clara Seippel, a doctor employed by the Morals Court, examined Frances. They signed a certificate: Frances was a man.

Frances was less upset by the doctors than by Mrs. Tesmer. "When I saw her," Frances said, "I felt sorry for her. Honest—I wanted to just put my arms around her. ... Then the damned fool went and tried to hook me for this. ... I was at home that night ... I know it was that night because I was sick [from drinking bad moonshine] the day before. I had to leave the [Windsor] theater in the middle of the movie because I was sick. ... I never shot a revolver in my life. All I ever done was drink. ... I was never out on the streets. And look what comes to me. . . . I'm going to fight this damned mess. . . . 'Fair heart ne'er won fair lady.' "[17]

Police arrested Frances's husband the next day. Lieutenant McCarthy and Sergeant Cusack searched the Carricks' apartment: wigs, hairpieces, face paint, and powder; a pair of frayed Russian boots, several expensive corsets, hundreds of player piano music rolls; piles of lingerie; a bird's-eye maple dining room set—table, sideboard, and chairs; a huge victrola; a shelf of cookbooks; a recipe for chocolate fudge; an insurance policy naming "Frances Carrick, wife" as beneficiary; a draft board notice exempting Frank from military service because of "the dependency of wife, Frances." Frances's closets were packed with clothes, but she didn't own a single brown dress. There were hats, all sorts of hats, scattered everywhere, but not a single bonnet with a floppy brim.

"It'll take me a long time to listen to that racket about Mrs. Carrick being a man," said the lady who lived in a little house behind Frances's apartment building. No one in the neighborhood believed that Frances was the sort of person who'd carry a gun. "Not a chance," the lady said. "We'd've known if she was up to that kind of stuff." There was only one thing that people thought was strange about Frances: her beard. "But," the lady said, "I knew she drank a lot, and I thought that when she got crazy from cheap moon, she might've shaved her face, once. Then she would've had to keep on."[18]

Chief of Detectives Hughes and Assistant State's Attorney Jones decided to be nice to Frances. They didn't let her shave, but they did let her change her clothes. On her second day in jail, Frances appeared in a black dress with a low-cut, oval neck and short, slit sleeves. Frances told Hughes she had a sensitive stomach, so he had detectives get her a bottle of milk to drink while he questioned her. Frances took a sip, pulled up her stockings, and denied everything. "Believe me," she said, "I don't know a damned thing about this mess. You help me and I'll help you. We'll go through the dope joints and we'll get the girl who killed Tesmer. That Tesmer woman— she's crazy. Why don't she give me a white man's chance? Let me doll up, shave, wash my eyes, get my rainbow garden [of makeup] working—then see if she could recognize me. Not a chance."[19]

Frances may have had an ulcer—but Frank had a habit. After two days without a fix, and another day of nonstop questioning, Frank cracked. Hughes hoped he'd get a confession—instead he got "the ravings of a dope fiend. . . . The tiny, anemic, wild-eyed man didn't seem to know what he was talking about . . . he twisted in his chair. . . . Occasionally, he would cough, dryly. Sometimes, he trembled and startled at imaginary sounds. . . . At noon, taken back to his cell . . . the frail-looking man began to talk wildly of shots, bullets, guns, murders, and automobiles. His ravings were a cross-section of all the questions that had been shot at him. From them, he constructed a weird story of having seen the shots that killed Tesmer. . . ."[20] Police had a hunch that a tall man with wavy hair named Slim had been Frances's accomplice. " 'Yeah,' said Frank, 'Slim did it. Sure, Slim did. I seen him . . . The bullet grazed the side of the automobile . . . Then he ran down the alley like the cops said he did.' "[21] Hughes had Frank taken to the city's Psychopathic Hospital.

Meanwhile, Frances gave interviews. Social workers, socialites, psychoanalysts, and curiosity seekers "thronged the Detective Bureau to see the creature with the duplex psychology."[22]

All of Frances's visitors were women. They all asked her the same—eternal—question:

"A girl in a modish fawn-colored suit rushed up to Freddie [Frances] to ask him, 'Which gets away any better in this world, man or woman?' "[23]

"Believe me," said Frances, "a woman can get away with murder. You know what I mean, honey. She can get anything from a new hat to a new husband if she knows how."

Frances spoke as if she were sitting in her kitchen, chatting over coffee. A middle-aged social worker asked Frances what she'd learned from her experience: "If you had to do it over again, would you dress like a woman?"

Frances arched her brows, took a sip of milk, and answered without hesitating: "Not a chance . . . Look what it's brought me to. But it's [been] good for me. It's like driving. . . . You're never . . . careful until you have an accident."[24]

The newspapers published photographs of Frances in her male and female incarnations. The *Chicago Tribune* reproduced a copy of the marriage certificate issued to Fred Thompson and Marie Clark. The paper published a snapshot of Fred, wearing trousers and a T-shirt, next to a snapshot of Frances in a housedress. Every day, the papers published photos of Frances, before, during, and after her interrogations. A portrait of Frances made on the day she was arrested was striking: beautiful, dark eyes, a lovely mouth, a pale oval face framed by dark, hennaed hair. Frances was no blonde; her eyes weren't blue; she hadn't been a twenty-year-old girl for thirteen years.

Someone hired an attorney named Frank McDonnell to represent Frances. McDonnell served Chief of Detectives Hughes with a writ of habeas corpus. The result: three days after Frances's arrest, she made her first public appearance—in the court of Judge Joseph David, the same judge who'd presided over Carl Wanderer's insanity hearings.

People from every office in the County Building left their desks to get a look at Frances. Three times, Judge David ordered bailiffs to clear the crowd from the courtroom. Three times, they tried and failed. After fifteen minutes of shoving and shouting, the bailiffs cleared a small space in front of the bench.

McDonnell's writ had specified that "Mr. and Mrs. Fred Thompson" be produced to stand trial before a judge. Judge David reviewed the writ, looked at the defendant, whom the prosecutor referred to as Fred-Frances, and asked, "which is which."

"Stand up," Attorney McDonnell said to his client.

Police had let Frances freshen up for the occasion. She was closely shaved, freshly powdered and rouged; hennaed hairpieces framed her face. She wore the same black dress she'd worn since her second day in jail. A reporter noticed that Frances wore high heels. Size 5, the reporter guessed.

"Very well, be seated," said Judge David. An attorney from Mr. Crowe's office presented a warrant charging Frances with murder. Attorney McDonnell stepped forward to object to the warrant's $10,000 bail.

"That's preposterous," said Judge David. "If it's murder, there is no bail."

"That's the point," said McDonnell. "The state has no case."

McDonnell had been alternating pronouns as he spoke about his client—sometimes Frances was a "she," sometimes a "he."

"Which is it?" asked Judge David.

McDonnell said he didn't really know.

"Well," said Judge David, "whichever it is, take this man or woman—take her—before Judge Burgee within an hour, arrange for a hearing in Municipal Court tomorrow—and have the bail canceled."

Police escorted Frances and McDonnell through the crowd to Judge Burgee's courtroom. Burgee wasn't there. Frances's escorts were so flustered, they began to present their request to a bailiff. Fortunately, a judge named Walker stepped into the room. He'd been looking for his secretary. His secretary was in the crowd. Gaping at Frances. Walker took the bench, accepted the state's warrant, canceled Frances's bail, and ordered a Municipal Court hearing for the next day.

Police took Frances back to a holding cell in the Detective Bureau. Chief Hughes had agreed to keep her there since she refused to dress or behave like Fred.

The next morning, Frances shaved, curled her hair, applied fresh makeup, and stepped into the bureau's briefing room wearing a pink silk slip. The sergeant who'd been in the middle of roll call stopped in mid-sentence.

"Don't you know it's against the rules to parade around a respectable jail dressed in a teddy bear," he said.

"It isn't a teddy bear," Frances said. "It's a step-in. I'm saving my blue dress so it won't be wrinkled for the hearing. So much depends on making a good appearance."[25]

Frances needn't have gone to the trouble.

Frank Carrick and Marie Clark were brought to court and ordered to stand with Frances when her hearing began. A crowd filled the hallways outside the courtroom, but bailiffs wouldn't let anyone in. Judge Rooney looked at Frances and Marie and said they looked like sisters. Marie had been charged with disorderly conduct the night detectives arrested Frances. Marie had posted bail; she was expecting to be arraigned. Judge Rooney told her that would happen later. She was free to go—but Judge Rooney reminded her: when Frances's case came to trial, she would not be—she could not be—required to testify against her husband.

Frank was calmer than he'd been in days. There had been some talk about charging Frank with draft dodging—claiming Frances as his wife. Nothing came of it: as far as Judge Rooney and the federal government were now concerned, Frank had no spouse and therefore no spousal privileges. Judge Rooney told Frank he was free to go.

Attorney McDonnell announced he was prepared to call the widow Tesmer to testify. "I'll undermine the state's case; I'll force them to show their hand.[26] . . . The only evidence the police have is the identification of Mrs. Tesmer and she has identified half a dozen other girls."[27]

Crowe's office didn't give McDonnell a chance to undermine anything. An assistant state's attorney asked Judge Rooney for a "continuance to enable the police to make a complete investigation of certain important phases of the case which need to be cleared up."[28]

Rooney postponed the hearing until July 11. In the meantime, he accepted McDonnell's request that Frances be transferred from police custody to the county jail. "I want my client referred to as 'Miss,'" said McDonnell. "That's my defense."

Fred Thompson

Wesley Westbrook, the warden of the county jail, took one look at Frances and made up his own mind. If Frances was his responsibility, then Frances needed to act properly: off with the dress, the heels, the rouge, and the hairpieces. Fred was given a pair of prison overalls and a jumper and sent to the men's quarters. "And so it was that legal authorities restored Thompson to the masculinity he had practically discarded as a boy."[29]

Four days later, Oscar Wolff convened a coroner's jury.

Mrs. Tesmer came to the inquest, escorted by her brother, her sister, and her daughter. A crowd, twenty deep, pressed forward to see her. Women and children, some as young as five, some as old as eighty, fell silent as Mrs. Tesmer began to testify. She pointed at Frances and said in a voice so frail it was almost a whisper, "That is the person that killed my husband. God will help me. God is with me."

Frances sat at a table next to her attorney. Warden Westbrook had let Frances wear a dress and makeup to the inquest. McDonnell leaned over to her and whispered, "What do you think of this?" Frances answered, loud enough for everyone to hear, "Aw—it's awfully well staged."

McDonnell asked Coroner Wolff's permission to cross-examine Mrs. Tesmer. A deputy coroner and two assistant state's attorneys objected as strongly as if McDonnell had asked Mrs. Tesmer to disrobe. "This girl's life and liberty are at stake!" McDonnell cried as he pointed at Frances. "Is this Russia that a person can be accused and not permitted to defend himself?"[30]

McDonnell kept changing his pronouns.

The result: A debate began about the name and gender of the prisoner. Sergeant Cusack, who'd arrested Frances, took the stand. He said that Frances was a man. A man named Fred Thompson. "Frances Carrick" was nothing but an alias. "Freddie-Frances" was the way police referred to him. Attorney McDonnell asked Sergeant Cusack if he was a "sex expert" as well as a police detective. Coroner Wolff told Cusack he didn't need to answer.

The coroner's jury took less than a minute to return a verdict:

"Fred G. Thompson" alias "Frances Carrick" had shot and killed Richard Tesmer during a robbery. The jury ordered Thompson's case be sent forward to the grand jury. By the time the grand jury returned its own murder verdict, the Criminal Court had recessed for the summer.

Frances's murder trial began on October 1, 1923. Her case was the first on the court's docket. Her judge was Chief Justice John Caverly—the same judge who'd ruled against Harvey Church. The same judge who would, a year later, decide that Leopold and Loeb were juveniles whose youth spared them from the death penalty. (Leopold later remarked that everyone would have been saved a lot of time, trouble, and money if Judge Caverly had simply asked to see their birth certificates on the first day of their trial.)

"One of the largest [crowds] ever seen in the Criminal Court building"[31] packed the courtroom and overflowed into adjacent corridors. "The crowd was composed for the most part of women with a fair sprinkling of males of the so-called 'cake eating' type."[32]

Frances had grown stouter and stockier during her months in jail. Instead of a silk dress, hose, heels, and a hat with a veil, she wore blue-denim prison trousers, "a woman's georgette shirtwaist," and hairpieces over each ear.[33] A reporter wrote that Frances wore her blue jeans "with a feminine bearing as if they had been silken Turkish pajamas."[34]

Jury selection was uneventful. The trial began just after noon.

"With burning eyes . . . Mrs. Anna Tesmer . . . arose from the witness chair . . . and pointed out Fred G. Thompson as her husband's killer. . . . Thompson, the she-man with the Mona Lisa smile, bent a glance of withering scorn at his accuser, straightened his [hair] puffs, and cracked his gum. . . . 'The bunk,' he commented in a girlish voice. 'The poor thing is hysterical.'

"Mrs. Tesmer held to her identification despite a sharp cross examination by Attorney Frank C. McDonnell. . . . [McDonnell's] hint that the widow had not always referred to the murderer as 'the one dressed as a woman,' brought sharp objections from the attorneys for the state. The objections were sustained."[35]

The state called three more witnesses after Mrs. Tesmer, then it rested its case.

Attorney McDonnell began by calling character witnesses. Some had known Frances for twenty years. They spoke of a "thoroughly domesticated housewife," "a talented seamstress," "an exceptionally fine cook."

The trial grew even more interesting when McDonnell called Frank Carrick to the stand.

As soon as Frank was sworn in, Assistant State's Attorney William McLaughlin jumped to his feet.

"I ask the court to halt this questioning until defense counsel has asked what relation he has to the defendant."

McDonnell tried not to smile as he objected—strenuously.

Judge Caverly ordered McDonnell to ask Frank McLaughlin's question.

"Are you and the defendant, man and wife?" The state had just helped McDonnell convince the jury that Frances did more than just dress like a woman.

"Yes, sir," Frank answered. He didn't seem upset by the question. "Freddie and I were married May 23, 1913 . . . it was several months before I learned that my wife was a man."[36]

Judge Caverly intervened. "Not another word," he said. He ordered Frank to step down.

"The ruling, said to be without parallel in American jurisprudence, was based upon the law that no husband may testify in his wife's behalf at a murder trial. . . . Judge Caverly held that the fact that Thompson was a man did not affect his status as a wife in so far as the interpretation of the law is concerned."[37]

Frances took the stand the next day. She'd asked permission to wear a dress, but the state had objected. Judge Caverly told her to wear what she'd worn when the trial began. Attorney McDonnell made his objections public: "The state charges my client is a man who, when the alleged crime took place, was masquerading as a woman. The defense will prove the defendant is a woman." McDonnell said he had medical experts and a set of X-rays that would prove Frances was who she said she was.

In the meantime, Frances told the jury the story of her life. Tears and sobs interrupted her testimony. She spoke of her marriage to Frank Carrick—"My man," she said—and then her marriage to Marie Clark. She said she'd married Marie to save the girl's soul. She described how she and Marie left Chicago, bought land in Elmhurst; how they'd tried to farm it; how she'd tried to live as Fred. How none of it had worked. She laughed as she cried. She began to describe her boyhood. She spoke of how lonely and ashamed she'd been, how she'd dressed as a boy, then dressed as a girl, back and forth, until finally she ran away. To the streets of Chicago. She wept as she said this.

McDonnell asked her:

"Did you ever change your clothes to conceal a murder?" "No," Frances said. She turned to the jury. "Gentlemen," she said. All the jurors were men. "Gentlemen," she said, "I didn't kill Mr. Tesmer. I couldn't kill a cat or a dog." She broke down. Women in the crowd began to weep. For five minutes, the only sounds in the courtroom were their sobs and Frances's weeping.

The jury took two hours to reach a verdict. Their first ballot was 8 to 4 for acquittal. Their second was 9 to 3. Then it was 11 to 1. Then it was: "Not guilty."

"My God!" Frances screamed. "I'm glad!"

Judge Caverly had ordered extra bailiffs posted in the room, but they couldn't control the crowd. Women engulfed Frances, patted her, tugged at her, embraced her. A three-year-old girl fell to her knees and was nearly trampled by her own mother.

"I've got things wrong with me, sure," said Frances. "But—hell—that don't make me a killer. Just because a man has cross eyes don't make him a pickpocket. A guy can have adenoids and not be a murderer. What the hell's the big idea!"

Frances thanked each member of the jury, then she and Frank and Attorney McDonnell made their way through the crowds. Outside the courthouse there were more crowds.

"I've learned a lot," Frances told reporters. "Everybody's been swell to me—but, my goodness!—I'll be glad to get some hair pins!"

Back at McDonnell's office, Frances changed into a navy blue suit trimmed with lace. Someone asked her if she had any plans. All the ladies who'd visited her in jail had asked the same question. "Write a book or go into the movies" was what Frances had said, then. Now all she wanted was a new hat. "It was June when I went on my little trip and it's winter, now. Must have a new lid."

By State's Attorney Jones's count, Frances was the thirtieth woman in Cook County to get away with murder.

Julian "Potatoes" Kaufman

10 · Duffy Double Murder

Things began as they usually did: Someone shot someone else. This time it was Dean O'Banion himself who did the shooting. He shot Davey Miller in the stomach, in front of one thousand people, on an opening night, after a show, outside the La Salle Theater. Everyone ran. O'Banion liked that. His left leg was an inch shorter than his right. Better other people should run.

O'Banion began his career as a choirboy and a petty thief in a bad neighborhood on Chicago's Near North Side called "Little Hell." His mentor was a psychopath whose rages were calmed only by the sound of young Dean singing Irish ballads. By the time O'Banion was thirty-two, he was a florist with twenty-five kills to his credit. He was married to a doll-faced blonde, lived in a twelve-room apartment, and wore suits made to accommodate his gimp leg and the three guns he usually carried. Not the night he shot Davey Miller, though.

A jewel thief named Yankee Schwartz had roped Davey in, walked past him during intermission while Davey was standing with his wife, his brother Max, and Max's wife. "Aren't you gonna say, 'Hello'?" Yankee said. "I don't say hello to ingrates." Yankee knew Davey would say that. After the war, Yankee had been stranded, sick and broke, in Philadelphia. He was a capable young man—born in South Africa, he'd traveled the world as a boxer.

Times were lean, though, especially for a man who stole diamonds. Hirshie Miller—Davey's older brother—heard about Yankee and brought him to Chicago, one Jew helping another. Hirshie loaned Yankee money, hooked him up, gave him work. Yankee said thank you by double-crossing one of Davey Miller's friends, then offering his services to Dean O'Banion. That's why, after the show, Davey walked up to Yankee, to finish their conversation. O'Banion was waiting. Yankee handed him a .38.

Behind Dean, his back to Dean's back, stood Hymie Weiss. "Hymie the Polack" (Christian name Earl Wajciechowski), a lethal man and a sophisticated one; the police called him the "perfume bandit." Hymie and Dean had been partners since their days as safecrackers, lugging drills and fuses, and taps of nitro, blowing payroll safes. The two of them, together, had perfected the tactic—and invented the phrase—"take a guy for a ride." Now they were big-time bootleggers—not big enough to own distilleries or warehouses like Al Capone or his boss, John Torrio, but well enough connected to sell whatever they were allotted—and whatever they could hijack—to every speakeasy on the city's North Side.

Hymie watched the street, tracked the cars, scanned the crowd, ready to open a path once Dean did what he planned. "Why'd you call Dean an ingrate, you son of a bitch," Yankee said when Davey came close. Dean poked his gun into Davey's belly. Two shots; the crowd scattered; Davey went down.

Davey didn't deserve what he got. He was no angel—none of the Millers were (Davey's dad was a cop, but a dirty one, mixed up in narcotics)— but Davey wasn't worth such personal attention. He was just a west side bookie; he fixed fights and ran a joint—cards, craps, and bets—one flight up, above a restaurant at Roosevelt and Kedzie. Davey was a message O'Banion wanted to send to Davey's brother, Hirshie.

Hirshie Miller and "Nails" Morton were the self-anointed Protectors of the Ghetto—Jewish tough guys who stood up to any Polack who wanted a taste of Jewish blood. Nails was the best connected and most successful of the pair. Nails owned a bar and a garage, but what he was was a fence—stolen cars and stolen liquor made him rich. Back in 1922, Nails and Hirshie had gotten into a fight with two Irish cops at the Beaux Arts Café, a speakeasy, one floor up from a "black and tan" place (a club where the races mixed) called the Pekin. Hirshie and Nails had every right to be there; the cops thought they did, too. The cops died; Hirshie and Nails spent a fortune, over the course of two trials, buying acquittals. In May 1923, Nails went riding in Lincoln Park. Not a very west side thing to do. Worse yet, his horse threw him. Not a very Jewish way to die. (Nails had just bought the horse from Dean O'Banion. Years before, Nails had fenced O'Banion's first, small load of stolen whiskey. The two became partners: Nails the distributor, O'Banion the bootlegger. They made each other rich.) Nails's friends solemnly executed the horse.[1] Five thousand people—Hymie Weiss and Hirshie Miller among them—attended Nails's funeral. A rabbi said kaddish; representatives of the Fraternal Order of Elks joined an honor guard; members of the 123rd Infantry with whom Nails had served in France paid tribute to his gallantry.

Hirshie announced he was retiring from the life he'd lived: Nails's death had opened his eyes. From now on, he said, he planned to devote himself to his family (May and Marie) and to his business, the Acme Cleaning and Dyeing Company. All true—but there was so much money to be made selling booze, Hirshie couldn't keep away. He and O'Banion entered a whiskey deal together—whiskey, trucked in from Philly, paid, in part, with an IOU. Once it reached Chicago, O'Banion would hijack it; he and Hirshie would split the take. Unfortunately, the people who owned the whiskey found out that O'Banion planned to steal it. They put a gun to O'Banion's head. O'Banion handed them cash. Hirshie refused to pay what he owed.

Davey paid instead. He should have bled out on the sidewalk, or died of shock and sepsis. He was a tough guy. He also had good luck: it was late January, so his overcoat helped him, too. His family got him to University Hospital in time. He lived. Barely. A police lieutenant named Farrell questioned him. Davey was so weak, in so much pain, so full of drugs, he almost told Farrell who shot him. He stopped himself, though. "No," he said. "I'll take care of it, myself. Leave this to me."

Two days later, Davey's brother, Davey's wife, and his brother's wife went to the Detective Bureau and swore out a warrant against O'Banion and Weiss. The police went looking. A squad car, carrying a lieutenant named O'Connor, found O'Banion doing what he liked: hijacking a load of whiskey in broad daylight. O'Banion was accompanied by a solid citizen named Dapper Dan McCarthy (McCarthy was a business agent of the Plumbers' Union. He'd been tried—and acquitted—three times for murder); McCarthy and O'Banion had just forced a truck, carrying 251 cases of whiskey, up onto a curb at Indiana and Nineteenth Street, when O'Connor interrupted them. (By 1923, O'Banion's annual income from selling booze—not flowers—was estimated at $1 million.[2] No matter: O'Banion loved taking what belonged to other people. Bootleggers who were more ruthless and more powerful than O'Banion soon grew tired of his tricks.)

The whiskey on the truck was the legal property of the Corning Distillery. Corning had a federal permit to transport its property to its warehouse in Peoria. O'Banion and Dapper Dan had presented themselves to Corning's drivers as police detectives; they'd asked the men to step into their Studebaker to answer a few questions. While the men made themselves comfortable, two other "detectives" got out and drove the truck away. O'Banion was climbing back into his car when Lieutenant O'Connor came around the corner. The whiskey truck went one way; the Studebaker, driven by Dapper Dan, went the other. O'Banion was left on the curb. O'Connor had to choose between chasing the truck with its $30,000 load of whiskey (worth ten times as much today) or chasing O'Banion's Studebaker. He decided to arrest O'Banion, then go after the Studebaker. O'Banion pleaded with him and his men not to shoot. "Don't fire," O'Banion kept saying. "They'll give up." He was right, of course.

Back in 1921, Dean and Hymie and a master safecracker named Charlie Reiser were caught by a police sergeant, standing in the smoking ruins of an office, in front of a safe they'd blown in the Postal Telegraph building. At trial, O'Banion told the jury that he and the others had been at a restaurant, next door, eating chocolate éclairs, when they'd heard the explosion, put down their forks, and rushed over to see what had happened. Despite the testimony of a watchman who'd seen the men climb in a window before the safe blew, the jury acquitted everyone.

As a consequence, O'Banion had come to trust Chicago's courts, juries, and judges. Even though he had the greatest respect for Chicago's police, he felt sure that he and Mr. McCarthy would be able to explain the true nature of the event that Lieutenant O'Connor believed had been a hijacking. O'Banion and his associates maintained large reserve funds, set aside for such purposes. He and McCarthy were released on bail. Police immediately arrested O'Banion for shooting Davey Miller. O'Banion posted another bond and went back to his flower shop.

Seven months later, on the same day that court-appointed psychiatrists concluded their evaluation of Nathan Leopold and Richard Loeb, the driver of the Corning Distillery truck—a man named Charles Levin— announced to the world that he had suffered an almost complete loss of memory concerning the traumatic events that had occurred when his truck was hijacked. Since Levin was the prosecution's principal witness against O'Banion and McCarthy, state and federal lawyers did everything they could to help Levin regain his memory. "When confronted with statements he had made shortly after the hold up, Levin told the court he was dazed and didn't remember having been questioned or giving any of the answers credited to him in the transcript. The driver said his mind was a blank from the time a closed car headed off his truck. . . . until long after he had been questioned by the police. The next dazed spell hit him weeks later, he said, when he was summoned before a federal grand jury."[3] After twenty-three hours of deliberation, the jury announced it was unable to reach a verdict.

All this hadn't happened, yet. Charles Levin still had his memory. The crime he forgot had just occurred.

For the moment:

O'Banion was out on bail, charged with shooting Davey Miller and hijacking a load of bottled-in-bond whiskey.

One month passed.

Early one morning, in February, a driver, heading north into the city, noticed a body sprawled on a snowbank, at the edge of a stretch of open prairie. The night before, the conductor of a "night owl" trolley had noticed a Ford parked there, with its motor running. "The occupants of the Ford seemed to be carrying a large object from the car."[4] The spot was fifteen miles southwest of the city; bootleggers had been dumping bodies there, on and off, for years.

When detectives arrived, they found a dead man dressed in an expensive suit, with a gold watch and a roll of money in his pockets and three bullet holes in his head. The bullets had come from a .38; one shot had been fired so close to the man's left ear, it might have begun as a whisper. Two shots in the head were professional. The third was personal. A tailor's mark in the man's jacket had the name "Duffy" and the address "1216 Carmen Avenue."

Two detective sergeants, Eisen and Baynes, drove to Carmen Avenue and waited for someone to go in or come out. No one did. A bag of groceries, delivered the day before, sat on the back porch. After sunset, the men could see a light through one of the windows. They waited until seven, then they jimmied the door. The lock sprang, but the door wouldn't open. They kicked it in. Someone had nailed the door shut from the inside. "Hello, you folks," Eisen called. No answer.

The place smelled of cigarettes and whiskey. There'd been a party, but no one had cleaned up. An electric lamp on the hall table was the only light in the place. The men stepped into the front room. Eisen turned on the ceiling light. Trays full of cigarette butts, a bottle with a few fingers of scotch still in it, an empty wine bottle, three liquor glasses, smudged and smeared. A davenport, an expensive one, wicker and thick cushions, covered with a bloody sheet. The wall behind the sofa had a big hole—maybe a bullet hole—in it. On to the kitchen: three chairs, three plates, two of them empty, one with a cup of coffee, untouched, next to it. Two bedrooms—one, neat, clean, fresh sheets. The other, rumpled, stale, littered. One bathroom—cosmetics in the cabinet, women; urine stains around the commode, men. Back to the living room. Back to the davenport and its bloody sheet.

"See what's under it," said Eisen. Baynes lifted a corner, then pulled it back. A young, very pretty dead woman. Twenty-five, maybe. Diminutive. Brown hair. Bobbed. She was dressed in pink silk underwear; she'd draped a pink and black shawl around her shoulders. She'd been shot—once— "with a .45, from a distance of five feet," the coroner's physician said. She'd been lying on a sofa when she died. "Probably asleep," said the physician. The bullet had entered under her chin, exited at the base of her skull; it was in the wall behind her. She was the same temperature as the room. Dead a day, but not much longer. The bureau's fingerprint specialist found four sets of prints on the glasses on the table.

On the dresser in the rumpled bedroom were pictures of the dead woman and the man who'd been left in the snow. The woman had been more than pretty—fresh-faced, alert, refined. The man appeared neither happy nor unhappy—big, tough, stone-faced. A lout.

Once a coroner's physician and the bureau's fingerprint man arrived, Eisen and Baynes began opening drawers. Letters, telegrams, and bankbooks identified the woman.

Mrs. John Duffy had several very large savings accounts in her name. Letters to and from her mother showed she was from a small town in Ohio. She'd gone to Stanford University for a year, then moved to Louisville. She worked for a while as a manicurist, then met a man named Irving Zollin. Mr. Zollin was a pimp. She changed her name from Leahbelle Exley to "Miss Virginia James" and started turning tricks. Unfortunately, Zollin was arrested in Columbus for "defrauding an innkeeper." He wrote Leahbelle letters from jail: if he ever found out she was with another man, he'd kill her. Leahbelle changed her name to Maybelle and got a job in the best whorehouse in Louisville. She and a girl named Ruby Downing became lovers. It was through Ruby that Maybelle met her future husband: in October 1923, John Duffy came to Louisville with a buddy of his from Chicago. His buddy had come to visit Ruby. Maybelle and Duffy fell in love. In January 1924, Duffy proposed; they were married on Valentine's Day. One week later, some men in a Ford dumped Duffy in the snow. One day later, Eisen and Baynes kicked down Duffy's door and found Maybelle.

The bureau matched prints from one of the liquor glasses to a set it had on file. That match, plus Mrs. Duffy's bankbooks, plus John Duffy's tailor's mark, plus neighbors' gossip, plus a tattoo on Duffy's right arm (a nude with a *J* on one side and a *D* on the other) confirmed that John Duffy was a thug from Philadelphia named Jack Daugherty. In Philadelphia, Daugherty had committed at least one hundred robberies and at least one murder (an African-American minister). Duffy liked .45s; he bragged about killing a cop. A few weeks before he was dumped, he'd been part of a $100,000 (equivalent to ten times that amount today; all dollar figures in this chapter are denominated in 1924 dollars: a 1924 dollar bought what $10 now buys) jewel robbery in Atlantic City. Yankee Schwartz, the jewel thief, had known Duffy in Philadelphia. He'd brought Duffy to Chicago to work for him. Yankee said he'd been double crossed in a beer deal and needed someone to help him even the score. Duffy's problem was that he was a drunk. Booze made him "crazy." "You'd be talking to Duffy, quiet and peaceable, and the next minute, you'd be picking yourself up with a black eye and half your teeth knocked out."[5]

So much for the bride and groom.

What about the other bedroom? The one with the clean sheets. There'd been three glasses, three plates, and four sets of prints. Who else was at the party?

More neighbor gossip:

Mr. and Mrs. Jack Horton shared the apartment with the Duffys: "Orlando Jack" Horton and his lovely blonde wife, Cecil. Jack told the neighbors he worked for the Chicago and Northwestern Railroad, as a claims investigator. That's why, he said, he came and went as often as he did; home for a while, then off to Indianapolis or St. Louis or Milwaukee. Freight claims, personal injury claims. People asked about his Cadillac, Jack said in his line of work he needed a good, heavy road car. He and Cecil were friends with another couple—the Curtises: Freddy and Betty. They visited the Hortons, often. They tried to stay clear of John Duffy and his temper. Everyone wondered how Maybelle put up with him. She was a good sport, though. For such a pretty little thing, she could drink anyone under the table. With all the parties that went on there—and all the people coming and going—neighbors got used to the noise. Laughter, hammering, even; once, what sounded like a gunshot—it was just the way the Hortons and the Duffys were.

The police knew more about Jack Horton than his neighbors did. The only thing Jack had ever done for the Chicago and Northwestern was work as a switchman. The only freight he'd ever investigated was booze; the only personal injury claims he ever settled, he settled with his .38. As to Freddy Curtis: the police knew him, too. Bootlegging was hard on cars. Freddy was Jack's mechanic.

Just before detectives found Duffy in the snow, the Hortons and the Curtises had decided to drive down to New Orleans for Mardis Gras. That's why the Hortons' bedroom was so neat and clean when Eisen and Baynes broke down the door.

Because of the letters Irving Zollin had written to Maybelle, police thought he might have killed her. Columbus police told them otherwise: Zollin was in jail. For lack of any other suspects, Chicago police decided to charge Jack Horton and Freddy Curtis with the murder of "Mr. and Mrs. John Duffy." They were almost right.

When New Orleans police arrested Jack and Freddy, the men were glad to admit they were bootleggers—but not murderers. Both men carried .38s. Both weapons had been recently fired. Two shots from Jack's gun; one from Freddy's. "We took pot shots at signs on the drive down," Jack said. Besides, they were all in New Orleans, unpacking their suitcases, in an apartment on the Esplanade when detectives found Duffy's body.

Back at the bureau, detectives read and reread the documents from the Duffys' apartment. The Detective Bureau had a new chief—a veteran officer, a captain named William Shoemaker. The city's new mayor, William Dever, had appointed a new police chief—Morgan Collins—and told him to sweep the stables clean. Dever believed in the power and purity of the law; Collins hated dirty cops. Shoemaker needed to do more than just find out who shot whom. Maybelle and Duffy were less important than the "how and why" of their deaths.

Duffy's account book showed that he and Horton had been in business together. In the last few months, they'd cleared $8,000 from selling booze. The Cadillac that Horton drove to New Orleans was half owned by Duffy. Interesting, but nothing special. Duffy's address book was more promising. It listed the names and phone numbers of clients—a man who ran a pool hall, a doctor who treated gunshot wounds and fractures—a dozen people worth interrogating. Then detectives saw the name Julian Kaufman. Kaufman was too rich and too well connected to have been Duffy's customer. Why was Julian Kaufman in the phone book of a dead man like John Duffy?

Captain William Shoemaker

Julian "Potatoes" Kaufman was the son of a millionaire commodities commission agent. Julian didn't have to work, but he did, buying and selling wholesale lots, side by side with his father. Julian traded in potatoes—but he specialized in criminal underwriting and deal making. An agent, a producer, an impresario, a middle man, a lender of first and last resort—Potatoes knew everyone and everyone knew Potatoes. Who was "everyone"? Nails Morton, when he'd been alive. Hirshie Miller, Yankee Schwartz, Hymie Weiss, Dean O'Banion. Top to bottom, Potatoes was connected. Shoemaker was pleased. Duffy could lead them to Potatoes; Potatoes might lead them to O'Banion. Shoemaker told Collins; Collins told Dever; Dever told State's Attorney Crowe. Mr. Crowe issued two warrants: one charged Julian Kaufman with the murder of John Duffy; one charged Julian Kaufman with being an accessory to the murder of Maybelle Exley.

While Julian's lawyers made arrangements for him to surrender himself to Mr. Crowe, a woman named Jean Mason decided to tell police who they really needed to arrest: William Engelke.

Engelke was barely twenty. Slender, fine-featured, almost pretty, a bit "nervous," Engelke had been a "handyman" for John Duffy and Jack Horton. The men treated Engelke like an errand boy but—said Jean Mason—Engelke knew what happened to Maybelle—and to Duffy. How did Jean Mason know this? Because: Duffy had wanted to sleep with her before, during, and after he married Maybelle. Jean didn't visit Carmen Avenue every day—but she visited often enough. She knew Jack Horton; she knew Cecil. Duffy had hit Cecil; he'd threatened to kill Jack. Everyone was afraid of Duffy and his temper. She knew Engelke not just because he worked for Duffy: Engelke had moved in with Jean's sister, Dora. Promised to marry her. Hadn't treated her right. Engelke was there when Duffy shot Maybelle. Police needed to talk to him. Find him and talk to him.

Police started with Engelke's mother and father. He hadn't been home, they said, since the day Duffy's body was found. Will had sat in the kitchen, reading the paper, talking to himself, saying how bad things were and how bad things were going to get. They didn't know where their son was now; they were worried about him.

The next day, Julian Kaufman, accompanied by his wife, the beautiful Marion, presented himself to Mr. Crowe, in his office. Captain Shoemaker was there to ask a few questions. He'd just begun when he noticed the broach Marion was wearing. "Beautiful," he said. "Thank you," Marion said. "Diamonds?" he asked. "Yes," she said. "May I ask where you purchased it?" "Yankee Schwartz sold it to us," she said. "Along with two rings." "Yankee Schwartz?" "Yes," she said. "Yankee is a frequent guest in our house. He has such beautiful things." "I hope you'll pardon me, Mrs. Kaufman," said Shoemaker, "but do you happen to recall how much you paid for the broach?" "Yes," she said. "I believe it was $550." Marion looked at Julian. Julian looked pained.

Yankee had given the Kaufmans a good deal. The person who owned the broach—a Mrs. Elsa Richmeyer—had told police it cost $2,000. She'd been wearing it on January 31, when two men had taken it—and two diamond rings—from her, at gunpoint, while she, her two children, and her mother

Morgan Collins

were in their car, waiting for her brother, outside the company where he worked.

Captain Shoemaker explained this to Marion, then he confiscated the broach and charged her husband with receiving stolen property. Shoemaker released Marion—but only after she'd promised to return with the rings Yankee had sold them. Julian went to jail.

Of course, Julian didn't know anything about John Duffy. He "maintained an air of sullen bravado."[6] "It's all a damn lie," he said. "I never heard of any of the guys you fellows are talking about."[7] At a hearing before Judge Lewis, Julian complained about the noise in the bureau's holding cells. "They won't give me no decent place to sleep," he said. "You got as good as the rest of our high class boarders," Shoemaker answered. "This man is entitled to rest," said Judge Lewis. "I direct you to take him to a quiet station."[8]

The same day Shoemaker noticed Mrs. Richmeyer's broach on Marion's blouse, detectives found William Engelke. He was hiding in the apartment of a married couple—a Mr. and Mrs. Philip Goldberg. Police arrested Engelke, then asked Mr. Goldberg what he did for a living. The Goldbergs

Philip Goldberg

lived quite comfortably, so comfortably that when Mr. Goldberg made a vague reference to his "luck as a crap shooter,"[9] detectives arrested him, too.

Engelke was so relieved that it was the police who'd found him, Shoemaker didn't need to interrogate him.

"I was in the flat at . . . Carmen . . . on the night of the murder of Maybelle," Engelke said.

"Duffy accused Maybelle of going out with other men. . . . He said, 'I'll kill you if I find out for sure.'

"Duffy and I went into the kitchen to eat some lunch. Duffy asked Maybelle to come with us. She refused and went to lie on the davenport. Duffy and I sat down to eat. Then Duffy went to tell Maybelle to come and eat with us.

"I heard Duffy tell her to come out; Maybelle said she wouldn't. Duffy pulled out his gun and said, 'Damn you, I'll croak you if you don't,' Maybelle said, 'Oh, you wouldn't do that.'

"Then I heard a shot. . . . I had taken one bite out of my sandwich. I ran to the front room. Duffy . . . threatened to kill me. I talked my way out of it. Then he made me stay with him for the next 24 hours."[10]

Police kept Engelke locked up. The next day, he told Shoemaker an even better story. It helped explain why Duffy was so angry: Jack Horton had double-crossed him. Jack had left town with the money he and Duffy had made, driving the car they owned.

"Duffy called me up and asked me to come over. . . . He'd broken his hand a few days before in a fight. . . . Duffy said he had to meet some guys downtown. . . . We got a cab . . . down to North Clark. Duffy . . . went to Richardson's poolroom. . . .

"He brought a stranger back with him—he called him 'Harry.' . . . We all got into Harry's Cadillac and drove back to Carmen Avenue. . . .

"Duffy was boiling over mad . . . about Jack Horton . . . Jack Horton had run away with his car and his money. . . . Duffy said he wanted to get another car and trail Horton and Freddie Curtis and kill the whole bunch. He said Richardson, the poolroom fellow, had advised him to cool down and content himself with . . . beating up Horton the first time he ran across him . . ."[11] (When Jean Mason, the woman who'd turned in Engelke, read this part of Engelke's story in the paper, she remembered something else: "Duffy said, 'I'll do worse than that. I'll kill Horton's mother so he'll have to come to the funeral—then I'll kill him, too.' ")[12]

Back at Carmen, Duffy, Maybelle, Engelke, and Harry started drinking. Harry had some gin in his car; the Duffys had some wine and some scotch. At one o'clock in the morning, Harry drove home.

"Duffy and Maybelle were in their room, kidding . . . then they began to quarrel. Maybelle got sore and called Duffy a 'punk.' Duffy hit her a lick across the head. I quieted him down, but then him and Maybelle started quarreling again. Maybelle was lying on the couch. She had on a pink chemise . . . and little slippers.

"I looked and saw Duffy draw his gun and shoot her. . . . Then Duffy whirled around. . . . 'I'll kill you, too, if you ever tell. If I shoot you, nobody'll ever know who did kill Maybelle.' " Engelke talked him out of doing that.

"After a while, Duffy calmed down a little. . . . He went over and kissed Maybelle's face and carried on terrible, saying he was sorry. . . ."[13]

Duffy told Engelke to call Kaufman. Engelke called Kaufman at home.

Shoemaker was pleased: He now knew that something—he didn't know exactly what—had made Horton double-cross Duffy. And he had a name—"Harry"—to connect to the fourth set of prints from the apartment.

Engelke kept talking.

"Kaufman answered the phone and I told him Duffy wanted to see him. Duffy spread a sheet over Maybelle and we slipped out the back door. We got a cab, then we stopped to get a bite to eat at a lunchroom, then we drove to Kaufman's house. It was about four o'clock in the morning when we got there.

"Kaufman let us in and took us to the parlor. Duffy told Kaufman he wanted to use one of his cars. 'What do you want a car for?' 'I went crazy last night,' Duffy said. 'I killed my wife . . . I need the bus to haul away her body.'

"Kaufman seemed a little flustered, but he didn't say anything.

"We dismissed our cab. Kaufman took us downtown in his Ford . . . Kaufman left us; Duffy and I got something to eat; at eight o'clock we met Kaufman at the Sherman Hotel.

"Duffy begged Kaufman for a car, but Kaufman said his Paige was in the shop and he needed his Ford for business. We went with Kaufman to order some potatoes, then Duffy and I drove over to . . . the Broadway Arms and got a room and stayed there until the next night.

"Duffy wanted to know if I knew of a 'night undertaker' who could handle a body, but I told him no. He got desperate and threatened to go back to the flat and blow his own brains out. Then he called up Kaufman again and made a date to meet him.

"At nine o'clock that night, we met Kaufman at 23rd and Wabash."

Shoemaker became very attentive when Engelke said that. Half a block away, at Twenty-second and Wabash (Two-two-two-two Wabash) was the Four Deuces. Al Capone managed the place. John Torrio, Capone's boss, owned it. There was a bar on the ground floor (a shot of common stuff cost 25 cents; Canadian whiskey cost 75 cents). On the second floor was a bookie joint and Torrio's office. (Torrio was a small, edgy, thoughtful man who'd made a fortune running brothels, large and small; he'd made an even greater fortune operating breweries and selling beer, wholesale and retail.) On the floor above Torrio's office was a casino—roulette wheels and card games. On the top floor was a standard Torrio sex shop—cubicles and cots (a simple lay cost $2; for $5, a customer could watch two women having sex). Twenty-third and Wabash was at the center of a criminal neighborhood as distinct as the Financial District in New York.

Engelke continued:

"Kaufman was standing beside a big Lincoln or a Cadillac car as we came up. His Ford was parked across the street.

"Kaufman took Duffy aside for a long conference, leaving me alone beside the big car. When they got through talking, Duffy went across to the Ford. Kaufman started to bawl me out for calling him up. 'What the hell is the idea—getting me mixed up in such a dirty mess,' he yelled at me. 'This Duffy is just a wild maniac.'

" 'If you had a .45 up against *your* stomach, you would do what you were told, too,' I said.

" 'Well—it was a dirty trick to do what that rat did,' Kaufman said. 'A man that'd do a thing like that ought to get smoked off.'

"Then he said to me, 'You go on home. And don't you rap and get me mixed up in this thing . . .' As I was walking away to catch the El, I saw Kaufman crossing the street toward the Ford. . . ."[14]

Shoemaker was so pleased with Engelke's new story that he ordered Kaufman brought in. He wanted Julian to hear the whole thing himself. Engelke repeated everything. Kaufman roared his denial. "I NEVER SAW THAT FELLOW BEFORE," he said, pointing at Engelke. "HE LIES. IT'S ALL A PACK OF LIES. HE'S TRYING TO FRAME ME BECAUSE HE THINKS MY FOLKS HAVE MONEY."[15]

"But you know I'm telling the truth," Engelke said. "You know you and

I were the last to see Duffy alive. I don't know who knocked him off, but I wish to hell I did."[16]

Kaufman glared at him. Detectives took Engelke back to his cell. Julian's lawyers presented a request for bail to a Municipal Court judge named Schulman. Since there was no proof their client had done anything but talk to Duffy, he should be permitted to post bail. They knew—and Judge Schulman knew—that murder, even accessory to murder, was not a charge that was subject to bail. But Julian Kaufman was the son of a prominent and very wealthy man. Judge Schulman set Julian's bail at $30,000. Julian posted it and left the courthouse by the time police tried to rearrest him for receiving stolen property.

Detectives went looking for Yankee Schwartz; they couldn't find him. Friends said he was out of town on business. In fact, Yankee was in New Orleans, arranging for a shipment of Cuban rum. When detectives went looking for Hymie Weiss, they had no better luck: Weiss suffered from migraines. He'd left town, weeks before, to recuperate. He was in Hot Springs, Arkansas; he wasn't well; no one knew when he'd be back.

Shoemaker explained this to reporters. Meanwhile, said Shoemaker, his men were still searching for Dean O'Banion. If and when they found him, Shoemaker said, he had a long list of questions he wished to ask him.

O'Banion read the papers like everyone else in Chicago. That Saturday, O'Banion called a *Chicago Tribune* reporter and invited him to visit his flower shop. O'Banion had been there, conducting business, since he'd posted bail for the Collins whiskey truck hijacking. "The police don't have to look for me," he said. "I'll go look for them."

The reporter found O'Banion at his desk, doing his books.

"I saw in the papers," O'Banion said, "that because Yankee Schwartz was mentioned with me in regard to that affair at the La Salle Theater, people consider him to be a pal of mine." O'Banion spoke calmly, earnestly. "Schwartz is only a casual acquaintance.... You hear someone called 'Slim' or 'Shorty' or 'Yankee' when he's introduced to you—and the name sticks in your memory.... That's how I know him—just to nod and call him 'Yankee' when I meet him somewhere in the Loop....

"I also saw that Schwartz's name was connected with the Kaufmans.... Everybody knows Potatoes. But my acquaintance with Kaufman is only of the theater lobby kind of thing. When he'd see me going into some show or I'd run across him in a hotel lobby, I'd shake hands and nod.... I know

Kaufman about as well as 100 other casual acquaintances. . . . I wouldn't be fool enough to get myself mixed up in a criminal affair for him or anyone else. . . . Whatever happened to Duffy is out of my line. . . . I don't mix with that kind of riff-raff."

"But," said the reporter, "did you know Kaufman well enough to do a favor for him?"

O'Banion looked pained. Not upset, just impatient. As if he'd tried to explain things as clearly as he could, but his guest had been unable, for some reason—inattentiveness? inexperience? imbecility?—to understand. O'Banion abandoned all delicacy. Simple truths, bold statements, unadorned facts were called for.

"I can tell you, candidly," O'Banion said, "that I can count on the fingers of one hand the men I would do a favor for. The floral business—more than any other business in the world—certainly teaches you who your friends are."[17]

The *Tribune* reporter was chastened. He felt privileged. To be addressed so candidly, so forthrightly, by such an important individual. O'Banion's remarks were reproduced in print that very day.

Chief Collins, State's Attorney Crowe, Mayor Dever himself spent Sunday pondering the lessons that the flower business taught. Not Captain Shoemaker, though. He had Engelke brought from his cell.

Detectives had found a fully loaded .38 in a trunk Engelke had stored at a railway baggage company. Engelke had told police he had never, ever, owned a gun. Was that gun his? Yes, Engelke said. Police had also learned that, back in March 1923, Engelke had held up a big typewriter company and made off with its payroll. Two thousand, two hundred dollars in cash. Was that true, as well? Yes, said Engelke. Then, said Shoemaker, is there anything else? We'll find out, you know. If you tell us now it'll be better for you. All right, said Engelke. There is something else. Yes? said Shoemaker. It's about Duffy, said Engelke. What about Duffy? The car Duffy got into. What car? said Shoemaker. The car parked across from the Four Deuces, said Engelke. Yes? said Shoemaker. It wasn't a Ford, said Engelke. No? said Shoemaker. It was a big Studebaker, said Engelke. Dark brown. A "Big Six" as a matter of fact.

What a coincidence.

A dark brown "Big Six" was very much like the car (the papers called it a "limo") that Dean O'Banion had been in when he and Dapper Dan had hijacked the Corning Distillery truck, back in January.

Mr. and Mrs. Julian Kaufman

"The more we talk to Engelke, the more thoroughly he convinces us he has lied in no particular," said an investigator for Mr. Crowe's office.[18]

On Monday, the Kaufmans, man and wife, accompanied by their lawyers, presented themselves to Judge Schulman. Marion had never returned with the rings they'd bought from Yankee, as she'd promised. That wasn't mentioned, though, when an assistant state's attorney read the warrants, charging the Kaufmans with receiving stolen property. The young couple posted bail, higher than the one Julian had posted for being an accessory to murder; then they left the building.

Two hundred people—everyone in Chicago who'd been robbed at gunpoint of expensive jewelry during the past six months—were invited to the Detective Bureau to view a lineup of suspects. Orlando Horton and Freddy Curtis, back, in custody, from New Orleans, and William Engelke, still in jail and still doing his best to remember more about his time with John Duffy, stood before a crowd of women (and a few men) who'd been robbed of their diamonds.

"I'm pretty sure that's the man," one woman said when she saw Horton. "He didn't have that coat on, and he wore a cap. About two weeks before Christmas, two men came into my store. They had handkerchiefs over their faces. They took my diamond ring and $23 from my stocking. The ring cost $1,000."[19] A woman who ran a millinery store also identified Horton as the man who'd walked into her shop, pointed a gun at her, and taken two rings valued at $2,800. Mrs. Richmeyer identified Engelke as one of the men who'd held her up while she sat in her car with her children and her mother.

The people who'd lived at Carmen Avenue seemed to have been jewel thieves as well as bootleggers.

Julian's stolen property case headed for the grand jury. Julian was ordered to appear before Judge Francis Borelli, prior to the grand jury hearing evidence against him. Julian didn't come to court. His lawyers said he had tonsillitis. Marion presented a doctor's letter that certified Julian had a temperature of 101 degrees. Judge Borelli ordered Julian's case be continued. The grand jury went on to other business.

State's Attorney Crowe lost his patience. Shoemaker's dog and pony show of robbery victims and jewel thieves, Dean O'Banion's flower shop platitudes, Julian Kaufman's tonsillitis and Hymie Weiss's migraines—the point and counterpoint of criminal evasion and official impotence made Crowe so angry he called a news conference. State's Attorney Robert E. Crowe— born and bred in Peoria, educated at Yale, the youngest *ever* chief justice of the Criminal Court—was fed up. The public needed to know. Reporters were summoned.

Mr. Crowe stood behind his desk, pursed his lips, sucked in a breath, and began.

"The murders of John Duffy . . . and his so called wife, Maybelle Exley, occurred nearly two weeks ago. . . . The streets are alive with gossip coupling the names of known gangsters with the execution of Duffy.

"It has been reasonably well established that Duffy killed the Exley woman. Who killed Duffy? The recurrent jest, accompanied by . . . laughter, is that the gang made its own arrest, held its own trial, and carried out its own execution. . . . Who is to be next? What assurance is there that any self respecting citizen may not be killed on his door step because the gang tried and sentenced him?

"For the last two weeks, every known gangster has been walking the streets of Chicago with a smile. . . . Bootleggers, with their huge limousines and chauffeurs, clad in evening clothes and tossing bills about at waiters, have inhabited theaters and cafés . . . The police know them and have failed to question them. . . .

"If . . . high officials have interfered with arrests, police should present that information to the State's Attorney's office. I promise it will be acted upon. I should like to know more about the iron band of crime that has hushed the mouths and palsied the hands of the police. There is no palsy in the State's Attorney's office. . . .

"One man, William Engelke, has told the police the names of two men who, knowing that John Duffy killed Maybelle Exley, took him away in a curtained automobile.

"The police know that Duffy was antagonistic to certain plutocratic bootleggers. . . . Those bootleggers executed Duffy. Has the iron band of crime prevented the arrests of Dean O'Banion and Yankee Schwartz? . . .

"I want these persons brought to my office. . . . I shall insist they be brought in:

"Dean O'Banion, a man with a record as a bootlegger and gunman.

"Hirshie Miller, long an underworld character and concerned with the killing of two policemen.

"Dan McCarthy, labor slugger and killer.

"Yankee Schwartz, whose name has long been mentioned as a bad man from the East.

"Earl Weiss, handyman for Dean O'Banion, booze peddler, and suspicious character.

"John Torrio, long a kingpin in the underworld . . .

"These men are rapidly nearing the millionaire stage through the peddling of contraband liquor. . . . It is foolishness to say that the State's Attorney's office—with 35 men at its disposal—should do the duty for which 5000 policemen are available.

"The State's Attorney is willing to try. It is my duty to *prosecute*—not to conduct a police force. If the police force has declared a complete breakdown in efficiency, I shall try to demonstrate that Justice has not broken down."[20]

Mr. Crowe may have honestly believed he knew the facts of Duffy's murder, knew the suspects, knew their motives. Perhaps he did, perhaps he was just pretending. The reality was:

The gangsters Mr. Crowe said were "nearing the millionaire stage" had passed that mark long ago. For example:

John Torrio owned at least three breweries, either outright or in partnership. One of those breweries—a brewery Torrio owned in secret with a member of a respected "Gold Coast" family—netted $12 million (a sum worth ten times that now) per year.[21] In addition, Torrio's 1921 gambling income, in Chicago alone, netted an estimated $4 million. His 1921 income from prostitution—again, in Chicago alone—netted an estimated $2 million.[22] In 1925, Torrio retired, after Hymie Weiss and Bugs Moran almost killed him in revenge for the assassination of Dean O'Banion. Al Capone inherited Torrio's criminal assets, just as Torrio had inherited the assets of his predecessor, Big Jim Colosimo (killed by one of Capone's first employers, Frankie Yale). By 1927, Capone's gross annual income, as estimated by the U.S. Attorney's office in Chicago, was $105 million. (As noted: equivalent to ten times that amount today.)[23]

Further, the murder suspects Mr. Crowe identified—Yankee Schwartz and Dean O'Banion—had never been named by William Engelke. Engelke hadn't named them because he hadn't remembered them. Mr. Crowe's press conference helped Engelke recall what he didn't even know he'd forgotten.

Finally: the motives Mr. Crowe attributed to the men who killed Duffy—Schwartz and O'Banion supposedly killed Duffy because he'd murdered his wife—were so absurd that, one day after Mr. Crowe's press conference, Jean Mason phoned the Detective Bureau and arranged a meeting with Captain Shoemaker.

"Duffy and Horton were . . . members of O'Banion's outfit," Jean said. "Johnnie Duffy often told me how friendly he was with Hirshie Miller. One day, Johnnie and I drove to Hirshie's house and Johnnie went in and when he came out, he had a fine diamond ring. He said he bought it for $300.

" 'That Miller is a swell fellow,' he told me. 'I can get anything I want from him, even $1000 if I ask him.'

"After O'Banion shot Davey Miller, Duffy and Horton went to see Hirshie. They were always trying to get an 'in' with Miller. . . .

"Duffy offered to kill O'Banion and Schwartz if Hirshie wanted him to. Horton was present and heard him say he would. Miller said, 'No'; he didn't want any trouble; he said he was a respectable businessman and didn't want anybody killed. . . . Miller was sore about having a proposition like that made to him. Duffy swore Horton to secrecy about it."[24]

Horton didn't keep Duffy's secret.

One night, a few weeks before Duffy died, Horton called Jean Mason and told her to get over to Carmen Avenue as quick as she could. "What's wrong?" Jean asked. It was one o'clock in the morning. "You better come over here if you want to save two lives," Horton said. "Johnnie's trying to kill Cecil and me." "So," said Jean, "I went upstairs and I saw Cecil's eye—it was black. I said, 'Johnnie, you best apologize.' " Duffy did as he was told. " 'Cecil,' Duffy said, 'I'll get on my hands and knees and apologize if you'll ever forgive me.' " Cecil wouldn't forgive him. She wouldn't forgive Jack, either. Jack should have defended her. Husbands were supposed to defend their wives. The trouble was, the only way Jack could have defended Cecil was to have killed Duffy. Jack was afraid to try. Jack's solution: Let someone else kill Duffy.

Jack told O'Banion about Duffy's offer to Hirshie Miller. That's all Jack had to do—except for packing his bags. Jack took all of Duffy's money, loaded everything in their Cadillac, and drove off to New Orleans with Cecil, Freddy, and Betty.

Duffy was killed because he'd offered to do Hirshie Miller a favor. Shoemaker's detectives had been only half right about Jack Horton: He'd killed Duffy—but he hadn't shot him himself.

William Engelke's lawyers thought that since Julian Kaufman—arrested for being an accessory to murder—had been released on bail, their client might be released as well. They filed a writ of habeas corpus and came before Judge Joseph David. Judge David was surprised when Engelke's lawyers told him about Julian's release: "Who admitted him to bail?" Judge David asked an assistant state's attorney from Mr. Crowe's office named Smith. "Judge Schulman," said Mr. Smith. "On what theory could he accept bail on a murder charge?" asked Judge David. "He just did, that's all," said Mr. Smith. "Well—if I were State's Attorney, I would have rearrested the man," said Judge David. Smith made no reply. Instead, he summarized his "accessory to murder" evidence against Engelke. When Smith finished, Judge David turned to Engelke. "Tell the court when you last saw Duffy," Judge David said. Engelke recited his recent recollections:

"It was Thursday night, about a quarter to nine, at Wabash, between 22nd and 23rd Streets," Engelke said. "We were waiting, Duffy and myself. First we met Julian Kaufman—then a large sedan pulled up, and Mr. Dean O'Banion got out."

Engelke had never said anything about seeing O'Banion before.

Duffy walked over to O'Banion. "I need a car—and I need money," Engelke heard Duffy say. "I've got a job for you," O'Banion said. "I'll give you a grand or more." "They talked for a few seconds," Engelke said. "Then they started toward O'Banion's car, and I went the other way."

Judge David turned to Mr. Smith. "You have no case against this man," he said.[25]

Engelke wasn't happy about the possibility of being released.

"You might as well drag my carcass to Roosevelt Road and Newberry Avenue and bury it," he said to Mr. Smith.[26]

Mr. Smith agreed. "Engelke really is the only material witness we have."

"Either indict him or release him." Judge David said. Mr. Crowe's office hurriedly presented its evidence to the grand jury—which obliged by voting a "true bill" charging Engelke with being an "accessory after the fact" to the murder of Maybelle Exley. Prosecutors decided they didn't have enough evidence to ask for a similar indictment against Julian Kaufman. The grand jury did indict Julian for receiving stolen property. The state abandoned its efforts to link him, in any way, to John Duffy's death.

Al Brown—otherwise known as Al Capone—walked into Mr. Crowe's office, the next day, accompanied by his attorney. "I am a respectable man," Mr. Brown said. "I do not own, nor do I have any connection with 'The Four Deuces.' I own a furniture store adjoining the place, and, for no real reason at all, somebody is always trying to drag me into something."[27] Mr. Crowe asked Mr. Brown if he knew Dean O'Banion. "Yes I do—but I haven't seen him since the first of February." Did Mr. Brown know Julian Kaufman? "Only by sight." Did he know John Duffy? "Never met him." William Engelke? "Never heard of him."

Three days after Capone met with Mr. Crowe, Dean O'Banion telephoned the State's Attorney's office to say he could be found at his flower shop. Mr. Crowe sent an investigator named Geary to take O'Banion into custody. "I don't know Orlando Horton or Freddy Curtis," O'Banion said to Geary. "I don't know William Engelke, even though he says I rode away with Duffy just before he was found dead. . . . I'm not the man who got into the automobile on Wabash."[28]

Geary took O'Banion to the county jail. Two assistant state's attorneys escorted O'Banion to Engelke's cell. Engelke was waiting.

Dean O'Banion surrounded by a large crowd in a courtroom. O'Banion is bareheaded,
in profile; behind, to the right, O'Banion's companion covers his face with his hat.

"If that's O'Banion," said Engelke, "he ain't the fellow I thought he was. . . . I never met O'Banion, but I understood he was the man I saw climbing into the sedan with Duffy. . . . This ain't the guy, though."[29]

O'Banion smiled, but Geary didn't take him home. O'Banion's trial for shooting Davey Miller was about to begin. The state's attorney installed him in a suite in the Hotel Sherman, under guard.

A day passed.

Hirshie Miller kissed his wife and his daughter good-bye and drove to work. Five men in a Cadillac pulled up next to him and opened fire. They had handguns. Miller dove to the floor and lived. Witnesses reported two men in police uniforms stood on the Cadillac's running boards as it sped away.

In the afternoon, a woman called Hirshie's shop. She sounded frightened. "Hurry up out of there," she said. "They're going to blow up the place." Hirshie thought it was a joke. He went home to May and Marie.

One minute after midnight, a black powder bomb went off inside Acme Cleaning and Dyeing. It destroyed the shop.

Dean O'Banion was in his suite at the Hotel Sherman at the time. He'd been talking with a reporter while enjoying a shave. An investigator from Mr. Crowe's office was also in the room. "Well," said O'Banion, "you can't get anything on me. I have an ironclad alibi—a barber, a manicurist, a detective, and a reporter—you can't beat that."[30]

By some coincidence:

O'Banion's trial for shooting Davey Miller began the next day. "Davey Miller will not be present. He is in California. There are rumors that Miller accepted $9000 in lieu of appearing as a prosecution witness."[31]

Beulah Annan

11 · Belva and Beulah

Belva shot her lover in March; Beulah shot hers in April. Belva wasn't married at the time; the man she shot, Walter Law, was. Walter met Belva when he sold her a car (a Nash). Belva's ex-husband paid for it. Her ex was thirty years older than Belva—and he was rich. He liked to buy Belva things—nice things—married to her or not.

The man Beulah killed wasn't married, but Beulah was—to a mechanic, an older guy, named Al. Al worked overtime—ten-, twelve-, sixteen-hour days—to buy things for Beulah. "I was a sucker," Al said. "Simply a meal ticket."[1] He stuck by her, though. He even said *he* killed the man. The police didn't believe him. The man Beulah killed was an ex-con named Harry. She'd met him at work. Harry delivered laundry. He kept up a good front, though—wore nice clothes, said his parents had money. The fact was he'd been in jail in Michigan. He'd deserted his wife—his pregnant wife.

Belva had an interesting face, but Beulah—Beulah was drop-dead beautiful. Red hair, pale, porcelain skin, wide-set blue eyes. She had a son—a seven-year-old—from her first marriage. The boy lived with his father's folks in Kentucky. Beulah's mother stood by her; her father said he'd seen it coming.

Beulah and Harry had been drinking when she shot him. They both had the day off. Al was at work. Beulah and Harry got into a fight. She shot him in the back. It took him nearly four hours to die. It took her that long to decide to call her husband. Beulah remembered what she'd done and regretted it. Not Belva.

"Why it's silly to say I murdered Walter," Belva said after she was arrested. "I liked him and he loved me—but no woman can love a man enough to kill him. They aren't worth it . . . There are always plenty more."[2] In fact, Belva and Walter had been drinking—just like Beulah and Harry. The

195

difference was that Belva was an alcoholic—she was so intoxicated she blacked out, had no memory of shooting Walter. She was telling the truth when she said, "I don't know what happened. I was drunk."[3] What happened was that she and Walter were sitting in the front seat of her car when she shot him in the head.

Beulah went on trial first. There were—as usual—no women on the jury. There were four bachelors, though. The men decided Beulah was innocent.

Three days before the jury acquitted Beulah, a Polish mill worker found the body of little Bobby Franks, stuffed in a culvert, twenty miles south of the city. Nathan Leopold and his boyfriend, Richard Loeb, had kidnapped Bobby, killed him, stripped him, poured acid over his face and his private parts, then left him, facedown, in muddy water.[4] The young men's ambition was to commit a perfect crime. Unfortunately, Leopold dropped his glasses while they were dragging Bobby to the ditch. Beulah's trial and acquittal shared the front page with the first installments of what the papers called "The Crime of the Century." By the time Belva went on trial—and was found not guilty—her story shared the headlines with news of Nathan Leopold's confession. Printed verbatim.

What Belva and Beulah had in common—other than lovers, infatuated older husbands, handguns, and too much to drink—was a *Chicago Tribune* reporter named Maurine Watkins.

Watkins had gone to college, done graduate work at Radcliffe, then taken a job writing ad copy for Standard Oil. When Watkins applied for work at the *Tribune*, the paper's managing editor sent her over to the city desk. A "girl reporter" named Genevieve Forbes had covered the Orthwein murder, as well as the trial of Fred Thompson (Frances Carrick), with such panache that the *Tribune*'s city editor—a man named Robert Lee—didn't need to be convinced that women could write about crime. Lee sent Watkins to cover Belva, then Beulah.

Belva had been in the papers, on and off, since 1917, when she sang in cabarets dressed in breast plates, pantaloons, and a feathered headdress; she went by the name of Belle Brown. Beulah was so astonishingly pretty that a newsreel crew came to Chicago to film her, her mother, and her faithful husband, Al. Watkins knew a good thing when she saw it.

Once Belva went free, Watkins—and every reporter in Chicago who could breathe and move a pencil—covered Leopold and Loeb. After they were sentenced in September, Watkins moved to New York and got a job as a newspaper drama and movie critic. She enrolled in Yale's new Drama School

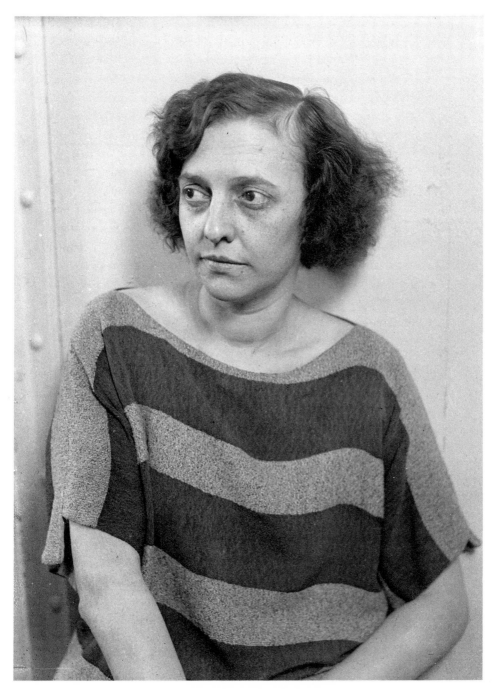

Mrs. Belva Gaertner sitting against a jail cell wall

workshop. Students were required to write plays. Watkins called hers *A Brave Little Woman*. Belva became "Velma"; Beulah became "Roxie Hart." Watkins's professor gave her an "A." It was the first "A" he'd ever given.

A Brave Little Woman became *Chicago* when it opened on Broadway in 1926. *Chicago* turned into a 1927 silent film called by the same name. (Cecil B. DeMille directed it. He cast a dark-eyed blonde named Phyllis Haver as Roxie). DeMille's *Chicago* led to a 1942 Ginger Rogers movie called *Roxie Hart*. Almost thirty-five years later, Bob Fosse turned *Chicago* into a musical. *Chicago*, the musical, became *Chicago*, the movie (Renée Zellweger played a blonde-haired Roxie).

Maurine Watkins became a born-again Christian. She wrote screenplays for twenty years, then retired, and moved to Florida to live with her mother. She wrote verse for Hallmark cards and stayed out of sight. She paid a yearly fee to the company that owned the rights to *Chicago* to prevent it from being revived. She regretted she'd written it. She was ashamed she'd turned what Belva and Beulah had done into a comedy.[5]

This is how things really began:

A patrolman named Fitzgerald and a sergeant named Quin were walking their beat along Forrestville Avenue, at one o'clock in the morning. There was a call box at the end of the block; they'd check in ("pull the box" is what they called it), go on to the next box, work their shift. Easy work: it was a nice, quiet neighborhood, young families, good salaries, big, solid apartments. Halfway down the block they saw a woman climb into a car; a man was at the wheel; the car's motor was off. The officers kept walking. Just as they were about to pull the box, they heard three shots. They ran back to the car. The woman was gone. The man was slumped over the wheel. He had a hole in his head. There was fresh blood on the floor. In the blood: a bottle of gin and an automatic pistol.

The officers called their station, then waited for a coroner's assistant to arrive. The coroner's assistant lifted the pistol out of the puddle on the floor: three shots had been fired from its magazine. The assistant fished the man's wallet out of his pants: Walter Law. A car salesman. The station checked the license plate of the Nash. The car belonged to a woman named Gaertner. Belle Brown Oberbeck Gaertner. Belva. She lived down the block.

Belva answered the door wearing a bathrobe. The officers followed her into the living room. The place was packed with furniture. Belva resumed what she'd been doing before the officers arrived: pacing and smoking, pacing and smoking. There was a pile of bloody clothes on the floor: a green velvet dress, a caracul coat (a lamb's wool coat), a pair of silver slippers.

Belva answered their questions, but she didn't stop pacing. Of course, she said, she knew the man in the car. "We went driving," she said. "Mr. Law and I . . . we went to a place on 55th and Cottage Grove and got a quart of gin. Then we went to the Gingham Café and had some drinks and lunch. We left . . . about midnight. Then we drove up Forrestville, right near where I live. Mr. Law said something about hold up men . . . said he was afraid of them. I don't know what happened next. I remember that I saw blood on his face. I was frightened. He didn't say anything and I didn't hear any shots. I just got out of the car and ran away."[6]

Fitzgerald and Quin had both seen Belva climb into the Nash. They asked her about that. She said they were wrong. She'd never left the car. They pressed her: Had she gone inside to get the gun, then come back with it? No, she said. She always carried the gun. The gun was hers. She was afraid of robbers. Her husband—her ex-husband—had given it to her. "He gave me that coat, too," she said, pointing with her toes at the caracul on the floor.

Fitzgerald and Quin took Belva to the station. They kept asking her about Law, about the blood on her clothes, about the gun. "I don't know," Belva kept saying. "I don't know. I was drunk." They locked her up. "Call William," she said. "William will know what to do." William was William Gaertner. "Wealthy manufacturer of scientific instruments." Belva's ex.

William was fifty-five and Belva was twenty-six when they met in 1917. Belva was married to a man named Oberbeck; William was lonely. William owned horses and rode in Jackson Park; Belva rented horses and rode there, too. The papers called their courtship "a romance of the bridle paths." The *Chicago Tribune* printed pictures of William and Belva on horseback dressed in riding togs.

Belva got a divorce. She and William eloped to Indiana, to Crown Point, a town that specialized in quickie marriages. Three months later, William sought an annulment. Illinois law required that a year elapse between a divorce and a marriage. The interval between Belva's divorce and her marriage had been less than three months. William wanted out. Belva wanted alimony. William compromised: he remarried Belva, then hired private detectives to spy on her. Belva hired her own detectives to spy on William. William countered by hiring detectives to spy on Belva's detectives. Belva hired a set of her own. The papers kept track: by the time William and his detectives found Belva in the arms of a man named Lusk, the Gaertners had a total of eight detectives following one another as they spied on their respective employers. The Gaertners' marriage ended in 1920.

Belva settled for $3,000, most of William's furniture (including his billiard table), and a car. Since the car was—at that moment—Belva's only productive asset, she installed a taxi meter in it, bought a green uniform, pinned livery badges to her lapels, and went looking for fares. The papers interviewed her. She posed for pictures seated behind the wheel. A woman in uniform. A liberated woman. "I just can't take orders from anyone," she said. "I must be my own boss. . . . I shall not drive at night and I won't make trips into the suburbs. There are too many hold up men. I can change a tire and do all that . . . but, tell me: is there anything I can do to get the squeak out of these leather puttees?"[7]

William answered the phone when the police called. He'd been expecting to hear from Belva: she called him every night. He still had a painting of her, dressed in her cabaret outfit, hanging in his study. "What has happened to her now?" William said.

Belva was right about William. He immediately hired three of the city's best criminal defense attorneys. He acknowledged that he'd bought the gun that Belva said was hers. He admitted that he'd paid for the car that Walter had sold to Belva, the car Walter drove to Belva's place. All this was true. But everything would be resolved: "I hope for a reconciliation just as soon as possible."[8]

Belva came to the coroner's inquest wearing clean clothes—and seven diamond rings. Walter's widow, Freda, was there; Freda's elderly father sat beside her; Freda's aged mother was at home, looking after the Laws' baby boy.

Freda testified that Walter was a faithful and devoted husband. Belva testified that he wasn't: "Sometimes he'd take me out three evenings a week. . . . Walter never did get along with his wife. . . . He often told me that if it weren't for his little boy, he'd never live with her. . . ."[9]

"Curly" Brown, the manager of the Gingham Café, testified that Walter and Belva had come in around ten o'clock, ordered three eleven-ounce "family size" bottles of ginger ale, then spent the next two hours there—presumably mixing the Gingham's ginger ale with the gin that Belva had carried in, hidden in her coat. That gin, according to a chemist employed by the city, had been a mixture of water, juniper juice, and alcohol. "Forty-two and twenty-six hundredths percent alcohol."[10] The Gingham's Mr. Brown said that the café had charged the couple $4.30 for their ginger ale. When they left, said Mr. Brown, they seemed perfectly sober.

The state called officers Fitzgerald and Quin, and the coroner's assistant who'd examined the crime scene. Then it called its star witness: a car salesman named Paul Goodwin. He and Walter worked together. They were friends. Goodwin's testimony made Belva very upset:

"Walter told me, Monday, that he planned to take out more life insurance. . . . Mrs. Gaertner threatened to kill him. . . . Three weeks before—he told me—she'd locked him in her flat with her and threatened to stab him with a knife unless he stayed there. . . ."[11]

"That's just a frame-up on the part of the automobile people," Belva said. "Me? Threaten him with a knife?? That's crazy. Why should I ever be angry with him? . . . I'll tell you the truth about that insurance: A few weeks ago, Walter told me, his wife had her fortune told—and the woman warned her that her husband would die inside of seven weeks. Walter took out the extra insurance just to humor her. . . ."[12]

It took the coroner's jury twenty minutes to decide that Belva had killed Walter Law.

The assistant state's attorney whom Mr. Crowe's office had sent to the inquest made a statement:

"The motive which the state believes lies behind this case is this: Mrs. Gaertner had ensnared Law. He tried to break away to stick to his wife and family. She killed him rather than lose him. When Law and Mrs. Gaertner returned from the café, she tried to make him enter her apartment. He remembered the time she'd held him there at the point of a knife. He refused. . . . She pulled the gun. . . . He tried to stop her—but couldn't."[13]

(In 1921 the attorney hired by Herbert Ziegler's widow used a similar argument against Cora Isabelle Orthwein. Said Attorney Dwight McKay: "It was the old, old story of selfish, insane love . . . she clung to him like a leech . . . she killed him before he could return to his home as husband and father.")

The *Chicago Tribune* ran a picture of Walter's pretty widow sitting with her white-haired father. Belva stood in a picture printed beneath them; she wore her cabaret costume, an Indian maiden dressed like a hoochie-koochie dancer. To Belva's right, in a picture all his own, sat Mr. Dean O'Banion. Three assistant state's attorneys stood around him. Everyone looked happy to see one another. The caption: "O'Banion surrenders and denies he ever knew Duffy."[14]

Belva went to jail.

Beulah told three different stories at three different times about how— and why—Harry ended up dead, in her apartment. She told her first story after Al—and then the police—arrived. She told her second story after she was interrogated; she told her third when she took the stand in her own defense. A police stenographer had written down Beulah's first two stories as she told them. The prosecutor read the transcripts aloud at her trial. Beulah told her third story—in her own, little-girl, trembly, southern voice—to the jury. She shed tears and cast sorrowful glances as she spoke. The judge declared that all three of Beulah's stories were admissible.

Beulah's first version of events was:

Harry invited himself over. She hardly knew him. She was "greatly surprised" when he walked in, took off his hat and coat, and put his arms around her. "He had a look in his eyes. 'Gee, Ann. I'm crazy about you,'" Harry said. "He tried to make me love him."[15] Beulah begged Harry to leave; he refused; she fled to the bedroom; he followed. Al kept a .38 under his pillow. She reached for it, and, as Harry approached her, she closed her eyes and fired.[16]

"But he was shot in the back," police said.

They took Beulah to the station, let her calm down, and sober up. Then, two assistant state's attorneys and a police captain took Beulah back to her apartment. "What about the blood on the phonograph record? What about the wine and gin bottles and the empty glasses? How come Kronstadt was shot in the back?"

Out came version No. 2:

"You're right," said Beulah. "I haven't been telling the truth. . . . I'd been fooling around with Harry for two months. This morning—as soon as my husband left for work—Harry called me up. I told him I wouldn't be home, but he came over anyway."[17]

Beulah gave Harry money to buy some moonshine. He came back with it after lunch. Half a gallon of it. He was already a little drunk. Beulah told him to leave. He said he would—but first they had to have a little drink. Beulah put on a record. A foxtrot called "Hula Lou." "Hula Lou has more sweeties than a dog has fleas."[18] "We sat in the flat for quite a while, drinking," Beulah said. "Then I said, in a joking way, that I was going to quit him. We had an argument. . . . I heard he'd been in jail and I asked him about it. He said he had. I told him he'd always told me he had a lot of money. . . . He jumped up. He said, 'To hell with you.' I told him he was a jail bird and didn't have any money. . . . He said he was through with me and began to put on his coat. When I saw that he meant what he said, my mind went into a whirl and I shot him. Then I started to play the record again. I was nervous, you see."[19]

Four hours passed.

Just before five, Beulah called Al at work. "I shot a man, Albert. He tried to make love to me." Al rushed home. Harry wasn't quite dead yet. Al called the police. Beulah tried to stop him. A desk sergeant named O'Grady answered the phone. Beulah heard O'Grady's voice; she grabbed the phone and shrieked, "I just killed my husband." Harry died thirty minutes later.

Admirers began sending Beulah presents in jail. Flowers, a good steak dinner, a few marriage proposals. Someone even bought her a pair of criminal defense lawyers—a matched set, William Scott and his partner, W. W. O'Brien. At Beulah's inquest, O'Brien outlined the story that Beulah would later tell jurors: Mrs. Annan and Mr. Kronstadt were in the bedroom when they started to argue. In fact, they were sitting on the bed. Both noticed Albert's .38 under the pillow. Mr. Kronstadt went for it; Mrs. Annan was quicker. Mr. Kronstadt stood up to leave. Mrs. Annan shot him in the back. "Both went for the gun," said Mr. O'Brien. "Both sprang for it."[20]

Belva was waiting for Beulah when she walked into jail.

So were Elizabeth Unkafer and Sabella Crudelli.

Mrs. Unkafer had just been sentenced to life for killing a streetcar conductor named Sam Belchoff. Belchoff had made the mistake of telling Mrs. Unkafer—while he was sitting in Mrs. Unkafer's bed—that he was "through with her." Mrs. Unkafer's attorneys claimed that she had a "subnormal mind" due to "a social disease." During her trial, Mrs. Unkafer had talked and mumbled to herself. She hated the way her lawyers described her. "Think I'm going to say I'm crazy? Not much!"

Beulah and Belva tried to ignore her. Mrs. Unkafer didn't care if they did or not. "If I was crazy," she said, "they'd have locked me up with some that are worse than I am—no telling what would have happened! I wanted them to shoot me! At State and Madison. Why not? Make a big day of it. . . . Give everyone a front row seat. They gave me life instead."[21]

Sabella Nitti Crudelli didn't talk as much as Mrs. Unkafer. She didn't know as much English. She and her husband, Peter Crudelli, had both been sentenced to hang, then been granted new trials. Mrs. Crudelli had originally been married to a farmer named Frank Nitti. Peter Crudelli had been Frank's hired hand. Peter and Sabella had fallen in love, then plotted to kill Frank. Peter had beat Frank to death with a hammer, then he and Sabella had chopped Frank into pieces and thrown them in a river.[22] The Illinois Supreme Court decided that there hadn't been enough evidence to convict the Crudellis.

Sabella knew all about Belva and Beulah. She didn't think either of them would go to prison. She wasn't so sure about herself. "Me-choke," Sabella said. "Me-no gun, no shoot. Me here over a year."[23]

Neither Beulah nor Belva stayed in jail very long. Beulah went free one month after she'd killed Harry. Belva walked out of court three months after she shot Walter.

When Belva went on trial, her attorneys decided that silence was their best policy. Since Belva was the only witness—and since Belva really, truly couldn't remember anything—why complicate matters? Belva's lawyers made no opening statements, called no witnesses, made no closing arguments. They did, however, make a motion of *nolle prosse*: they contended—out of the hearing of the jury—that the state had no case. Said the judge: "I haven't the power to tell the State's Attorney[24] what to do, and therefore deny the motion. But, if the jury should bring a verdict of guilty, I am confident the Supreme Court will reverse the decision, as the evidence is circumstantial: strong enough to arouse suspicion of guilt—but not enough to convict."[25]

When Beulah took the stand in her own defense, she added to the story her lawyer, Mr. O'Brien, had told at the inquest: When she and Harry had both reached for the gun, she was fighting to save not just her own life—but the life of her unborn child. She'd told Harry about her "delicate condition" when he came over carrying the liquor. She'd told him—but it hadn't made a bit of difference to him. She had to shoot Harry—to protect herself and her baby.

Beulah divorced Al in July 1926. She said he'd left her the day she was acquitted.

The day Belva was acquitted, she announced that she and William planned to marry again. "Married him once and that was annulled; married him again and got a divorce; third time's the charm!"[26] The Gaertners' third marriage lasted eighteen months. In August 1926, William sued for divorce. He said Belva had started drinking again—heavily. He'd reproached her; she'd hit him over the head with a mirror. A few months later, he caught her with another man. She threatened to kill him. William locked himself in his room, then moved out of the house. The judge granted William a divorce.

Six months after Beulah divorced Al, she met a man named Edward Harlib at a party. Ed had been a boxer; he and his brother owned garages. Edward's family knew who Beulah was and didn't want him to marry her. The two eloped to Crown Point, Indiana, and were married in January 1927. Edward's brother, Peter, said Edward was still married to his first wife. Edward and Beulah went to Los Angeles for their honeymoon. Five months after Beulah married Edward, she sued him for divorce. She claimed cruelty—and bigamy. She settled for $5,000 alimony. (As noted: equivalent to ten times that amount today.)

Beulah died ten months later. She gave her name as Dorothy Stevens (Stevens was the name of her first husband) when she checked herself into the Chicago Fresh Air Sanitorium. She had tuberculosis. Beulah's mother accompanied her body back to Kentucky, where she was buried not far from her family home in Owensboro.

Al moved to Louisville after he left Beulah. Louisville was where he and Beulah had first met. Al got married again—to a woman named Otilla Schaefer. Louisville police arrested Al in October 1934; they charged him with killing Otilla. Al denied it. He said he and Otilla had been home, all day, drinking. He said he went out on an errand; when he came home, Otilla was sick. He called two doctors. Otilla died an hour later. The coroner performed an autopsy. Otilla had been beaten to death.

(Left to right) Attorney Thomas D. Nash, Attorney Pat O'Donnell, John Scalise, Albert Anselmi

12 · Assassins

O'Banion was a trickster, a wit, a serious joker, a man fond of irony. The story goes he once broke into a warehouse full of whiskey, the real stuff, *uisgebeatha*, as the Irish called it, the water of life. O'Banion took two thousand barrels of it, emptied them, brought them back.[1] Jesus turned water into wine; O'Banion did the reverse. He filled the barrels with water, then rolled them back in place.

One joke led to another; success excited him. O'Banion kept trying to top himself. In May 1924, he made a little mistake, then he made a big one: he played tricks on people who didn't share his sense of humor.

O'Banion's first mistake was to hijack a $30,000 load of rotgut that belonged to a Sicilian family known as the "Terrible Gennas." It wasn't that the Gennas were humorless: they owned a license to warehouse and sell something called "industrial alcohol." "For external use only." Perfume and cosmetics manufacturers used small quantities of it in their formulas. The Gennas added coal tar to it, bottled it, and, depending on the label, sold it as whiskey, bourbon, or rye. The humor of what the Gennas did came from the location of their warehouse: four blocks from the Maxwell Street police station. So many cops came and went from the warehouse—to pick up bribes, single bottles, or case lots—that the locals called the place "the police station."

The Gennas' bookkeeper later gave a deposition that described the way the warehouse did business: "Each month said warehouse was visited by 400 uniformed police and by squads. . . . It was visited, moreover, by representatives with stars [badges] but not in uniform . . . representatives of the State's Attorney's office of Cook County . . ."[2]

So many officers, detectives, and deputies came and went, all with their hands out, that the Gennas had trouble distinguishing honest cops from moochers. "That police might not impose upon the Gennas by falsely representing themselves as assigned to the Maxwell Street station, each month there came, by letter or by messenger, a list for all stars [badge numbers] worn by officers and men with the Maxwell Street station . . . the entire list of [badge numbers] was run off on [our] adding machine. . . . As each man came in for his pay, his [badge number] was observed. If his [badge number] was on the list, he was paid. . . ."[3] The Gennas grossed $300,000[4] per month; police payoffs cost them $7,000.[5]

The rotgut that O'Banion hijacked came from the Gennas' other source of alcohol: homemade copper stills, hidden in hundreds and hundreds of apartments in the Sicilian parts of Chicago's Little Italy. The Gennas paid each family the princely sum of $15 a day to tend and store the distillate for weekly pickup. The Gennas' network of alky cookers produced 350 gallons of moonshine per week. Each gallon cost no more than 75 cents to produce. The Gennas added caramel color and fusel oil to the brew and sold it to speakeasies for $6 a gallon. Retailers were responsible for removing organic (rats, mice) and inorganic (metal shavings, wood chips, household refuse) matter from the product before dispensing it. Blindness and paralysis sometimes resulted—but only rarely. The real problem was that the speakeasies that bought the Gennas' homemade stuff were on the north side of the city. The North Side was O'Banion's territory—territory that had been assigned to him by Al Capone's boss, John Torrio, who presided over the activities of Chicago's gangs like a feudal lord. O'Banion thought he had a perfect right to hijack the Gennas' load of domestic solvents. The Gennas thought otherwise.

There were six Genna brothers. Two ran bars; one fancied himself an architect and a poet; the other three were killers. Sam was the eldest, raised in Marsala, practiced in the courtly ways of *La Mana Nera*, the Black Hand, elaborately polite letters of extortion, decorated with little skulls and daggers. To ignore them was to invite kidnapping, disfigurement, and death. The murder of innocents usually brought people to their senses. Sam made all such decisions, but it was Angelo—"Bloody Angelo"—and Mike—"The Devil"—who executed them. They would have nailed O'Banion's private parts to a wall long before he hijacked their load of home brew—would have considered such revenge an obligation and a pleasure—but they were restrained by a man of probity, Mike Merlo, the head of Chicago's *Unione Siciliane*.

The *Unione* had begun as a fraternal, benevolent society; it became a clearinghouse and overseer, delivering votes and extorting money from the people it "protected." No one, Sicilian or Italian, crook or cop, civilian or politician, crossed the *Unione*. Merlo understood O'Banion: "The man's as crazy as a fox." What's more, the fox had friends, volatile friends, cunning and relentless people, people like Hymie Weiss. Killing O'Banion would lead to reprisals; reprisals would lead to more reprisals. Revenge was always the most expensive dish on the menu.

O'Banion might have lived long enough for Mike Merlo to convince him to make amends, but O'Banion wasn't playing to the crowd. The applause he heard came from inside his own head. He pushed past the limits. He played a trick on John Torrio.

O'Banion owned a one-third interest in a brewery—a big, profitable place called the Sieben. John Torrio and Al Capone owned the other two thirds of the operation. Six weeks after an armed convoy of Chicago detectives (led by the same detective sergeant who'd helped the widow Tesmer positively identify Fred Thompson as the girl who'd shot her husband) had killed Frank Capone in Cicero, on Election Day, O'Banion asked to meet with John Torrio and Frank's grieving younger brother, Al.

Torrio and Capone were prepared for O'Banion to do one of two things: either offer to compensate the Gennas or ask them to take his side. Instead, O'Banion announced his retirement: Frank's killing had unnerved him. He'd prepared and delivered the flowers—thousands and thousands and thousands of dollars' worth of funeral wreaths and bouquets and tributes; Frank's death had hit home. He himself had had three close calls with the cops: the Davey Miller shooting; the Corning Distillery truck hijacking; the unsolved murder of John Duffy. Sure, he'd managed to stay a few steps ahead of the law—witnesses left town or suffered amnesia or recanted their testimony. No matter: O'Banion knew things were going downhill. The mayor and the state's attorney were out to get him. They were the ones who'd sent that posse to kill Frank. What a guy! Cut down in his prime! Since when was it a crime for a citizen to get out the vote? O'Banion knew he was next. He had a beautiful wife; they were planning to move to Colorado. Make a fresh start.

O'Banion wanted out. Torrio and Capone were surprised. Surprised—but glad to help:

What do you want for the Sieben? said Torrio.

I'm a reasonable guy, O'Banion said. We're friends. How does $500,000 sound? Fair?

Done, said Torrio.

O'Banion didn't know what to say. Capone nodded. O'Banion flashed a shy little smile. He tried to change the mood.

Listen, he said. Tell you what—I'll give you guys a hand. For old time's sake. When is it? May 19? Count on me. I'll be there. Me and my guys. We'll help load.

Torrio smiled a tight little smile. He wrote O'Banion an IOU. Business was business. The Gennas smelled like garlic. This was Chicago, not Palermo.

The fact was, O'Banion had people inside the chief of police's office. He not only knew that Chief Collins was planning to raid the Sieben on May 19—he also knew that Collins and Mayor Dever had no intention of turning anyone they arrested over to Mr. Crowe. Crowe was nothing but words. His office was dirty. From the bottom up. The Sieben bust would be a federal bust, directed by the city's U.S. attorney. John Torrio had been arrested in 1923 for violating the Volstead Act. A second arrest on federal charges would tie Torrio in knots: fines, mandatory jail time, headlines, his picture in the paper. Everything Torrio hated.

The only thing O'Banion loved about Colorado was easy access to military surplus Thompson submachine guns. He planned to be the first one in Chicago to use them.[6] Torrio would end up in jail; O'Banion would be $500,000 richer. He'd go to the Sieben; he didn't mind getting arrested. He wanted to see Torrio's face when the feds arrived.

The Sieben bust happened just as O'Banion knew it would. One hundred and twenty-eight thousand gallons of beer, thirteen trucks, full crews of drivers and warehouse men, four limos, a half dozen well-dressed crooks (including one well-known, local Democratic politician). Police found a ledger under a loading dock: names, dates, and payroll schedules; six police sergeants on two-man, eight-hour shifts had protected the place twenty-four hours a day.[7]

All the prisoners—O'Banion among them—went straight to the Federal Building. O'Banion greeted the police who guarded him by name. Torrio figured out what had happened by the time he was taken before a judge. He peeled off $7,500 from a roll in his pocket and bailed himself out.

O'Banion lived as long as Mike Merlo did. Merlo had cancer. "Six months, maybe," said the doctors. Merlo was tough, though. Torrio, Capone, and the Gennas counted the days and made their plans.

The first thing they did was consult with Frankie Yale, the president of New York's *Unione Siciliane*. Yale had been Capone's first employer:

Mayor William Emmett Dever

Capone had worked as a bouncer in Yale's club—the Harvard Inn—on Coney Island. One night, Capone got into a fight with a man armed with a four-inch knife. Capone had said something inappropriate to the man's sister. The man turned Al into "Scarface." Yale had also been Torrio's business associate in Brooklyn before the First World War—Yale was an undertaker; Torrio was a pimp; Yale wholesaled ice; Torrio ran numbers.

In 1909, Yale had recommended Torrio to Chicago's Big Jim Colosimo, a labor extortionist, pimp, and political influence peddler who ran the biggest network of bars and brothels in the city. By 1920, Colosimo had grown sloppy: he'd divorced his wife—a madam who'd become his business partner—and married a girl named Dale Winter, who sang in his nightclub.

Yale had been watching Torrio grow richer and more powerful as Colosimo became more sodden and distracted. In May 1920, Yale invited himself to Chicago to do Torrio a favor: he shot Big Jim in the back of the head in the lobby of his own club one afternoon, as Big Jim was leaving for an appointment.

After that, Yale and Torrio had made plans whenever it was in their interest. Killing O'Banion and replacing Merlo with a man who suited them served them both. They decided that Angelo Genna should succeed Merlo. Angelo wasn't as old-fashioned or as independent as Sam; he wasn't as impetuous and bloodthirsty as Mike. Killing O'Banion required preparation, though.

Since O'Banion had made fools of Torrio and the Gennas while everyone watched, they decided that O'Banion should be killed in as public a way as possible—in a way that confirmed their right, and their power, to execute him. They decided to kill him in broad daylight; kill him face-to-face; kill him where he worked, where he felt most at ease; kill him in his own shop on North State Street, across from Holy Name Cathedral, where he'd been a choirboy. No ambushes, no going for a ride, no bullets in the back of the head. Yale said he'd do it, but he'd need help. O'Banion carried a .45 and an extra magazine in his back pocket. He was young, quick-witted, cunning. He knew Yale by reputation, but not by sight; O'Banion wouldn't recognize him the way he would Mike Genna or Angelo. Yale wanted two more men. Out-of-towners would be good.

Torrio asked the Gennas for names.

Mike said he knew some people.

Guys from Marsala, he said. Very good with shotguns. Very good. Very steady. The kind of guys who always finish what they start. You tell them to do something, it gets done. They take a stand, they're like rocks or trees. They get hit, they don't go down. One of them's been in town for a while. John Scalise. O'Banion's never met him. Speaks a little English. Nice-looking guy. Young. Wall-eyed, though. When he looks at people, it's like he's looking at them and around them. Spooks people. Which is OK; people ought to be spooked. Because when John shows up, he's there for only one reason. The other guy . . . the other guy . . . I know him from home. Albert Anselmi. Doesn't know much English, but the work he does, he doesn't need to talk. He's older. Not much to look at. Married, though. Wife and four kids. He was in Chicago during the war. Worked in a woolen mill, then a powder mill. Sent all his money home. Went home after the war. Kept goats. Made cheese. He would have stayed where he was, but the Italian police were after him. They wanted him for murder. One murder. What did they know.

Scalise and Anselmi; Anselmi and Scalise. Imagine Tweedledum and Tweedledee, carrying shotguns. Skilled men. Lethal men. Assassins. People said when they used handguns, they rubbed their bullets with garlic to keep them true. Everyone started imitating them.

Shotguns and handguns. Those two never failed. Torrio offered them $10,000 each, plus a diamond ring. They and Yale did the job. From then on, straight through past Valentine's Day 1929, those two tracked a trail of blood. They survived the Gennas; they survived Yale. Capone eventually put an end to them—tied them to chairs, beat them with a club, then shot them full of holes. A county coroner said that in thirty years of practice, he'd never seen bodies torn up like that. No one remembers them now.

Merlo died in early November. People began ordering flowers from O'Banion right away. Capone's people called in an $8,000 order; Torrio's office called in a $10,000 one. There were orders for floral banners that spelled out Merlo's name; there were orders for floral topiaries shaped like hearts, horseshoes, archways, and pillars. Trade associations, unions, and benevolent societies ordered wreaths and baskets trailing golden ribbons. "Our Pal." "Padrone." "Gone but not forgotten." A total of $100,000 worth of flowers.[8]

O'Banion, three of his assistants, as well as his business partner, a florist named Schofield (who'd once owned the business outright), worked Saturday, all day Sunday, and into Sunday night. Early Sunday evening, while O'Banion was out on an errand, Jim Genna, one of the more harmless of the Terrible Gennas, came in to place an order. O'Banion was puzzled when he came back: Genna wanted $750 worth of red and white carnations delivered to Merlo's home. Nothing special. In fact: a little cheap. Why had a guy like Jim Genna even bothered to come in?

Just before closing, Schofield answered a call from Frankie Yale. Yale introduced himself. Schofield said, of course, he knew who Mr. Yale was. Yale was polite. Said he'd just come in from New York for the funeral. He hoped it wasn't too late to place an order. Not at all, not at all, said Schofield. OK, said Yale. I want a wreath of red roses. A nice big one. Say, $2,000? Fine, said Schofield. We can do that. I'll come in to pick it up tomorrow, Yale said. Around noon, Yale said. Noon is fine, said Schofield. I'll have a couple of guys with me to help carry the thing. We can deliver it, if you want, said

Schofield. No, said Yale, this is something I got to do myself. Of course, said Schofield. Glad to oblige. He thanked Yale for his business. He called O'Banion about Yale's order, then went home to bed. Next day was Armistice Day. Schofield had to be at Mount Carmel to help decorate graves.

O'Banion went out drinking that night. He didn't understand: Jim Genna had come to the shop to scout it. Frankie Yale didn't need help to carry his wreath. O'Banion got four hours' sleep, then came in at nine o'clock Monday morning, to work on the rest of the Merlo orders. He was bent over his worktable, cutting and pruning, when a big blue touring car rolled up in front of the shop. Three men climbed out; the driver stayed where he was, motor running. A short visit. A kid who was playing on the sidewalk watched: two of the guys looked like foreigners—short and dark. The man in the middle was taller and lighter-skinned. Inside the shop, O'Banion's janitor, an African American named Crutchfield, looked up from his sweeping. The men were all well dressed; two of them looked like Italians. They moved like they weren't used to wearing suits; the man in the middle was some kind of rich guy, a Greek or a Jew. Crutchfield had nothing against such people, but he didn't like the combination—three guys and a big car with its engine running. He headed for the backroom. O'Banion looked up, smiled, and limped forward, clipping shears in one hand, the other out for a handshake. "Hello, boys," O'Banion said. "Here for the flowers?" Yale took O'Banion's hand and drew him in. O'Banion tipped a bit and laughed. Crutchfield made it to the backroom and shut the door behind him.

Fifteen minutes went by. Chitchat. A couple of laughs.

Then: six shots. Then, a seventh.

The first shot went wild. The next five were fired so close, O'Banion's clothes had powder burns. The last shot was a head shot. A coup de grâce. Crutchfield ran in as the three men ran out. O'Banion lay on his back in a puddle of blood and flower petals. His hands twitched; his eyes stayed open. The Gennas had a sense of humor. This time, the joke was on O'Banion: he was fixing flowers for his own goddamn funeral.

That funeral was one of the most extravagant and heavily attended in Chicago's history.

Thirty thousand people mobbed the funeral home where O'Banion's body lay in state. The man who owned and operated the place—a man named Sbarbaro—specialized in dead gangsters; he not only knew how to fill in cuts and sew up holes, he also worked for Mr. Crowe as an assistant state's attorney. He'd been expecting O'Banion for weeks.

O'Banion's casket of silver and gold cost $10,000; its makers had sent it from Philadelphia by express train in a private baggage car. Musicians from the Chicago Symphony Orchestra played "Ave Maria" as five Municipal Court judges and an alderman offered condolences to O'Banion's widow. She wore black satin and a full-length mink. She spoke from behind a black veil. "He was not a man to run around nights," Viola said. "He never left without telling me where he was going."[9]

Mrs. Dean O'Banion

Hymie Weiss wept loudly. Dapper Dan McCarthy (the union agent who'd been at the wheel during the Corning Distillery hijacking) and George Moran (known as "Bugs" because of his crazy temper) tried to console him. Maxie Eisen, a labor racketeer and friend of the late Nails Morton, sat grim-faced and silent. Eisen and Weiss had both told O'Banion to make peace with the Gennas. Eisen (like Merlo and Torrio) understood crime was a business—"conducted by other means." He knew—and disapproved of—what Weiss would do next.

The musicians played the "Dead March" from Handel's *Saul*; O'Banion's friends lifted his casket from its bier and slowly, slowly, carried it to its hearse. Two hundred Chicago police officers cleared a path through the crowd. O'Banion's cortege was a mile long—24 cars and trucks full of flowers; 124 cars of mourners. Ten thousand people walked behind them; three brass bands played solemn music. Ten thousand more people stood waiting at Mount Carmel, as O'Banion's casket was lifted onto a catafalque and borne to its grave. A priest who'd known O'Banion as a boy delivered a eulogy; another priest read from the liturgy, then recited a Hail Mary and the Lord's Prayer.

The cardinal of Chicago refused to let O'Banion be buried in consecrated ground. Five months passed. As soon as the ground thawed, O'Banion's friends had him dug up and moved: his new grave was eighty feet from the tomb of a bishop.[10]

PART TWO

The war of revenge that Merlo and Eisen feared began less than two months after O'Banion was shot. It lasted from January 1925 until February 1929. During the first ten months of 1926 alone, there were forty-two criminal combat deaths in Chicago; there were another fifty-four in Cook County. Police killed an additional sixty gangsters in skirmishes, ambushes, and counterattacks.[11] Albert Anselmi and John Scalise had plenty of work. "Are we living by the code of the Dark Ages, or is Chicago part of the American Commonwealth?" asked Mayor Dever just before he was voted out of office.[12]

Weiss made his first attack on Capone in the middle of January 1925. Weiss, Moran, and a small-time thief with big ideas named "Schemer" Drucci found Capone's Cadillac parked outside a restaurant at State and Fifty-fifth. Weiss and his two friends attacked the limo with shotguns— and one of O'Banion's new Thompsons. "They let it have everything but the kitchen sink," said a police sergeant who inspected what was left of the car.[13] Capone's cousin nearly died; Capone's chauffeur was shot in the back. Capone himself had just gone inside to have lunch. When he came out and saw what the Thompson had done, he took the lesson to heart: the new Cadillac he ordered had steel body armor, bulletproof glass, and doors with combination locks to stop anyone from slipping a bomb under a seat. Capone changed the way he traveled: a scout car preceded him; a chase car with armed men followed him. At the office, Capone installed a new desk chair with an armored back; outside his office, he began to deploy guards in wider and wider defensive perimeters. Some of his guards watched for outsiders; some of his guards watched other guards. A local hardware store began to sell Thompsons to people who asked for them.

John Torrio detested machine guns. He never carried a weapon. Gentlemen never carried guns—and never called attention to themselves. Violence was measured: one shot, one kill. Torrio knew his work was dirty, but it was other people's dirt, not his. It was other people's sins that made him rich. He lived a sober life. His home was a clean, calm, and quiet place. No whores, no booze, no guards, no guns. Which is why there was nothing but a front yard between him and safety when Weiss, Moran, and Drucci ambushed him outside his house, twelve days after they shot up Capone's Cadillac.

It was late afternoon when Torrio and his wife Anna came home from shopping. There was just enough light left in the sky to see the ground. Anna walked to the front door, arms loaded with packages. Torrio and his driver began to unload the rest. Anna turned to look just as a blue Cadillac pulled up behind their town car. Drucci was at the wheel. Weiss and Moran jumped out. Moran had a .45; Weiss had a shotgun.

Moran shot out the passenger-side windows and the front windshield; Weiss fired into the car's backseat. Torrio's driver was hit in the legs and went down. Torrio dropped everything and ran for the front door. He was still in his forties, small and agile. Moran might have been able to kill him if Torrio had been standing still, but Torrio was running for his life, and Moran wasn't a very good shot. The bullet aimed at Torrio's back took a chunk out of his arm. The impact spun him around. Weiss fired—buckshot shattered Torrio's jaw, made holes in his neck and chest. The load of shot knocked him down. Moran stood over him. First, he shot Torrio in the shoulder; say good-bye to your arm. Then he shot him in the groin; say good-bye to your balls. Torrio never lost consciousness. Anna screamed and kept screaming.

Moran put the muzzle of his .45 to Torrio's head: one coup de grâce deserved another. Click. An empty chamber. Click. An empty magazine. Moran hadn't been counting his rounds. He dug out another magazine. He was shaking; the air was freezing; Moran had never reloaded in low light. A laundry truck came around the corner. Drucci hit the horn. Moran and Weiss ran back to the car.[14] Anna dragged Torrio inside; their driver called Capone; an ambulance took Torrio to the hospital. Torrio's jaw and his arm were shattered; he still had his balls. Surgeons dug out as many pellets as they could find. They cauterized his wounds. Infection could still kill him.

Capone feared what might happen next: Weiss would call in some favors, then come after Torrio in the hospital. Weiss did exactly that. The police ordered Capone downtown to answer some questions. Where Capone went, so did his guards. Weiss sent three cars of men to the hospital. One man went with a bouquet. The ward nurse asked the man who he was. He gave her a name.

You're not on the list, the nurse said. What list? the man said. Let me see that list. There are police guards everywhere, she said. You keep talking to me like that and I'll call them. Anna had warned her. The nurse and the man looked at each other. Go on now, she said. And take those flowers with you.

When Capone came back and heard the news, he ordered a cot for himself. He slept next to Torrio's bed after that. His guards stood watch outside Torrio's door. Two weeks later, Torrio was well enough to stand. He hobbled down a back fire escape into Capone's car. A few days later, he stood before a federal judge, bandaged up to his ears, his right arm and shoulder in a cast. The judge sentenced him to nine months in a Lake County jail. Torrio made friends with the county sheriff. The sheriff let Torrio move a brass bed, a bookcase, a radio, and a record player into his cell. Torrio liked to listen to opera. The sheriff assigned two deputies to guard him; he hung shutters over Torrio's windows to keep snipers away. By the end of Torrio's sentence, he was eating dinner at the sheriff's house.

Once he was released, Torrio announced his retirement. He moved most of his money to Italy. Then he and Anna left the country. Capone took over.

Weiss and Moran went after the Gennas next. Angelo had been appointed the new president of the *Unione Siciliane*. He was Torrio and Capone's puppet. He'd just gotten married—married up, married into a family of gentrified Italians. The papers covered his wedding—three thousand guests; a two-thousand-pound wedding cake. The papers described Angelo as a "young importer."[15] He and his wife moved out of Little Italy, rented rooms in a fancy hotel on Sheridan Road, and began looking for a house in the suburbs. By May 1925, they'd found one.[16]

Angelo couldn't have been happier. He folded $9,000 cash into an envelope, climbed into his new roadster, and drove off to make a deposit on a bungalow in Oak Park.[17] He'd been lucky at craps that week—$35,000 lucky. Money in his pocket; hair blowing in the wind; he was on his way. A sedan pulled out of a side street and began to follow him. Drucci, Moran, and two other guys.[18] Angelo speeded up; they speeded up. Sixty miles an hour. Moran's car pulled up next to Angelo. Angelo began shooting; they fired back. Angelo had never driven and fired a weapon at the same time. He swerved left, lost control, hit a lamppost. He died in the hospital: twelve slugs and a concussion. The police found a little black book in his car. Liquor deliveries from Philadelphia. His wife said she didn't know anything about that.

Mike did. He understood blood for blood. He still had a sense of humor, though: he sent one of his own guys, a big-mouthed, fancy dresser named "Samoots" Amatuna, to make a deal with Moran. Amatuna told Moran he had a grudge: he deserved to be the next head of the *Unione*. He'd talked to Mike. Mike had laughed at him.

So, said Samoots, here's the deal: Mike wants to kill you and Drucci. You want to kill Mike. If you kill Mike, there's nothing between me and the presidency. I know where Mike goes. You be there; you wait. He'll drive by; you nail him. Deal?

Moran had guts, but Weiss had brains. Unfortunately, Weiss was in jail when Amatuna showed up. Two years after the police interrupted the Corning Distillery hijacking, a jury had finally sentenced Weiss—and Dapper Dan McCarthy—to six months in a county jail.

Moran didn't keep track of people the way Weiss did. Weiss knew that Amatuna was partners with John Scalise in a café called Citro's. Weiss knew that Amatuna was too loyal, and too scared of Mike Genna, to offer him up. Weiss also understood Mike's sense of humor: Mike loved surprises.

Moran didn't understand any of this. Deal? said Amatuna. Deal, said Moran. Amatuna went back to Mike. Mike told Scalise and Anselmi to get ready. Shotguns, this time. Tell Moran, said Mike to Amatuna: Be at the corner of Sangamon and Congress. Nice, said Amatuna. He told Moran.

Moran and Drucci and two other men were in Moran's Hupmobile, traveling west on Congress, headed for Sangamon, when Genna ambushed them. Anselmi, Scalise, Genna, and two other shooters stepped out of an alley and opened fire with shotguns. Things didn't work out the way Genna thought they would. Anselmi and Scalise did well: they'd fired at moving targets before. Moran's Hupmobile was shredded down to its doorframes, but only Drucci was wounded.[19] Moran doubled back and caught Genna's crew in the open. The Hupmobile was losing oil, but it was like a gunboat. By the time Genna pulled everyone back to his Cadillac, two of his guys were staggering. Drucci and Moran didn't come back for more. They drove the Hupmobile until it stopped, then Moran and Drucci ran. Genna's two guys were in bad shape. He dumped them in an alley, then turned onto Western and headed south. Fast. Genna was furious; Anselmi and Scalise were rattled.

What happened next, no one could have predicted.

Genna's Cadillac was going fifty when it passed another Cadillac, a big black one, headed north. There were four men in that Cadillac: two detectives, two patrolmen. The detectives—Conway and Sweeney—had just been assigned to the zone. The patrolmen—Olson and Walsh—knew the territory: vacant lots, building lots, a few houses, some stores, empty prairie. None of the police were in uniform. Their car had a gong (a kind of fire bell, used like a siren) attached to it, but it had no police markings. Olson drove; Conway sat next to him. Walsh sat beside Sweeney in the back.

Conway recognized Genna. South on Western meant south to the rail yards; the rail yards meant deliveries; fifty miles per hour meant something big. "Follow 'em," said Conway. Olson made a U-turn. Genna saw it. A U-turn like that meant trouble. Genna speeded up. "Catch 'em," said Conway. Olson sounded his gong.

By Fifty-ninth, a mile south of where Olson made his turn, both cars were going seventy. The sound of Olson's gong traveled sideways and backwards. Genna had just come out of a firefight. Anselmi and Scalise checked their weapons.

The police carried .38s. None of them had had much practice. They didn't know that Genna's car was an arsenal: four double-barreled shotguns;[20] two pump shotguns;[21] four revolvers. Conway and Sweeney thought they were about to catch a big fish. Their fish was a shark.

Genna hit his brakes to jackknife his car. He planned to be half a block away, heading north, picking up speed, by the time the black Cadillac realized what had happened. Genna managed to make his 180, but his tires didn't hold. The back of his Cadillac kept moving south; the car jumped the curb and crashed, tail-end, into a lamppost. Olson locked his brakes, aimed his car, and skidded in, nose to curb, next to Genna's car.

Olson didn't even have both feet on the ground when Scalise killed him with a head shot. Walsh had his weapon out but not up when Scalise shot him in the chest. Conway and Sweeney dove, ducked, and backed away, weapons out and up. Conway fired. Anselmi shot him in the chest before he could take cover. Sweeney dragged him back behind the Cadillac. Olson and Walsh were dead. Conway was still breathing. "Get in the fight," Conway said.

Sweeney ran forward. He grabbed Olson's .38 and moved in, firing, a gun in either hand. A streetcar stopped, half a block away. Everyone in the car had seen what was happening. An off-duty patrolman named Rickert jumped off and sprinted up the street. Anselmi and Scalise and Genna saw Sweeney, saw Rickert; they turned and ran. A crowd of men stood in front of a garage a block away and watched. Rickert reached Sweeney, passed him a handful of shells. Sweeney reloaded and began the chase. Rickert followed him.

Scalise, Anselmi, and Genna ran across a vacant lot, headed for a cluster of houses and stores. Genna was limping; his pants leg was bloody. Anselmi and Scalise ran ahead of him. Sweeney came closer. Genna stopped, turned, leveled his shotgun, and fired. Nothing but air. Out of ammo. Sweeney took a shot. Genna pulled out a .38. Sweeney dropped back. Anselmi and Scalise ran down an alley, then disappeared around a corner.

An old cop named Oakley was just getting out of bed when his wife called up to him: "George, there's a shooting." Oakley was sixty, white-haired, good for nothing except sitting at a desk, at night, in the hall outside the State's Attorney's office. Oakley pulled on his pants and came out just as Rickert stopped in front of his house. Anselmi and Scalise had thrown their shotguns into some bushes. Oakley picked one up, snapped it open: one shell left. He cocked it and followed Rickert.

Genna was shouting, cursing, limping worse than before. He knocked out a basement window of a house and rolled himself in. Sweeney told Rickert and Oakley to cover him, then he went in, shooting. Genna had a blue steel Spanish revolver in his hand, but he was too weak to use it. Conway's shot had hit an artery. Genna was bleeding out, but he was still alive. An ambulance arrived; the crew lifted Mike onto a stretcher. "Take it easy, you son-of-a-bitch," one of the men said. Genna kicked him in the face. He died on the way to the hospital.

Sergeants ordered patrolmen into whatever cars they had and sent them into the neighborhood. Anselmi and Scalise had run into a dry goods store at Fifty-ninth and Rockwell. They were dirty, out of breath, and bareheaded. No one—no respectable person—walked around bareheaded. "A couple of guineas," is what the owner of the place, a man named Issigson, thought. Scalise pointed at his head, then to a pile of caps, then at his head. "We want to buy," he said. Issigson threw them out. Police caught them, still bareheaded, trying to board a trolley headed west.

The shoot-out had lasted ten minutes. A high-speed car chase, followed by a gun battle. No one had ever seen or heard of such things. Public officials stood in line to make speeches.

"Never before in this city—perhaps never before in this country—has the law been so wantonly flouted," said State's Attorney Crowe.[22] He ordered raids and mass arrests. "This is the worst outbreak of lawlessness since the throwing of the Haymarket bomb," said Chief Collins.[23] "We have reached a time," said William Shoemaker, the city's chief of detectives, "when a policeman had better throw a couple of bullets into a man first, and ask questions afterward. It's war—and in war, you shoot first and talk second."[24]

Mayor Dever told the papers he was thinking of having Chief Collins organize a special police "strong arm squad." Chief Collins said the era of the foot patrolman was over. He told the mayor what he really needed: He needed cars. One hundred and ten new cars. "Flivvers" he called them.[25] Mayor Dever replied to his chief in print: "I have every confidence in Chief Collins," the mayor said. "This is only a sporadic outburst of lawlessness. The administration has no special drive on against the criminals."[26]

Detectives began to interrogate Anselmi and Scalise. Anselmi didn't know English, so Scalise answered for them both.

Genna? said Scalise. Sure, I heard of Genna. Mike Genna. Bad, very bad. Detectives pointed at Anselmi. What about your friend? they said. My friend? said Scalise. We don't know each other. The first time we met, we were waiting for the trolley. We both just got to town. He was looking for work; I was looking for work. We were both looking for a job and a place to sleep. A boardinghouse, or something.

Anselmi looked at the ceiling, then at the floor, then at the wall. Tell us about Genna, the detectives said. Anselmi shook his head and yawned. The detectives turned back to Scalise. Tell us about Mike Genna, they said. What do you want? said Scalise. I don't know anything. He pointed at Anselmi. I don't even know him. Why don't you ask him?

Mr. Crowe decided to take reporters into his confidence. We have reason to believe, Mr. Crowe said, that the two men we have in custody were directly responsible for the murder of Dean O'Banion, last November, in

Robert E. Crowe, Cook County state's attorney

his flower shop. Papers printed Mr. Crowe's remarks as if he'd made them at a press conference.

Torrio (who was still in jail) and Capone began to raise money for Anselmi and Scalise. Within a month, they'd raised $100,000 and hired the best criminal defense lawyers in the city: Michael Ahern, Thomas Nash, and Patrick O'Donnell.

Ahern and Nash were the men who'd defended Belva Gaertner. Ahern believed in keeping things simple: If his client didn't remember anything, then there was nothing to remember. Nash had made a name for himself back in 1920, part of the legal team that had successfully defended the Chicago Black Sox. Ahern was a handsome, well-tailored, open-faced

Irishman. Nash favored cutaways and cravats and carried himself like an English barrister. O'Donnell was his own man: trim, silver-haired, slightly stooped, with fine features, dark eyes, and a temper. He used to give bottles of whiskey to court clerks and bailiffs before a trial began. To show his appreciation. "For Christmas," he'd say.

Mr. Crowe let it be known that he looked forward to the fight. He named as his "Special Assistant" for the "War on Crime" a gentleman named Colonel Henry Chamberlain; Chamberlain was head of the Chicago Crime Commission, a civic organization of businessmen, bankers, and lawyers who were very alarmed by what was happening to their city. Mr. Crowe made stirring proclamations: he called on every Superior and Circuit Court judge and on the Bar Association of the City of Chicago to select forty of their number to devote themselves, full time—forswearing vacations—to clearing the hundreds and hundreds and hundreds of criminal gang cases that filled the courts' dockets.

"We are at a crossroads," Mr. Crowe said. "There have been other reigns of terror, but the gangs and guns have never ruled with such an iron and abandoned hand."[27] "I promise here and now that I will personally go into court in this case. Not only is this case complete, it is one of the most open and shut cases I have ever seen."[28] "We are not going to let these gangsters and killers continue to flourish. Scalise and Anselmi will be hanged as an example."[29]

Mr. Ahern had his doubts. A court case in Montana had caught his eye: A Montana sheriff had entered a grocery store, where he believed moonshine was being sold. An argument ensued. The proprietor of the store told the sheriff to leave. The sheriff began to search the place. The proprietor shot him dead. During the trial, the prosecution presented evidence that the sheriff had been right about the moonshine. He had been killed, said the prosecution, doing his duty. The defense argued that—moonshine or not—the sheriff had no right to enter the store and search it without a warrant. The jury decided that the sheriff had violated the law—he had no warrant—and that the proprietor had not done anything illegal. A citizen had the right to defend his person, his personal property, and his home.[30]

Mr. O'Donnell took a somewhat different approach.

The police claimed they'd chased Mike Genna. Chased him because he fled. Fled because Genna knew he'd broken the law and feared arrest. Mr. O'Donnell said he was prepared to present evidence to the contrary—not only were the police as guilty of violating the Volstead Act (the law, passed in 1919, to enforce Prohibition) as Mike Genna—they were guilty of taking bribes. Mr. O'Donnell was prepared to prove—in court, in public—why Mike Genna had no reason to fear the police: he'd paid hundreds of them thousands of dollars in bribes every month. Patrolmen, ranking officers, detectives, investigators, even assistant state's attorneys—they were all on Mike Genna's payroll.

Mr. O'Donnell deposed Mike Genna's bookkeeper, Francis Golfano; he leaked Golfano's deposition—and the contents of his ledger—to the press. "BRIBED 300 POLICE Monthly Graft Called $8000."[31] Mr. Crowe was able to keep Golfano's deposition and his book of bribes and badge numbers from being admitted as evidence, but O'Donnell was not deterred. "I intend to give this little book and its list of names to Uncle Sam, and I'm not bluffing," he said. "When you do," answered Mr. Crowe, "be sure to take whatever booze tickets and bottles you have left in your office." When reporters questioned Mr. Crowe about O'Donnell's allegations, Mr. Crowe said, "We concede that Mike Genna feared policemen less than policemen feared him. But how ridiculous to take the word of a bootlegger, supported by rewards, that anyone could forge and try to blacken the name of 300 policemen."[32]

Mr. Crowe decided to try Anselmi and Scalise first for the killing of patrolman Olson, and then for the killing of patrolman Walsh. The "Olson trial" began in October 1925. The "Walsh trial" began in February 1926. Mr. Crowe was wrong—very wrong—about his case being either complete or "open and shut." Mr. Crowe was right, though, about the city being at a crossroads. By 1928 Capone's people felt at liberty to plant bombs in a public market (seventeen sticks of dynamite in the Water Street Market), blow up the houses of a U.S. senator (Senator Charles Deneen) and a judge (Judge John Swanson), threaten the life of a U.S. Attorney (George Johnson), and murder an opposing candidate on Election Day (Twentieth Ward candidate Octavius Granady).[33]

More than two hundred prospective jurors were summoned for the Olson trial. It took three weeks—an unusually long time—to find twelve men who could and would serve. "It's surprising," said an assistant state's attorney, "how many highclass men who come into the jury box talk themselves out again."[34] People had good reason to make excuses: Detective Sweeney's house was bombed before the trial began; once the trial started, two members of the jury received threatening letters. Police were sent to guard their homes.

The trial itself took four days. Testimony of bystanders and ballistics experts, accusations and denials of police corruption, challenges and rebuttals about legal jurisdiction—all were less important than who fired first, who fired what, who fired when. Anselmi and Scalise never took the stand—but attorney Nash spoke on their behalf: all the weapons in Mike Genna's car belonged to Mike Genna. He'd loaded the weapons into his car to take them to his brother's house. On the way, he'd offered Anselmi and Scalise a ride. It was their bad luck to be in the car when the police began shooting.[35]

Montana had annexed Chicago.

Mr. Crowe was appalled.

"If the law is to be supreme instead of the gang and the sawed-off shotgun, your verdict must doom Anselmi and Scalise. . . . The theory of Ahern, who tells you that the police may be shot down if they question a suspected criminal, is propaganda as dangerous as that which led to the Haymarket riots. . . .

"How can the police capture the men who murder, who rob, who burglarize, who rape, if they may not arrest without first running to a judge to obtain a warrant. Must the police take a judge with them . . . call upon the judge to join them in pursuit while he pens a warrant?

"These men, when they jumped into that gun-laden automobile, had murder in their hearts. They were out to kill!

"When they saw the pursuing polic car, these wanton killers feared punishment for past murders. . . . They resented interference with some plan they were bent on in the killing of others.

"This talk of self-defense is rot! The defense asks you to throw away the sworn testimony of the state's witnesses . . . and to take, instead, the unsupported word of these two men, bathed in the blood of innocent policemen. Will you do that? Not if you cherish life. Not if you respect the law of God and man."[36]

The judge instructed the jury: the defendants were charged with murder, not manslaughter. Murder was the "sole charge" against them. Fourteen years was the minimum sentence that could be imposed for such a crime.

The jury took a straw vote after four hours: ten "guilty" votes, two "not guilty." "Guilty of what?" someone asked. "What are we voting about anyway?"[37] The jury took another vote: eight voted "guilty of murder," two voted "guilty of manslaughter"; two voted "not guilty." The jury asked the judge for instructions. The judge repeated himself: The defendants were charged with murder. A manslaughter verdict would be "worthless."

"Worthless" offended some jurors. "Fourteen years is too much," said one of the "not guilty" jurors. "These men didn't do anything so terrible that they ought to serve fourteen years for it. We ought to give them a manslaughter verdict for it—it carries a sentence of one year to life."[38]

"These men are killers," said a "guilty" juror. "They weren't going to sell cheese with those shotguns."[39] "Chicago is infected with gunmen. It's worse than the old frontier days," said another.[40]

It took another six hours for the jury to reach a compromise: Anselmi and Scalise were guilty of killing Officer Olson, but they weren't guilty of murdering him. "Manslaughter, with a sentence of fourteen years." Anselmi and Scalise smiled at each other.

"I hope to God we have a jury of decent, God-fearing men for the next trial," said Mr. Crowe. "I hope they will do their duty and hang these killers." Attorney Nash heard him. "What do you know of decent people," Nash shouted. "I associate with them," said Crowe. "Not with gangland, as you do."[41]

Michael Ahern appealed the verdict.

In February 1926, while Ahern's appeal was getting under way, Anselmi and Scalise were brought back from Joliet to stand trial for killing Patrolman Walsh. Ahern, Nash, and O'Donnell decided to blame everything on Mike Genna. They found two witnesses who agreed with them. Mike did it all: he shot Olson; he shot Walsh; Conway and Sweeney shot back. Mike got what he deserved. Anselmi and Scalise were guilty of nothing but being in the wrong place at the wrong time.

The jury acquitted them. The defendants jumped up when they heard the verdict. They cheered; they shouted; they embraced; they did a little dance.

"I would have to carry a gun for the rest of my life if I found those two guilty," said a prospective juror before the trial even began.[42] Police took them back to Joliet.

Ahern's appeal reached the Illinois Supreme Court in October 1926, just before Christmas. The court surprised everyone: it threw out the manslaughter verdict and ordered a new trial. In the court's opinion: "The judgment in this case of fourteen years in the penitentiary was a travesty of justice from whatever angle viewed. If plaintiffs . . . were not guilty, or were guilty of manslaughter only, sentencing them for murder was an injustice. If guilty of murder, a sentence of fourteen years, the least penalty under the circumstances in this case, is but a mockery of justice."[43]

The judge who presided over Anselmi and Scalise's new trial was William Lindsey—the same judge who'd presided over Belva Gaertner's and Beulah Annan's murder trials. Ahern, Nash, and O'Donnell once again represented the defendants. Mr. Crowe sent two assistant state's attorneys—Harold Levy and Emmet Byrne—to try to do what he couldn't. Byrne and Levy had fifteen death penalty convictions to their credit. Ahern took the opposing counsel very seriously.

Ahern screened prospective jurors more carefully, more pointedly, than he had before. He asked each of them three questions.

First: "Do you believe in the principle of law that no person should be deprived of his liberty without due process of law?" If the answer was yes, Ahern asked a second question: "Do you also agree with the principle of law that any person has the right to resist unlawful arrest? The law says that under those circumstances, force may be resisted with force. Do you accept that as law?" If the answer again was yes, then Ahern asked his last question: "The law also says that in this resistance, a person would have the right to kill if he believed his own life was endangered. Will you apply that principle of law to the facts if you are accepted as a juror?"[44]

It took the defense and the prosecution seven days to screen one hundred prospective jurors. The papers listed the professions of some of the men selected: a cattle broker, a roofing contractor, an insurance agent, a real estate salesman, a butcher, a streetcar motorman, and a telephone repairman.

Emmet Byrne presented the state's case: "The evidence will show that the policemen were ringing their gong [during the chase]. When they got out of their car, they announced that they were policemen. The evidence will further show that Anselmi and Scalise each leveled a [sawed-off] shotgun at Olson and Walsh and that both officers, without firing a shot, crumpled to the gutter."[45]

Ahern's reply was:

The police never rang their gong. They never said they were policemen. They pursued Genna's car because they were suspicious—not because they knew, for a fact, that anyone in the car had committed a crime. Such an intervention was "a willful, wanton act of oppression"; in fact, said Mr. Ahern, it was "an assault with intent to kill." Whatever the defendants did, they did to defend themselves. Their response to the "police assault" was "justified."[46]

The state called witnesses who said they'd heard the police ring their gong. The defense called witnesses who said they'd heard nothing.

Ahern decided to put both his clients on the stand. Scalise spoke broken English: "The other guys shot first," he said. He didn't know who they were. He thought they were gangsters. Other gangsters. Mike Genna pushed a shotgun into his hands. He took it; he fired once, then he ran. Mike Genna did all the rest of the shooting.

Anselmi spoke through an interpreter. He told the same story as Scalise. No one in Genna's car knew who was chasing them. After they crashed, the shooting started. Mike Genna grabbed a shotgun and a revolver and shot back. Anselmi said he was so frightened, he threw himself on the ground; when the shooting stopped for a minute, he ran for his life.[47]

The jury took two hours to acquit them.

Mayor William Dever

A year passed.

Capone found something for Anselmi and Scalise to do: in July 1928, he sent them to Brooklyn to kill Frankie Yale. Twice, Yale had come to Chicago to kill important people: Colosimo in 1920, Dean O'Banion in 1925. Capone didn't intend to give Yale a chance to come to Chicago a third time.

There was one other reason to kill Yale: for years, Torrio and Yale had done business together whenever it suited them. After Torrio retired, Capone continued the relationship: He bought alcohol in New York. Bought it from Yale or with Yale. Yale transported it to Chicago. By 1927, Yale had begun to hijack his own trucks on their way west. Capone understood the insult; since Yale knew he could double-cross him, Yale probably believed he could kill him. Long term, short term, Capone's strategy was to kill Yale first.

There were two men riding with Anselmi and Scalise when they went hunting for Yale. Both men were machine-gun experts. One was a very cunning, very handsome man named Vincenzo Gribaldi. Gribaldi called himself McGurn, "Machine Gun Jack" McGurn. The other shooter was one of Capone's golfing buddies. He wasn't as imaginative or as good-looking as McGurn, but he was big and lethal. Big, lethal, and ugly: Fred "Killer" Burke. The four of them were in a Buick (with Illinois plates), cruising the streets of Brooklyn, when they spotted Yale.

Yale—like Angelo Genna—was taking the morning air, at the wheel of a new car. Angelo had been on his way to buy a new house when he died; Yale was coming home from Mass. Unlike Angelo, who drove his roadster with the top down, Yale drove a Lincoln that was fitted with body armor. Unlike Capone's Cadillac, though, Yale's town car didn't have bulletproof glass.

Yale saw the Buick pull up behind him. Yale was forty-two; he'd survived three assassination attempts, including, early on, a bullet in the back. He recognized the signs. He rolled up his windows, swerved onto Forty-fourth Street, and floored the Lincoln. Forty-fourth was a nice street in a nice neighborhood: brownstones, sidewalks, trees. The Buick pulled up next to him. Scalise aimed at Yale's head, and blew out the Lincoln's windows. Yale collapsed against the steering wheel; the Lincoln kept rolling; the Buick kept pace. McGurn emptied his Thompson into Yale. A whole drum of steel-jacketed .45s blew through the Lincoln as if it were made of balsa wood. Yale's car jumped the curb and slammed into the steps of a brownstone. The Kaufman family was inside, celebrating their son's bar mitzvah. Yale's body spilled out, dressed in church clothes. The Buick drove away. The police found it later, abandoned along with its weapons.[48]

Seven months went by. Capone found something else for Anselmi and Scalise to do. Jack McGurn did the planning for the job. McGurn was someone Mike Genna would have liked, someone Dean O'Banion would have
appreciated. McGurn was a serious practical joker. A trickster who always
had the last laugh.

The war of revenge that had begun when O'Banion was killed continued. Weiss was dead; Bugs Moran and his crew were still alive. Their
dumb luck. Moran had sent two brothers, Peter and Frank Gusenberg,
to kill McGurn. They'd ambushed him one night while he was standing in
a phone booth, making a call. They'd blasted him with a Thompson and
a .38. McGurn went down; dead, they thought. He'd just collapsed. Too
bad for them. McGurn had personal as well as professional reasons to kill
Moran.[49]

The lure was a load of Canadian whiskey. The man who offered it to
Moran worked for McGurn. The first load was so good and so cheap (Capone
underwrote it) that when McGurn's man offered Moran a second load,
Moran agreed.

Ten-thirty in the morning on the fourteenth, the man told Moran. You
know the SMC garage up on Clark? Moran knew the place. Be there, said
the man. Moran made a little joke. The fourteenth? he said. You want me
to bring roses and a box of chocolates? Cash, said the man.

Moran had something else to do that morning. He sent his business
manager and his brother-in-law instead. They brought five other people
with them. One of them was a man named Weinshank; he ran a bar. Weinshank looked—and dressed—enough like Moran that when he walked
into the garage, McGurn's lookouts sent the signal to close the trap.

A delivery truck was driving slow, looking for an address on Clark,
when a Detective Bureau car—a big black Cadillac with a gong, a siren,
and a gun rack—came fast around the corner at Webster; it clipped the
truck's front fender.[50] The truck driver pulled over and climbed out. The
Cadillac stopped; a plainclothes detective stepped out. The driver braced
himself; he could see four other cops in the car; two of them were in uniform. Trouble. The detective looked at the truck's fender, then he looked at
his own. "Be careful next time," he said. The driver looked down, touched
his cap. Lucky this time. He drove off; the detective climbed back into his
car. The Cadillac drove away. Headed for the SMC garage.

The two cops who were wearing uniforms were Anselmi and Scalise.
They never did like suits.

Hymie Weiss's funeral

13 · Hymie Weiss

Hymie Weiss got out of jail in April 1926.[1] He decided to make O'Banion's flower shop on State Street his new headquarters. Weiss made deals with bootleggers in Cleveland, rumrunners in Miami, wholesalers in Quebec. Big slot-machine operators from Cicero, bootleggers from Chicago's South Side—any and all enemies of Capone became Weiss's new friends.

By July, Weiss was ready to resume his war of revenge. He planned an ambush. He began by kidnapping Capone's driver. The man knew Capone's daily schedule, but he wouldn't talk. Weiss had him tortured. Burning cigarettes, branding irons, the man endured the torments of a holy martyr. Not a word. Weiss shot him in the head, then dumped him in a cistern.[2] Capone was appalled. People said that he and Torrio used to torture people in the basement of the Four Deuces on Wabash. No matter. Capone was outraged: his driver was *his* driver.

Three months passed. In October, one of Weiss's new allies—an over-the-hill South Sider named Joe Saltis—went on trial for murder. Weiss raised $100,000 for Saltis's defense. The first day of the Saltis trial, after court ended, Weiss told his driver to take him to headquarters. Weiss had a list of Saltis jurors in his pocket and a list of state prosecution witnesses in his safe. He was eager to get to work. He jumped out of his Cadillac and crossed the street. He never made it to the shop's front door.

Capone would have killed him sooner, but he'd been out of town. Not on vacation, but in hiding. All because of something that had happened the same month Weiss got out of jail. The three months Weiss spent rebuilding his connections, Capone spent working out a deal—from a safe distance—with state and federal prosecutors. Capone returned to Chicago in July. Six grand juries met, fretted—and decided nothing. Capone's problem faded away, like a stain in a rug.

Capone's problem started one night in late April. Capone had been having dinner at his headquarters in Cicero—a hotel called the Hawthorne Inn—when one of his watchers interrupted his meal: the O'Donnell brothers—gang leaders from the South Side—were wandering around Cicero, drunk and disorderly, as if they had nothing to fear. The O'Donnells knew they were targets; they were tempting fate. Capone decided to relieve them of their lives. He sent three men to kill them. He sat in his own car and watched.

Unfortunately, no one told Capone that the O'Donnells weren't drinking alone. A well-known public official, an assistant state's attorney named McSwiggin, had made the mistake of joining them. Maybe the O'Donnells thought that with McSwiggin along they were safe. Maybe McSwiggin thought that he was too well connected to die. Capone's men attacked the O'Donnells with machine guns. The O'Donnells ducked; McSwiggin didn't.

A prosecutor shot dead in Cicero would have been embarrassing enough, but McSwiggin was no ordinary prosecutor: his father was a veteran Chicago police detective; his mentor was Mr. Crowe himself. McSwiggin had won so many death-penalty convictions that the papers called him "the hanging attorney." Back in October 1925, Mr. Crowe had tried—and failed—to convict Albert Anselmi and John Scalise of killing Patrolman Olson. When those two were brought back from Joliet to stand trial for killing Patrolman Walsh, Mr. Crowe chose William McSwiggin to prosecute them.

Capone's real problem was that on McSwiggin's way up the ladder—on his way to becoming the prosecutor—Mr. Crowe asked him to do what he couldn't do: McSwiggin had tried, very publicly, to indict Capone himself. Not for bootlegging or pimping or election fraud, but for personally killing a man in front of witnesses in a bar back in 1924.[3]

The shooting made headlines. Capone's picture appeared in the papers. William McSwiggin saddled up and went after him. William Dever had just been elected mayor. Crime and corruption would end. Justice would prevail.

Nothing came of the case. Witnesses forgot or rearranged their memories. Capone presented himself to McSwiggin and offered to explain everything: He was a businessman; he'd been out of town; he'd never met the dead man. The coroner's jury ventured a guess: the dead man had died because he'd been shot. End of story. Except, Capone and McSwiggin met. They took a good look at each other. They were both on their way up. Capone would inherit Torrio's world; McSwiggin would inherit Crowe's. Why not live and let live? Maybe even do business.

McSwiggin's body was still warm when it was found. The O'Donnells had emptied McSwiggin's pockets, ripped the labels out of his clothes, and dumped him on a prairie road. Mr. Crowe—and all the papers in the city— decided that William McSwiggin had died a martyr's death. The young prince had been killed while patrolling the streets of Cicero. Cicero— where not even the sun set without Capone's permission. Why McSwiggin was there was a mystery. Why he'd been in the company of bootleggers was also puzzling. He must have been on a mission.

Mr. Crowe announced a $5,000 reward—money from his own pocket— for information leading to a conviction. He deputized three hundred detectives and set them loose.

The president of Chicago's Union League Club spoke for many prominent people: "I have nothing against Mr. Crowe personally," he said . . . "but, obviously, he is unfit to [investigate] the beer racket. . . . It is mixed up, all down the line, with politics and politics only. . . . Citizens cannot expect Mr. Crowe to prosecute the kind of an investigation this city requires."[4]

Mr. Crowe was offended. Politics? "I am engaged in the investigation of the most brazen and dastardly murder ever committed in Chicago," he said. His deputies broke down the doors of gambling dens, tore brothels to ribbons, flooded speakeasies with beer from their own broken barrels. Whatever ledgers and account books they found, they brought back to Mr. Crowe and laid them before him like spoils of war.

"It has been established," said Mr. Crowe, ". . . That Al Capone in person led the slayers of McSwiggin . . . five automobiles, carrying nearly thirty gangsters, all armed with weapons ranging from pistols to machine guns were used. . . . It has been found that Capone handled the machine gun, being compelled to this act in order to set an example for fearlessness to his less eager companions."[5]

Capone left town. He thought he'd be shot on sight. In his absence, the city's newspapers, civic leaders, law enforcement officials, prosecutors, and coroners quarreled with one another. Who was in charge? Who was to blame? McSwiggin's death—and the investigations that followed— played out like primal scenes. Doors opened: no one wanted to see what they saw.

Three months later, when Capone returned (he'd been hiding in plain sight in Lansing, Michigan), he made a statement:

"I'm no squawker," he said, "but I'll tell you what I know about the case. All I ask is the chance to prove I had nothing to do with the killing of my friend, McSwiggin. Just ten days before he was killed, I talked with McSwiggin. There were friends of mine with me. If we had wanted to kill him, we could have done it then and nobody would have known. But we didn't want to; we never wanted to[6] . . . I liked the kid. Only the day before he was killed, he was up at my place, and when he went home, I gave him a bottle of scotch for his old man. . . . I paid McSwiggin and I paid him plenty—and I got what I was paying for."[7]

That settled everything: Mr. Crowe's protégé was just another cop who took money. Sleep with dogs, wake up with fleas.

Capone went back to solving the problem of Hymie Weiss.

One week after some boys found the body of Capone's driver, Weiss met "Schemer" Drucci at Drucci's hotel. They had breakfast and talked business. Business and politics; they had an appointment that morning with a ward boss named Morris Eller. Eller was Weiss's connection to Mr. Crowe's

Morris Eller

office. Drucci handed envelopes to Eller; Eller would take what he needed, then pass the envelopes to John Sbarbaro (the assistant state's attorney whose funeral home specialized in dead crooks). Sbarbaro would take his share, then hand the envelopes to someone else. No one discussed who that someone else was.[8]

That morning, Drucci had an envelope with $13,200 in it.[9] It was such a nice day, and Eller's office was so close to Drucci's hotel, Weiss suggested they walk there. Eggs and bacon in their stomachs, money in their pockets, Weiss and Drucci strolled down Michigan to the Standard Oil building.

Four men attacked them with handguns just as they reached the front door. Weiss threw himself down; Drucci took cover behind a mail box and fired back; two men charged him; Weiss ran; the men disappeared in the crowd. Drucci commandeered a car. "Take me away and make it snappy," he told the driver. He didn't get very far: Police appeared, blocked the sidewalks, blocked traffic. So efficient, so vigilant. They arrested Drucci and one of the men who'd rushed him. Neither Drucci nor the other man gave their real names. No matter. The police knew Drucci by sight. They knew the other man worked for Capone. They presented him to Drucci for identification. "Never saw him before," said Drucci. "It was a stick up," he said. "They wanted my roll."[10] Thirty rounds had been fired; the front of the Standard Oil building had bullet holes in it. No one was dead; the only person wounded—slightly—was a pedestrian. The attack was a piece of theater. If Capone had wanted to kill Weiss and Drucci in as public a place as Ninth and Michigan, he would have.

Weiss didn't take the hint.

On September 20, while Capone was having lunch at the Hawthorne, everyone around him stopped talking. They listened: machine gun fire, distant, steady, then closer and closer. Capone's bodyguard pulled him down. Everyone in the restaurant hit the floor. The gunfire passed in front of the hotel, then faded away in the distance. Capone pulled himself up and headed outside to inspect the damage. His bodyguard preceded him. No broken windows, no bullet holes. Capone's bodyguard understood before he did. Blanks. A trick to draw people outside. The real show was about to start. Capone's bodyguard knocked him down, then covered him with his own body.

Six cars[11]—big ones—Cadillacs and Lincolns—drove slowly past the hotel, firing broadsides, like ships of the line. Hundreds and hundreds of machine-gun slugs tore chunks out of the Hawthorne's facade, ripped apart its lobby, blew holes through the front walls, windows, and insides of shops on either side of the place. Two more cars appeared. They turned and parked in front of the hotel. Screams, falling glass, masonry dust. A man in overalls and a work shirt—probably Moran—climbed out of the first car, carrying a Thompson. He knelt as if he were on a firing range, braced his weapon, and began. He went through two, two-hundred-round magazines. Deliberately. Methodically. He made long, parallel rows of holes, chest high, along the Hawthorne's inside walls. Then he stood up, turned his back, and walked to his car. The driver blew his horn three times; the two cars drove to the head of the line, paused, then led the convoy away. East. Back to Chicago.[12]

Capone had had enough.

He put two plans in motion. One was visible: he proposed a truce. One was hidden: he sent agents to rent rooms, next to and behind Weiss's headquarters. If Weiss agreed to a truce, the rooms would be blinds for watchers; if Weiss refused, the rooms would be sniper posts.

Capone didn't give Weiss the satisfaction of proposing anything to him personally. Instead, Capone ordered the president of *Unione Siciliane* to meet with Weiss and make him an offer. Samoots Amatuna had tried for the presidency of the *Unione*, but Capone wanted the *Unione* to obey him and no one else. In November 1925, soon after Mike Genna died in the shoot-out with police, Capone had Amatuna killed and Tony Lombardo made president.[13] Lombardo did as Capone wanted: He contacted Weiss and arranged a meeting.

He and Weiss met in a hotel room on October 4. Lombardo began by reminding Weiss of something that every police commander and every gang leader in Chicago knew: If the war continued, no one would be alive to enjoy the peace. There was plenty of money to be made. Plenty of money for everyone. Capone was prepared to be generous: he would give Weiss the exclusive right to sell beer to every speakeasy north of Madison Street in Chicago. Capone's offer was equivalent to Uncle Sam offering Weiss the Philadelphia mint. Weiss refused.[14]

Weiss didn't want territory; he didn't want money. Then what? asked Lombardo. Anselmi and Scalise, said Weiss. Yes? said Lombardo. What do they have to do with Mr. Capone's offer? Tell Mr. Capone, said Weiss, if he wants things to stop, he needs to give me Anselmi and Scalise.

Lombardo left the room to call Capone. Capone shouted into the phone, "I wouldn't do that to a yellow dog."[15] Lombardo told Weiss. Weiss left. No truce. No peace.

Steve Juranovich, the landlady's son

A week after the attack on the Hawthorne, a young man—blonde, German speaking—asked to rent a room in the boardinghouse next door to O'Banion's old shop. The young man said his name was Oscar Lundin.[16] The landlady showed him a back room; it faced a wall. Not so nice, but all she had. The young man said he'd been hoping for something with more light. The landlady said there might be a better one—nice view, looked out on Holy Name—there might be a nice room opening up, soon. Mr. Lundin said he understood. He gave her three weeks rent in advance. He hoped she'd keep him in mind. Sure enough, a week later, the young lady across the hall gave notice. Mr. Lundin moved right in. He worked nights, slept days. The people who owned the building sold it to someone else. No one—except the landlady's son, Steve—even remembered what Mr. Lundin looked like. Mr. Lundin did have friends, though. Steve remembered an older man, small, dark. Jewish, maybe. Or Italian. The man visited once or twice.

Attorney W. W. O'Brien

The same week that Mr. Lundin moved in, a pretty young woman—Mrs. Thomas Schultz was her name, came to the city all the way from Mitchell, South Dakota—rented a third-floor apartment on West Superior Street.[17] The apartment didn't have as nice a view as some people might have liked. Especially a person from South Dakota, used to all that sky. If you looked one way, all you saw was the intersection of State and Superior. Nothing but cars. If you looked the other, there was just an alley. Behind a flower shop. Mrs. Schultz said she was glad to find anything she could

Joe Saltis

afford. Beggars can't be choosers, she said. She paid her first month's rent in advance. She even paid her second month, right then and there. After that, hardly anyone saw her. She must have had relatives, though. Probably lent them her keys, the way they came and went.

While Capone's agents were renting rooms, jury selection began for the Saltis murder trial.[18] Weiss wanted to prove that he could bend the law as easily as Capone. The lawyer Weiss hired—W. W. O'Brien—was less polished than Thomas Nash or Michael Ahern, but O'Brien was experienced and he

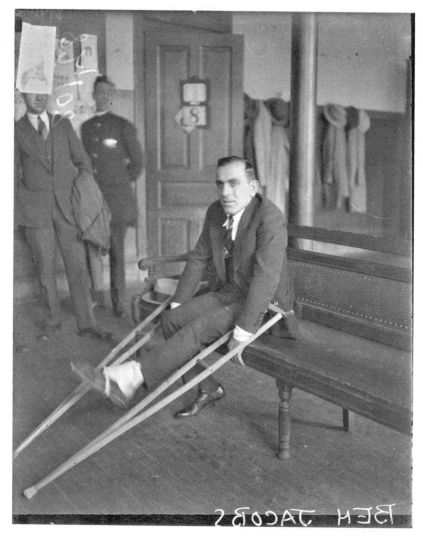

Ben Jacobs

guaranteed results. (Mr. O'Brien had been one of Beulah Annan's attorneys.) Morris Eller, the ward boss who'd been sitting, waiting for Drucci's envelope, supplied Weiss with other men who could help: an enforcer named Ben Jacobs became O'Brien's "investigator"; a drifter with a criminal record named Sam Pellar became Weiss's driver. Both men carried weapons; both men stayed close to Weiss and O'Brien when the Saltis trial began.

Jury selection ended on October 11. The Criminal Courts building was only a quarter of a mile from O'Banion's shop. Weiss and O'Brien could have walked there. Jacobs, Pellar, and another bodyguard named Murray would have screened them. Instead, they decided to drive. Better to be cautious. They parked next to Holy Name, then crossed the street together. Straight into the ambush set for Weiss.

Murray died where he fell. Weiss had enough holes in him—machine-gun and shotgun rounds—to have died there, too. A fire rescue truck took him to a hospital. He died on the examining table. O'Brien was hit in the arm, the side, and the stomach. He staggered into a nearby doctor's office and lived. Pellar was hit in the abdomen. When the shooting started, he thought Weiss had set him up.[19] He pulled his gun and fired a round. It hit Jacobs in the foot. Pellar lurched away; Jacobs hobbled after him. Machine-gun fire chased them around the corner onto Superior. Pellar threw his revolver down a basement stairwell. One of them spotted a doctor's office; they tumbled through the door and were saved.

Crowds gathered around Murray's body. Police found more than $2,000 in his pockets. Police searched Weiss's clothes: in one pocket, a rosary; in the other, a wallet with $5,000 in it. In his jacket, two envelopes: one had an unsigned check for $6,000 in it; the other had a list of jurors. Separate from all this: a shoulder holster with a .45 in it.

Almost as soon as the shooting stopped, two well-dressed men came bursting out a ground-floor window, behind the boardinghouse next to the flower shop. One man carried a machine gun; the other carried a revolver, muzzle up, in each hand. Neither of the men looked like Oscar Lundin. When they reached Huron, the man carrying the machine gun lofted it, two-handed, over a back fence. It landed on the roof of a doghouse. No one saw those two again.

Police searched the room where they'd been: days and days of cigarette butts;[20] shell casings from a machine gun and an automatic shotgun. The shotgun was still in the room. So was a nice, new, gray fedora from a shop in Cicero.[21]

A week later, a lady who lived below Mrs. Schultz's apartment on West Superior complained that Mrs. Schultz's radiator was leaking water through her ceiling. A janitor went to fix the leak; he discovered Mrs. Schultz had moved out. She left a golf bag with an automatic shotgun in it.

Chief Collins announced delivery of 215 new police cars. He planned to arm them with rifles and shotguns "to combat the winter crime wave." "These roaming fortresses," he said, "will cruise the streets, ready to pump lead into every bandit caught committing a crime."[22] Reporters asked the

Fred J. Weiss

chief about the killing of Weiss and Murray, and the wounding of O'Brien, Pellar, and Jacobs. "I don't want to encourage this business," said the chief, "but if somebody has to be killed, it's a good thing the gangsters are murdering themselves off. It saves trouble for the police."[23]

Reporters asked the chief whether the killings would delay the Saltis trial. "No," he said, "nothing will delay Saltis's swift prosecution." Attorney O'Brien spoke from his hospital bed; his wounds would not affect the trial. His law partner, Frank O'Donnell, was more than ready to proceed with the defense.

Three days later, a Saltis juror began talking to himself. A bailiff reported to the judge: "During the night, the man began to shout, rave, and whistle from an open window. . . . I asked him what the idea was, and he said he wanted to hear the echo. He also spoke of being in a coal mine. . . . Then he gathered up the cuspidors and tried to put them in a dresser drawer."[24]

The judge questioned the man's wife. She said her husband had been in and out of mental hospitals for the past four years. The judge asked a court psychiatrist to examine the man. "Circular insanity," said the psychiatrist.

The judge declared a mistrial.

The coroner convened an inquest. Steve Juranovich, the landlady's son, described Oscar Lundin. Two Salvation Army workers and two artists who shared a studio on Cass Street described Pellar and Jacobs staggering away from the shooting. A woman said she thought she saw Pellar turn back and fire at Weiss. A man named McKibben testified that he'd seen Pellar and Jacobs draw their weapons and fire them, point blank, at Weiss.

Pellar was brought to the hearing on a stretcher. He refused to say anything. Jacobs hobbled in on crutches. He refused to say anything. Finally, Hymie Weiss's brother Fred was called to testify. Fred didn't want to be there. "I saw him only once in twenty years," said Fred. "That was when he shot me three years ago."

John Sbarbaro patched up Weiss's body just as he had O'Banion's. O'Banion's widow, Viola, came to the service. She sat next to Weiss's mother and patted her hand. Eight cars of flowers followed Weiss's hearse. Morris Eller, John Sbarbaro, and a man running for county judge pinned political placards to Weiss's hearse to advertise their candidacies.

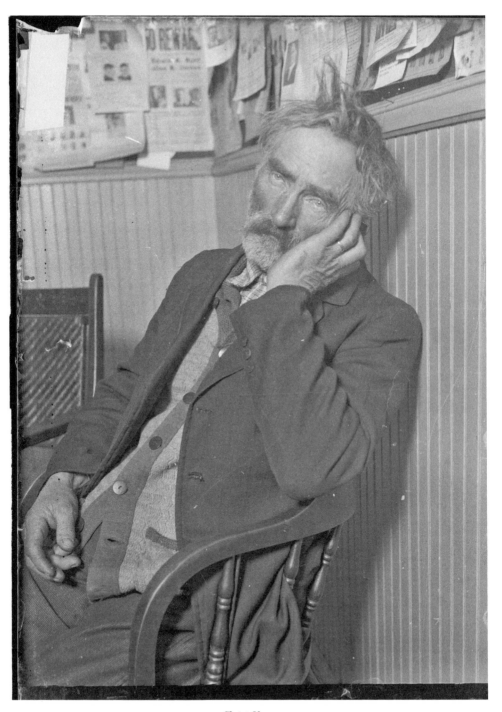

Christ Olson

14 · Christ's Dream

Christ's daughter came to him in a dream. "I've seen Clara," he said. He told everyone he met. "I've seen her . . . I know she's dead. I saw her buried on her face in a grave on a hill near Rising Sun."[1] People thought Christ had gone queer in the head. He was a sight: ragged hair, ragged beard, an old sheepskin duster that smelled of whiskey and hay. Anger and despair— the not knowing—wouldn't let him rest.

Clara was twenty-two when she disappeared. She wasn't the Olsons' oldest, wasn't their youngest. Six girls, two boys; Clara was Christ's favorite. She'd gone missing in September—stepped outside at midnight, "to get a breath of air," is what she said. Christ had just blown out the light; he'd been up, checking the cattle gates; he'd seen headlights coming up the road. Clara came downstairs, passed through the parlor; Christ called to her; she was headed to the outhouse. The next morning, her bed was empty.

Christ had money. Owned land. Hundreds and hundreds of acres. Rich land, expensive land, tobacco land. He and his sons farmed it. Christ went to the county seat in Viroqua and hired a lawyer; he went to the state capital, to Madison, Wisconsin, and hired a private detective. All he had was his dream. He started pestering the district attorney in Prairie du Chien. Fifteen times Christ visited him. The DA was a hardheaded man but Christ wore him down. Everyone knew about Christ's dream. Late in November, the DA drew up a warrant; Christ and his lawyer took it to a justice of the peace, had it properly sworn, had it issued.

Christ's family had been in Seneca for thirty years. Everyone knew everyone else or was related. Albertsons, Helgersons, Ericksons, Olsons. Norwegians. Christ's sons, Bernard and Adolph, took the matter to the American Legion post in Gays Mills. The post called for volunteers. One thousand men stepped forward. Snow was falling.

At sunrise, a posse of three hundred men, in small groups, walked north from Seneca, along Highway 27, toward Rising Sun. Six miles. Eyes to the ground. Clarence Allen, one of Clara's cousins, walked next to his friend Hillman Lee. They reached the crest of a hill called Battle Ridge. Chief Blackhawk and his band had taken a stand there, back in 1832. People still found bones there. Clarence stumbled on a root. The ground was stony, thick with the roots of red and black oak trees. Clarence stumbled, looked down, kept walking. A hunter named Charles Brown came up behind him. Brown looked down to see where Clarence had stumbled: yellow mud, frozen now, but a sign that someone had turned the earth. Brown poked the spot with a stick. He saw the bottoms of a pair of high-heeled shoes. "It's all over," he yelled. "It's down here."

Clara's grave was shallow and long. Someone had spent time, digging it. An hour just to get eighteen inches down; another hour to cover it with soil and shrubs. Digging it hadn't been quick, hadn't been easy. It may have been waiting for her. She lay in it, now, on her belly, facedown, just as Christ had seen her. She wore her nicest clothes—a new silk dress, a new wool sweater, a tan coat. Her favorite coat.

Searchers converged on the spot. Men stopped cars on Route 27 and sent them, north and south, to carry the news through the county. By the time Frank Holly, the coroner from Prairie du Chien, reached the place, two hundred men had gathered around Clara's grave. They'd laid bows and branches around it, framed it, out of respect. Night was coming on; a light snow was falling; the oaks rose into the sky. At the coroner's signal, the men lifted Clara up and laid her in a long, shallow wicker basket. They were careful not to brush the mud from her clothes. Her left hand was drawn up clenched, against her chest, between her breasts. A broken pearl necklace, a little purse dangling from the belt of her dress—the men were careful not to leave anything behind. In the gloom, they could see the lights from Albert Olson's farm, a quarter of a mile away. Albert's son, Erdman, had been Clara's boyfriend. Erdman had gone missing, too.

Erdman and Clara had been keeping company for more than a year. Erdman would call on her whenever he came home from college. He'd drive up to Clara's house—the Olsons' big white house with its gables and porches—and park in front. Wouldn't come in, wouldn't even walk up the steps to the front door. Just sit in his Ford and wait. Clara would come out, then they'd drive away. She never offered to introduce Erdman to her folks; he never asked.

Clara was older than Erdman. Four years older. She kept close to home, close to the farm. She was a good girl, a sweet girl, a dutiful daughter. Dark hair, dark eyes, lips like a Cupid's bow. Clara was closest to her middle sister, Alice. Alice was twenty-six; she lived at home, too. Clara confided in her. Alice told Christ who Erdman was, but that was all she told him. She and Clara kept each other's secrets.

Erdman was what some people called a "country Don Juan." Albert, Erdman's father, was as rich as Christ, but Erdman was Albert's oldest child and oldest son. Erdman knew he'd inherit everything—and behaved that way.

All the girls knew Erdman, and he knew all the girls. At dances, he always had a bottle in his pocket, always knew where a person could buy something for himself. The fact was, Erdman sold the stuff. No one knew where he got it, but everyone knew he had it. Erdman had a reputation for something else. Back when he was nine, he and a friend had been playing with a shotgun. The gun went off. Erdman's friend died. The county sheriff decided it was an accident, but some people thought it was Albert Olson and not the sheriff who'd decided that. Now Erdman was eighteen, went to Gales College; he'd been thrown out once, then readmitted. He sang in the glee club, played basketball, had a college sweetheart. Back home, though, Erdman spent time with Clara. When someone at school asked about Clara, he called her "a hick."

In August 1926, Clara wrote Erdman's parents a letter. Erdman had never brought her home, never introduced her. Never mentioned her.

"Dear Mr. and Mrs. Olson," Clara wrote. "I know you folks will be surprised to hear from me and what I have to say. Understand I am a good friend to your son Erdman and sorry to say we are in a pinch and have to get married if God is willing and you folks are willing to help us.

"I wrote Erdman a letter some time ago and told him I wanted to see him, but have not seen him come down. I saw him and you folks at West Prairie Missions, Sunday, but did not have the chance to talk with him. Tell Erdman to come down one day or night this week so I can talk with him and also let me hear a few words from you.

"I do not like to get Erdman into trouble so I hope you folks will help us before my folks find out what is coming. Please be good to Erdman. I know he never meant to leave me in this way. It is only four and a half months left now until I will be expecting so I hope Erdman and I can get married this month and make our life worthwhile. Will close with love and God's blessings. . . . P.S. Excuse scratching as I am in haste and hoping to hear from you and see Erdman soon."[2]

Erdman's parents showed him Clara's letter. Erdman shrugged it off. "I'd never seen the girl," Erdman's father said, "didn't know anything about her. I told Erdman to get a doctor to examine the girl and get the truth."[3] "Tell her to come see us," said Erdman's mother. Clara refused. She wouldn't go to see a doctor; she wouldn't come to see Erdman's parents. She knew what she knew. Erdman told his parents: "She got her dates mixed." They believed him. Clara had landed herself in a mess; she needed a husband. She was probably after Erdman's inheritance. It was a trap. She had enticed him. "He was no more than a child," Erdman's mother said. "He was a boy; he wasn't full grown yet."[4]

Erdman wrote Clara a letter:

"Dear Friend: I suppose you think me awfully neglectful, but I haven't. I have been to the hospital for a while. Had a couple of operations [on my throat]. I have decided the time is right for us to show some action. Now— we'll not leave for good, but will go and get the ceremony over with, and then come back in a week or so and let them know if they don't know. Of course, we'll have to disappear, you know, so I thought we could skip. You'll have to coax your brother to take you down to the dance in Seneca. . . . I will get you there.

"Then go to Hendrum, Minn., which is the same as Winona. Do not take any more clothes than what you wear and taking more will raise suspicion, but try to get as much cash as possible as that is necessary if you wish to make it a pleasant trip.

"I will be at Seneca between nine and ten o'clock and when you see me, leave the hall and walk up the street until I find you and remember that everything is on the QT. Also write a note and leave some place where it can be found in a day or so and say that you are going away for a while and not to worry as you'll be back some day, but don't mention why you are going or my name.

"If you can't come to the dance, sneak out of the house about 12:30 and come towards the road. If I'm not there, keep on going until I meet you. Don't let anyone see you. Please destroy this letter and my other letters and act hard toward me to your folks.

"Do as I have asked you to do and everything will be OK. If you don't, your chance will be shot and I might make a scarce hubby. So if you wish to avoid disgrace, do as I say and keep mum. See you tonight. As ever, as usual. Remember to do as I say and destroy all my letters."[5]

Erdman's letter was postmarked "Sept. 9, Ferryville, Wisconsin." It was delivered to Clara at two o'clock in the afternoon, the same day Erdman mailed it.

Alice was there when Clara opened it. Purple ink; the pages folded, thick. From Erdman. Clara read it, folded it into tight squares, then slipped it into her bodice. She went to the parlor, took a school geography book from the shelf, and began to look through it. Winona was on the Mississippi, north of La Crosse. Her sister Minnie, her oldest sister, asked her what she was looking for. "Oh—a place," said Clara. Then she went to her room and did what Erdman told her to do: burned his letters. Not the envelopes though; she left them hidden under her rug. Alice sat and watched.

Clara helped with the evening milking. At supper, she sat pale and silent.

At eleven-thirty, Erdman drove past the back door of the general store in Seneca. There was a pool hall next door, and a dance hall, one flight up. Two girls, cousins, Christine and Marie Anderson, remembered dancing with Erdman that night. Fox-trots. Christine remembered because Erdman couldn't keep step.

A farmer named Merle Murry was standing out in front of the pool hall. Erdman drove by, asked him if he wanted a drink. Erdman had a stranger with him. Never introduced him, though. The three of them went around back and passed around a bottle that Erdman had with him. They stood and drank for a while. Merle asked Erdman if he had another one; Erdman did indeed. The stranger climbed back into Erdman's car. Erdman and Merle walked into the pool hall; Merle paid Erdman. Park Moore, the proprietor of the Mount Sterling hotel, ambled over to say hello. The two men walked Erdman out to his car. Merle and Park got a look at the stranger; it was dark but they saw him there. Erdman drove away. It took twenty minutes to reach Clara's house.

"It was about five minutes to twelve when I blowed out the light," Christ said. "Clara went out just a couple of minutes after I went to bed. Then I seen a car. I didn't see no person. I looked through my front door and I seen him turn around this way. . . ."[6]

Christ dozed off. When he woke up, he turned to his wife. "Clara didn't come back, did she?" "Yes, I think she did," said Dina. Christ fell asleep; he had a dream. In the dream, he walked past Clara's room and looked in.

Her bed was empty. Christ woke up, frightened. He told Dina to go see about Clara. She did. Clara's bed was empty. The two of them went outside with a lantern. No Clara.

Christ woke up his sons. He told them Clara was missing. He told them about the car. Adolph and Bernard took a lantern and went down to the road. They found tire tracks; one tire had been patched. The tracks led north.

Clara had left a note under the lamp in her room. "I didn't know I was going until this afternoon, but couldn't make up my mind until now, when I'm leaving. Please don't take it seriously, as it will mean nothing, only a little surprise. I am taken good care of and will be back soon. Lovingly, your Clara."[7]

Albert Olson was awake when Erdman came home that night. The "chime clock" in the parlor struck the hour—one o'clock. Erdman walked into the kitchen, turned on the radio, made himself a sandwich. He ate while he looked through a catalog. Then he went to bed.

Albert Olson family

Clara's brother Bernard knocked on the Albert Olsons' door at six o'clock the next morning. Erdman's mother was cooking breakfast. Albert, Erdman, and the Olsons' hired man, Ed Knudson, had three days to bring in the tobacco before Erdman went back to college. "Well, good morning," said Bernard to Mrs. Olson. She nodded. "Pretty cold this morning," he said. "Yes it is," Mrs. Olson said. "I'm here to see Erdman," said Bernard. "He's asleep, but I'll see," she said.[8]

Erdman came in. "You were up pretty late," said Bernard. "Yes," Erdman said. Alice had told her father about Erdman's letter to Clara. Bernard and Adolph knew about it, too. "You wrote a letter to Clara the other day?" said Bernard. "Yes," said Erdman. He wasn't quite awake. "Last night you came after her and I came to know where she went." Erdman didn't answer. His mother handed him a cup of coffee. He looked out the window. "I didn't come after her," he said.

Bernard told him about the tire tracks on the road. "Those were your tires, all right," said Bernard. Erdman pulled on his boots and led Bernard outside. They looked at the tires on Erdman's car. New tires. "It must have been somebody else," Erdman said. Back inside, Erdman's mother asked what this was about. Bernard explained. Mrs. Olson led Bernard through all the rooms in the house. "So you can be sure your sister's not here."[9]

Bernard went home and told his father.

Erdman worked all day with his father and Ed Knudson, cutting tobacco, tying it and hanging it. Erdman worked all the next day and the next. Then he went back to college in Galesville.

Christ waited two weeks. "If Clara was alive, she would have written me . . . she was not afraid of me—no matter what was wrong."[10]

Christ and Dina went to see the Albert Olsons. Erdman's mother told them not to worry. "I'll remember what she said as long as I live," said Christ. "She said it would be just like a lot of other girls—Clara would be home after New Years with a kid and no man. . . . That was the first we knew anything about it."[11]

Clara was six months pregnant. Christ and Dina hadn't noticed.

Christ asked Oliver and Andrew Helgerson to drive him to Galesville to see Erdman.

"I asked Erdman what he done with Clara. I asked him if he seen Clara that night. He said he hadn't. He said he never went down to get her. I told him I could prove it. He said, 'You can't prove nothing on me,' and then he started to go away. I said, 'You gave that girl instructions to burn your letters. . . .' He kind of stopped and got kind of weak and asked me if I seen the letter. I said, 'Alice seen it.'

"I put my hand on his shoulder and I said, 'Erdman, I want to talk just a few minutes with you. You told her in that letter to meet you at the door at twelve o'clock, didn't you?' He said, 'I did.' I said, 'Now, you sent somebody else in your place to take her, because you called her out to the road.'

"He said he took her to Veroqua. I said I didn't believe it because I seen those auto tracks the next morning and they came from the south.

"Then he said she went to St. Paul. He said he gave her $50.

"I told him I didn't have any strings on the girl. She was of age and all I asked was that she write a few lines so we can see whether she is alive. He said he couldn't do that. I said, 'You got to bring her back so I can see if the girl is alive.'

"I said, 'Erdman, if there is anything between you and the girl that we don't know anything about, bring her back. I will help you all I can'[12] . . . I said, 'The two of you can go ahead and get married. I have plenty of room . . . I'll give you a nice piece of ground and you can grow some tobacco and start you that way.'[13]

"He didn't answer me. He told me: If I would give him a little time, he could bring her back Thursday morning. I told him, 'Now you go down to the car and tell them, Oliver Helgerson and Andrew Helgerson, what you told me.'

"He went down and told the Helgersons what he told me.

"I told him, if the girl didn't show up Thursday night, I would get the sheriff after him."[14]

Erdman's roommate heard him crying that night.[15] Erdman wrote two letters—one to Christ, one to his parents. He mailed them the next day (September 27, 1926). Then he left town.

To Christ, Erdman wrote:

"Just a few lines to let you know that I will no longer be at Gale after tonight. I am going to make myself scarce enough so you can not find me or Clara . . . Just where she is is my business at present, and after the bunch of lip I got from you, Sunday, I'm not caring a great deal, either. I believe she is all right, in health and such, but where she is, I cannot say. . . . I am leaving because I don't like the idea of the sheriff coming up here if I couldn't find her. I'll be back when she comes back."[16]

Place where Erdman Olson was said to have waited for Clara

To his parents, Erdman wrote:

"I suppose you have heard a lot of things already. I know I did. I had some visitors yesterday and they were real nice about some things. They seem to think they have me where I can't wiggle my toes, which is where they are mistaken, very much so.

"He, the old man, claims that he has absolute proof that I know where she is. . . . I haven't the least idea of her location, but I cooked up a story that she was in St. Paul and that I would have to have some time to get her back here.

"I am leaving tonight for some place no one knows. I shall not even tell you folks, though God knows how I feel. I have thought of finishing everything, but life is sweet and hard to part with, but . . . I would rather take death than captivity.

"Sometime I may write you, but I can't say that you will ever see me again, unless it may be in a coffin. Perhaps you may never want to see me again. I would not blame you if you don't. . . .

"I will never stay long in one place. . . .

"Mother, I suppose that your health will suffer tremendously from this and it might wreck Father, but don't let it do that.

"Live for Orvid [Erdman's younger brother]. He will repay you many, many times for what you sacrifice for him. . . . Forget me and live for Orvid. Send him to school and he will make you proud. . . .

"These people cannot prove anything definite although they will try. Do not let them try to pull anything over on you folks. . . . Please try to forget me as I am not worthy of your memory. Shut me out of your thoughts . . . as though I never existed. . . . You have not failed me as parents, but I have as a son."[17]

After Erdman's parents got his letter, they went to see Christ. "They told me I made a bad mistake when I went up to Gale College," Christ said. "They said I'd threatened the boy and scared him out of school. . . . The Dad came back later; he said, 'Between me and you, you had better drop this thing.' I said, 'I won't drop it. I'll find that boy and he'll tell me where the girl is if it costs me $1,000.' "[18]

The lawyer Christ hired told him he thought Clara was probably dead. The private detective Christ hired thought Erdman was probably staying with relatives: a grandmother in North Dakota; an aunt in Canada. Once Clara's body was found, the county sheriff and the DA sent telegrams to police in Milwaukee, Chicago, Minneapolis, and St. Louis. They asked the Canadian Mounted Police to be on the lookout for Erdman.

The story of Christ's dream—the way the details of the dream coincided with the facts—carried the news of Clara's disappearance, death, and discovery east, west, and south to the biggest city newspapers in the region. Editors in Chicago at the *Tribune* and the *Daily News* remembered a 1916 Wisconsin murder case that made news even in the *New York Times*. Chicago reporters and photographers began to converge on Prairie du Chien the way searchers had gathered on Battle Ridge.

The 1916 case, the "Orpit murder case," had involved a pretty high school girl from Lake Forest, Illinois, and a pale, handsome college student from the University of Wisconsin.[19] Now, ten years later, there was a new "pregnant girl/Wisconsin college boy" murder case. Had Clara really been pregnant?

If she had been pregnant, had she killed herself? Died after an abortion? Died because her college boyfriend thought she was nothing but a nuisance—a pregnant hick who needed a husband?

The Crawford County sheriff asked Dr. Charles Bunting, a professor of pathology at the University of Wisconsin, to autopsy Clara's body. The sheriff asked three doctors from Prairie du Chien to witness and assist with the autopsy.

As the doctors lifted Clara's body onto the autopsy table, the pearls from her necklace scattered across the table. A tiny bottle of perfume fell out of her purse. A thick wad of paper fell out of her bodice. Dr. Bunting retrieved the pearls and put them in a little pan; he tightened the cap of the perfume bottle and stood it in another pan; he used tweezers to lift the wad of paper up to the light. The doctors could see words written on it, written in purple ink. Dr. Bunting placed the wad on an enamel tray, set everything aside. He noted Clara's clothing: tan coat, greenish-black silk dress, red wool sweater. New shoes, new stockings, new undergarments. All noted. All set aside.

Dr. Bunting began his examination of the cadaver. "Terrific crushing blows to the head" were the direct cause of death. As Dr. Bunting rotated the head, a two-and-a-half-inch piece of bone fell from the left side of the skull onto the table. Multiple, severe fractures of the left temple; a single fracture of the right. It appeared that Clara had been struck from behind. A single blow from a heavy ax might have caused the head injuries but, more likely, "a series of blows had been struck."

There was no evidence of rape.

No evidence of abortion.

Clara had been six months pregnant when she died. The child she carried was a girl.

Dr. Bunting asked the county coroner to come in. Bunting wanted him to be present when he unfolded the paper that had fallen from Clara's bodice.

It was Erdman's last letter to Clara. The one that told her, twice, to burn all his letters.

The coroner convened an inquest. Family, friends, dance hall partners, drinking buddies—all called as witnesses. The coroner leaked news about Erdman's letter. The fact of it. No details. A letter found.

Albert Olson spoke to reporters. By now, newspaper readers in Chicago

Clara Olson's funeral

were beginning to know as much about Clara and Erdman as they'd once known about Carl Wanderer, Cora Orthwein, Belva and Beulah, and Harvey Church.

Albert Olson issued a statement:

"Dear boy of mine" was the way it began. "Come back, Erd boy. I'll stand by you until the last. I know you didn't have anything to do with the disappearance of Clara. Your mother is fine and knows you are innocent of any wrong doing. It may look bad for you, boy, but trot along home to me, kid, never mind how black it may look. Try your damnedest to get in touch with me and I'll do the rest."[20]

Five hundred people came in cars, in wagons, buckboards, buggies, and sleighs to the inquest. Most people thought, "Erdman ran so he must have been guilty." Albert testified; Christ testified. Alice took the stand. The DA held up the pages of Erdman's letter, sandwiched between panes

Clara Olson's funeral

of glass. Alice identified it. She told what she knew. Five minutes later, the
coroner's jury indicted Erdman.

They buried Clara the next day. They laid her out in a gray coffin. The same
people who'd come to the inquest came to her funeral. The service was in
Norwegian.

They buried her in the middle of a snowstorm, in a cemetery on a hill
next to the church where she'd been confirmed.

Christmas was two weeks away. No one ever found Erdman.

Diamond Joe Esposito

15 · Diamond Joe

The year 1928 began with three bombings.[1]

First, the home of the city controller Charles Fitzmorris was blown up. Fitzmorris had been Big Bill Thompson's chief of police, back in 1920. Fitzmorris's qualification for that job was having been city editor of the *American*. The circulation war that the *American* fought with the *Chicago Tribune* lasted ten years and killed dozens of people. Each paper hired its own gangs to stop delivery drivers, newsdealers, newsboys, and readers from getting their hands on the other's paper. (The *American* gave Dean O'Banion some of his first professional experience: O'Banion ambushed *Tribune* trucks, threatened *Tribune* dealers, and burned newsstands.) While Fitzmorris was chief, Carl Wanderer, Harvey Church, and Arthur Foster had been caught and convicted. After Big Bill was reelected in 1927, he hired Fitzmorris again—as controller. Fitzmorris's new job required considerable discretion: He presided over the taps that siphoned off the city's municipal revenues.

Next, the home and businesses of municipal judge John Sbarbaro were blown up. Sbarbaro had begun as one of Mr. Crowe's assistant state's attorneys. Sbarbaro still ran—and lived above—a funeral home that specialized in dead crooks. He also owned a garage where bootleggers did business—a place where trucks came and went and money changed hands. One bomb destroyed Sbarbaro's garage, the other blew up his funeral home—and tossed him and his wife out of bed. When reporters asked Sbarbaro why anyone would do such things, he answered: "I've been handling some criminals roughly in my court lately."[2]

Finally the apartment building where Mr. Crowe's brother-in-law, Lawrence Cuneo, lived was bombed. Mr. Cuneo served as Mr. Crowe's secretary. Cuneo's job required the same sort of discretion as Fitzmorris's:

Cuneo kept track of the envelopes that were passed, hand to hand, until they reached Mr. Crowe's desk.

By 1927, Big Bill and Robert Crowe had only one set of real rivals: other Republicans. Moderate, reform Republicans, led by a U.S. senator named Charles Deneen, and a Circuit Court judge named John Swanson. Swanson wanted Crowe's job; Deneen (who'd begun as state's attorney, then been elected governor, then been elected senator) had been trying to take apart Thompson's political machine for years. Thompson's machine included the governor, himself, a man named Len Small, who'd been in office since 1921.

A Republican primary was scheduled for April 1928. Mayor Thompson's job wasn't in jeopardy, but the futures of the state's attorney and the governor were at risk. If Crowe and Small lost to candidates loyal to Deneen, and if other, lesser Thompson/Crowe candidates also lost to Deneen's people—then, even though Thompson would remain in office, he'd be stranded, like a barge at low tide.

The bombs that blew up Fitzmorris's house, Sbarbaro's funeral home and garage, and Cuneo's apartment building were like notes played on a flute compared to the orchestral blasts that were about to begin.

After Thompson was first elected mayor, the only pro-Deneen Republican to win any municipal office was an illiterate, first-time candidate named Guiseppi "Diamond Joe" Esposito. Esposito was elected ward committeeman for the city's Nineteenth Ward, the "Bloody Nineteenth," carved out of Chicago's Italian ghetto.

A day before the 1920 municipal election, squads of police detectives swept through the Nineteenth, arresting Esposito campaign workers and political lieutenants, wherever they found them—in shops, on street corners, in apartments. "Thieves and crooks" was what Detective Lieutenant Hughes called them. "Disorderly conduct" was their offense. Esposito and his lawyer bailed everyone out. Anger and resentment elected Esposito to office.

The Bloody Nineteenth was ruled by the Genna family. There were so many "alky cookers" in so many apartments, in so many buildings, on so many streets in that ward that whole city blocks smelled like sour mash. Esposito did business with the Gennas—on their terms, not his. Joe's restaurant, the Bella Napoli, became the place where people met and made deals.

The city's Detective Bureau suspected Esposito had been connected

Mayor William Hale Thompson

with as many as fifteen murders since 1909. A shooting in a barbershop, a shooting in a bar. Joe was no little lamb—but he wasn't as fierce, as rich, or as powerful as the Terrible Gennas. Joe wore a diamond belt buckle; he wore diamond rings. He liked being called "The Diamond." He had political ambitions. Joe was a public man, not an outlaw.

Mr. Crowe sent prohibition agents to investigate and arrest Joe as often as the state's attorney needed to show he was doing something. The only booze Mr. Crowe's men ever found were thirty gallons of red wine; the only people they ever arrested were four waiters. Joe bailed out his waiters, just as he'd bailed out his campaign workers. Mr. Crowe's raids made Joe more popular.

During the 1922 State House elections Big Bill offered "The Diamond" a deal: Name your price, just tell your people to vote for us. "I told them to go to hell," said Joe. Joe was a candidate himself—a Deneen candidate for the County Board. "This is where I clean them up," Joe said. "The biggest inside politics in town is being played in my Nineteenth Ward.... I am afraid of none of them.... This is a finish scrap. Politicians, gunmen, or anything else will not frighten me away from my candidacy—or my friends."[3]

Surprise: Joe lost the election. Thompson's friends in the state capital merged the Nineteenth Ward with the Twenty-fifth. Joe lost his political base, but not his people. The International Hod Carriers, Building and Construction Laborers' Union elected Joe their business agent. The *Circolo Acerro*—an organization of immigrants from Joe's hometown, east of Naples—elected Joe their president.

Joe did favors, arranged deals, made contributions. Every year, Joe served Christmas dinner to eight hundred kids from his neighborhood. He sent baskets of food to hundreds of families. He paid people's rent, bought them coal, paid their doctor bills. "Dimey" they called him; "Don Peppe," they called him. "If Dimey wants, it can be done."[4] By 1926, the Terrible Gennas were no more. Joe thrived.

When Joe was forty, he married a sixteen-year-old named Carmela Marchese. Carmela's parents and Joe's parents—they were all from Acerro, all from the same town. Joe and Carmela had three children. Joe had big plans for their oldest, Joseph Jr.: college, university, law school, even. Their youngest, Charles, born in 1926, they named him after Senator Deneen. The senator and his wife attended the christening. Mr. Crowe attacked the senator for doing that. He called Joe an "alky cooker," a friend of criminals. Joe spoke back:

"I think Bob Crowe ... should taka shame to himself to make criticize my christening of my bambino.... I have my good fren Deneen and his wife and other frens, and they help me to celebrate. No-body shoulda steeka da knife een my ribs because my frens visit my christening.... I been a poor man all my life ... but nobody can say Joe ever do any-body a bad turn. My frens, are de beegest and highest men een da ceety of Cheecago, and I got more frens in my ward than any man in Eellinois."[5]

In 1928, Senator Deneen asked Joe for help: The primaries were coming. He asked Joe to run again. Joe knew he didn't stand a chance, but a friend was a friend. Joe announced: He'd be a candidate for ward committeeman. The Diamond wanted his old job back.

In the middle of March, a man named Mangano paid Joe a visit. Mangano ran a gambling house called the Minerva Athletic Club. He worked for Big Bill's ward candidate, a lawyer named Joseph Savage. Savage was a former assistant state's attorney. One of Mr. Crowe's men. "You can't beat Savage," Mangano said to Joe. "Why are you making us go to a lot of expense just to play safe? Get out of the ward. It'll be healthier for you."[6]

Joe heard what Mangano said. He knew what he meant. He shrugged. "I can't cross 'em," Joe said. "The senator's my fren. I can't throw 'em down."[7]

A few days passed. Joe got a call.

"Get out of town or get killed."[8]

Joe told his friends. "Leave," they said. "I can't go," Joe said. "My daughter just came down with scarlet fever." "You're a marked man," they said. "Go down to your farm," they said. "You're next."

Joe met with his precinct captains that night. He didn't say anything about the phone call; he didn't mention Mangano's visit.

Joe never carried a gun. His bodyguards didn't either. They walked him home. The Varchetti brothers. One was Joe's driver; the other was a precinct captain. A fruit wholesaler. Mangano had talked to him, too. Tried to convince him to come to work for Savage.

Joe lived two blocks from his office. That night, he stopped to talk with a neighbor. Rose Seego. Rose was an election clerk. "I guess I haven't much of a chance of winning," Joe said. "It won't make much of a difference. If I lose, I'll move out of the ward—then I'll be missed."[9] Joe walked another half block. He stopped to talk with another neighbor—Elizabeth Channing. Mrs. Channing wished him luck. Joe and the Varchettis passed the Varchettis' house. They'd walk him to the corner, then go home. The Varchettis made it; Joe didn't.

Joe died with fifty-eight shotgun rounds in him. A drive-by. The first load knocked him down. The rest were fired so close, Joe's clothes had powder burns. The Varchettis didn't have a scratch on them. Ralph, the precinct captain, said they thought—maybe—the first salvo was a tire blowout. He said they hit the ground. (The police checked their clothes: no dirt, no tears.) "I'm shot! I'm shot!" Joe yelled. Carmela came out. She saw the men—two men—standing over Joe. She ran at them, screaming. "Oh, Guiseppi! Guiseppi! Is it you?"

Seven squads of detectives converged on the scene. They questioned the Varchettis. Ralph said the killers drove a gray sedan. Other witnesses

Crowds at the home of Joe Esposito

said the car was dark green, maybe blue. "No question about it," said one of the detectives. "It's the booze game. Joe crossed somebody."[10] No one else thought so.

Two days after Joe died, John Infantino's landlady found him dead in his room. Infantino had seen what happened. (Infantino was no ordinary witness: He was a cousin of the late Samoots Amatuna, the man Mike Genna had used, back in 1925, to lure Hymie Weiss and Schemer Drucci into an ambush.) Someone had shot Infantino three times in the back. He'd been kneeling by his bed. His landlady thought he was praying.

Infantino's death was reported by the papers as a front-page, late edition bulletin. The *Chicago Tribune* headlined the news: ESPOSITO WITNESS IS SLAIN. Underneath that, the *Tribune* ran a report written by James O'Donnell Bennett. Bennett was the *Tribune*'s Special Correspondent.

Crowds at the home of Joe Esposito

Bennett's article read like a front-page editorial. It was titled:

"CHICAGO" WORD OF TERROR

ALL OVER WORLD

Evil Fame Blazoned Far and Near.[11]

James O'Donnell Bennett was one of the *Tribune*'s greatest writer/reporters. He'd begun as a drama critic, then became a war correspondent. His frontline dispatches described events as if they were scenes in a play or episodes in a novel. A Special Correspondent, indeed.

Bennett was more than a stylist. He did his homework: he traveled, took risks, watched, listened, read, talked to everyone. He wrote about the war as if he were describing a pageant, grand, comic, tragic, and grotesque. The *Tribune* gave Bennett the room to write what he wanted because his editors believed Bennett knew the truth when he saw it. Knew it—and knew how to tell it.

Bennett's " 'CHICAGO' WORD OF TERROR" began with some of the jokes Bennett had heard while traveling up and down the East Coast. "Well, I see you got out alive," a hotel clerk in Richmond said to him after Bennett signed the register. "Take care of yourself; you're going back to a wild town," a cashier in a restaurant in Baltimore said as Bennett paid his bill.

After the jokes came the serious stuff: Bennett strung together quotes from articles and editorials he'd read in newspapers on both sides of the Atlantic. North, South, East, and West: everyone was talking about Chicago's criminal anarchy. "Listen to what people are saying about us," was Bennett's message.

Bennett began with the *Washington Post*:

"The only effective rule in Chicago is that of violence, imposed by crooks and murderers. . . . The ill fame of Chicago is spreading through the world and bringing shame to Americans who wish they could be proud of that city. . . . They are forced to apologize for America's second-largest city and to explain to strangers that it is a peculiar place."

After the *Post* came the *London Evening News*:

"BOMB A DAY KEEPS CHICAGO GAY—300 POLICE IN A STATE OF SIEGE. . . . The situation has become so serious that many officials are planning to send their families out of the city."

"CHICAGO IS AMERICA'S WORST ADVERTISEMENT" was the lead editorial in Little Rock, Arkansas's biggest and best paper, the *Gazette*:

"Protected vice, fattened and strengthened by its protection, has gone wild. Today, the city's officials must have guards to protect them from bomb throwers . . . and lesser officials are whimpering in fear. Chicago's political overlords sowed the wind and are reaping the whirlwind. The whole country is humiliated by the spectacle of America's second city over run by hordes of dirty rats that would be thrown out within 24 hours by honest and courageous officials."

Bennett ended by quoting a Chicago businessman who'd been interviewed in Paris by the *Herald Tribune*:

"Everywhere I went," said the man, "in Italy, on the Riviera, I heard evil remarks about Chicago. . . . Judging from the reports in the papers, a European . . . would think every Chicagoan took his life in his hands when he stepped out-of-doors."[12]

Joe Esposito's casket

Four thousand people of every kind, class, and predicament attended the High Requiem Mass celebrated in Chicago's historic Holy Family Church in honor of Diamond Joe.

Crooks and magistrates, wealthy lawyers and poor widows, ward heelers and U.S. congressmen, a U.S. senator, a Municipal Court chief justice, an assistant U.S. attorney—all listened as Father William Murphy delivered the eulogy. Joe's silver and bronze casket lay on a bier before him. "This man, this kind and rugged man," said the reverend father, "was the victim of a most brutal, dastardly crime. . . . This community of four million has been inexpressibly shocked by the cruelty and cowardice of this dastardly deed. . . . The defiance of law with which the four million people of our county are frequently confronted must end. And it will. Surely, among the four million, there is a residue of decency which will rise and put an end to this defiance of the law. The decent element must awake—and awaken now."[13]

Outside the church, four thousand more people waited in sleet, snow, and freezing rain. Joe's casket was carried out; his cortege was formed: It was one and a half miles long. Two airplanes were to have flown above the procession, scattering red roses along the route.[14] The weather grounded them. Three hundred cars of mourners, twenty-five cars of flowers, hundreds of policemen, thousands and thousands of ordinary people accompanied Joe's coffin to Mount Carmel. His grave lay in consecrated ground. Senator Deneen and his wife offered their condolences. Joe Savage, Mr. Crowe's candidate for committeeman, paid his respects. Detectives moved through the crowd. They spotted a man wanted for killing two people in a cabaret. They arrested him as Joe's family and friends prayed by his grave.

Senator Deneen took a train back to Washington. Judge Swanson went to a campaign meeting and then a rally.

That night, two powerful bombs exploded outside their homes in Chicago.

The Deneen bomb was a black powder bomb. It went off on his front porch. It was loud and it was big, but it wasn't lethal—meant to frighten, not to kill. The Swanson bomb was a dynamite bomb. It was meant to kill the judge—and his family.

Deneen's neighbors reported seeing a man in a gray fedora get out of a moving car, run up the senator's front steps, then run back and jump in as the car was still moving. The senator's sister, Florence, was reading in her bedroom on the second floor; Florence's maid, Anna Rose, was asleep in her room on the third floor. The bomb blew apart Deneen's front porch, threw both women out of bed, broke every window in the twelve-room house.

Twenty minutes later, a night watchman, making his rounds, forty feet down the street from Judge Swanson's house, saw the judge turn into his driveway. "I was just coming back from a speaking engagement in Congress Park," Swanson said. The night watchman noticed a car trailing the judge. A dark sedan. It moved slowly, keeping its distance, then, as the judge turned in, it speeded up. Someone in the car threw "an object . . . about two feet long and round" at Swanson. The bomb exploded in the air. It blew in every window in the house, tore off part of the front roof, tore off the front dormer windows, blew a big hole in the front yard.

"Mother—Mrs. Swanson—was waiting up for me the way wives do," the judge said. "She'd gone upstairs for something and was on the second step from the bottom when the thing went off."[15] Two more steps up and a few feet forward and Mrs. Swanson would have died. Upstairs, the judge's five-year-old grandson and his baby granddaughter were asleep in their beds. Pieces of glass blew in and over and past them. They lived. "They're not quite old enough to understand yet," said the judge. "I hope when they are, things will be different in Chicago."

"There is no doubt who did this," said the judge. "It was some of the same crowd who are fighting against my election. It was done by the crooks I want to put out of business."[16]

The judge issued another statement at midday:

"The bomb was aimed at me by the crooks and thieves whose political machinations are creating the present crime situation. There is no doubt that the bomb was thrown by those whose criminal interests are opposing the election of an enemy of their political alliances.

"The reason is obvious:

"This is another illustration of the breakdown of law enforcement in this county. It has come to a pretty pass when a man cannot run for office without endangering the lives of his family. . . .

"I can blame this on no one but my political enemies. . . . If it had exploded three seconds earlier, it would have been within six feet of me."[17]

Senator Deneen spoke from Washington:

"The bombing of my home is the work of the organized and protected criminal classes of Chicago and Cook County in their desperate effort to retain control of the city and the county."[18]

Mr. Crowe was offended by what the judge and the senator said. He felt as if they were blaming him, *personally*. He turned the blame back on his accusers.

"Apparently the Deneen crowd has just started its campaign to elect a discredited county ticket. . . . They are resorting to desperate means to fool the public. . . . After having bombed the homes of friends of mine and made no headway, they are now bombing their own homes in an effort to create the impression that the forces of lawlessness are now running this town. . . . I personally offer $10,000 reward for information leading to the arrest and conviction of those guilty of this outrage."[19] "I am satisfied that these two bombings are the result of a conspiracy upon the part of a few Deneen leaders to win the primary elections on April 10th."[20]

In Washington, President Coolidge and his cabinet discussed the bombings in a morning meeting. At noon, Senator George Norris, Republican, of Nebraska, addressed his colleagues on the Senate floor. In light of the recent bombings, said the senator, "I urge the President to withdraw marines from Nicaragua and send them to Chicago." (Senator Norris was an isolationist. He'd been against American intervention during the Great War. He'd voted against American intervention in Nicaragua. The senator's colleagues knew all this—and appreciated his irony.) "It seems," continued the senator, "that American property is safer in Nicaragua than in Chicago. . . . Instead of sending the forces of the Army and Navy to Nicaragua, we should keep them at home and send them to that great patriotic, and windy city, Chicago."[21]

Back in Chicago, Mayor Thompson spoke in defense of his ally Mr. Crowe:

"I think Bob Crowe has the right slant on what is going on," said Big Bill. "Fake reformers, traveling in sheep's clothes in the daytime and operating with bombs at night and attempting to hijack public officials of Chicago because they can not dictate their political actions will be eliminated on April 10th. . . . The quicker Charles S. Deneen takes his fake reformers[22] the better it will be for our great city—and his political future—if he has one."[23]

Mr. Crowe was gratified by the mayor's remarks. He repeated his accusations—more emphatically:

"It is a sorry thing," Mr. Crowe said, "that a U.S. senator and his discredited, defeated, disgruntled crowd must resort to bombing their own homes in order to arouse enmity against Mayor Thompson and myself, the constituted authorities."[24] The audience to whom Mr. Crowe addressed these remarks was said to have been "startled" by them.[25]

The next day, Judge Swanson's daughter (the mother of the children who'd been asleep in their beds) received a threatening phone call: "You can tell the Judge that we will do a better job next time."[26]

That same day, the family of a Deneen candidate for committeeman in the Forty-sixth Ward received a threatening letter. The letter was addressed to the man's wife. "Evidently you do not know that there is a plot to get one of your babies before the primary. To you it may happen like Swanson's house or Senator Deneen's. Tell your fat husband to beware."[27]

A federal grand jury issued indictments against a Thompson/Crowe political ally—an alderman named Titus Haffa. Haffa and ten other men—

including a Prohibition agent and a city Parks Commissioner—were charged with conspiring to distribute alcohol. The indictment charged Haffa and the others with selling the output of two large stills—an output estimated to be worth $5 million. "This is the result of a big political plot to whip me into line," said Haffa. "I stand where I have always stood: For the 'America First' ticket [of Thompson/Crowe], for Governor Small, and for personal liberty. I'm not going to be whipped into line by a trick like this."[28]

The next day, federal marshal Palmer Anderson asked the U.S. attorney general to send federal marshals to Chicago to guard the polls on April 10. Anderson's memo was titled, "Danger to Free Expression of the Suffrage."

"I find," wrote Anderson, "that there are strong indications for a conspiracy to prevent honest elections in a very large number of precincts in various wards in Chicago and surrounding territory. . . . I fear that unless some strong protective measures are taken, serious trouble may occur. I recommend that you give me authority to appoint 500 Special Marshals."[29]

Eight insurance companies gave notice to Chicago churches and meeting halls that the companies would no longer provide riot insurance for political meetings held in their facilities.

Grace Missionary Church in Elmwood Park received a bomb threat. Judge Swanson was scheduled to speak there, that evening. The church's trustees voted to hire a detachment of armed guards to protect the place. The trustees asked Judge Swanson to personally guarantee reimbursement for any damages the church might suffer. The judge agreed, then delivered his speech.[30]

Mayor Thompson issued a statement: The senator and his allies had brought the roof down on their own heads. Said the mayor:

"The Deneen faction sent Prohibition men in here. . . . Then some of their own people ran for protection to Diamond Joe. . . . He couldn't give it. . . . They wanted their protection money back. Those birds are tough. You can't take their money and the next minute doublecross them. Esposito couldn't get back the large amount of money they paid—so they paid their respects to him and Deneen and Swanson."[31]

The next morning, a commodities trader at the South Water Street produce market discovered a bomb sitting on a loading platform next to

Mayor William Hale Thompson with William Cosgrave (president of the Irish Free State)

the market's front door. Sixteen sticks of dynamite, wrapped with black tape: enough dynamite to have blown up every building (and everyone in every building) in a half block radius. The bomb's fuse had been lit; falling snow had dampened, then doused it. A police lieutenant named Flynn told reporters, "The bomb was big enough and powerful enough to blow up a dozen buildings. There is no doubt it would have caused death as well as property damage."[32]

On April 5, five days before the primary, the mayor issued another statement. He made the most serious accusations he'd ever made against Deneen, Swanson, and their running mates:

Hidden from the eyes of the people of Chicago, said the mayor, Senator Deneen had cast a vote in favor of the World Court. Everyone knew who controlled that court—the British controlled it. Deneen's vote was a vote to place America—once again—"under the British yoke." Worse yet, the

Mayor William Hale Thompson

senator had publicly expressed a wish to permit a "British syndicate" to buy control of the huge hydroelectric plant at Muscle Shoals, Alabama. (During the Great War, the U.S. government had built the plant to provide power to factories that made nitrates—for high explosives. Since 1921, the government had been trying to sell the plant. Henry Ford himself had offered to buy it. Senator Norris of Nebraska had sponsored a bill that would have kept the plant in government hands.) Senator Deneen—the traitor—wanted *no one* in America to own it. Again, the British:

"Electricity from that plant produces fertilizer," said the mayor. "Fertilizer goes into the soil that produces the wheat from which flour is made, from which bread is baked. Every time you eat a slice of bread—if this English company gets ahold of Muscle Shoals—you can say, 'Good morning, King George!' "

Deneen's Tory schemes extended beyond the World Court, beyond Muscle Shoals.

"Because of Prohibition," said the mayor, "because of a law much favored by the Senator and his kind—bourbon whisky has increased in price from $1.50 to $15 a bottle. King George's rum-running fleet, 300 miles long, lies twelve miles off our coast. So, every time you take a drink, you ought to say, 'Here's to the King!' "[33]

The mayor made a pledge to the people of Chicago:

If King George ever tried to show his face in their great city, the mayor himself would keep him out. Remember, said the mayor:

A vote for Senator Charles Deneen is a vote for King George. A vote for Big Bill and his friend Bob Crowe is a vote for "America First." "Hit King George in the snout!"[34]

The Swanson campaign answered back: "Say It With Bombs!" became the new rallying cry of the pro-Deneen campaign.

The U.S. attorney general declined to provide special deputy U.S. marshals to oversee the polls on primary day. Chicago police commissioner Michael Hughes said he didn't have enough men to guard every one of the 2,690 polling stations that would be open that day.

Mr. Crowe lost to Judge Swanson.

Governor Small lost to Lou Emmerson, his own (pro-Deneen) secretary of state.

One man lost his life:

Octavius Granady, an African-American lawyer, a veteran of the Great War, had been a Deneen candidate for committeeman in the city's Twentieth Ward. Morris Eller—who'd been waiting in his office in the Standard Oil building, back in 1926, for Weiss and Drucci to hand him an envelope full of cash—was Granady's opponent.

On primary day, Granady and two of his supporters pinned pro-Deneen banners to Granady's car and went on a tour of the neighborhood. Two cars, with a total of nine men in them, began to chase Granady. The men in the first car were police detectives; the men in the second car were crooks. Someone shot at Granady with a handgun. Granady fled.

Granady's car took a corner on two wheels, jumped a curb, hit a tree. The police car sped off; the men in the second car stopped and climbed out. Point blank, they killed Granady with machine guns.

Morris Eller won the primary.

The county coroner, Oscar Wolff, convened an inquest. The late Mr. Granady was represented by a pro-Deneen judge named Trude. The

Judge Swanson

Chicago Bar Association and the Cook County Bar Association sent lawyers to assist Judge Trude. Coroner Wolff was a Thompson man; the jury
he'd selected was packed with Thompson and Eller people. Judge Trude
objected. Coroner Wolff took offense. "I don't want you to make a political issue of this inquest," Wolff said. "Well," said Trude, "it is a political
inquest—and it was a political murder."[35]

The case eventually went to trial. The five detectives who'd chased
Granady and the four crooks who'd killed him were acquitted.

No one was ever charged with the killing of Diamond Joe.

The day after the primaries, the *Chicago Tribune* declared itself satisfied:

"Chicago can again walk proudly among the cities."[36]

The four young men (center, foreground) involved in the Eggleston murder case.
Stanley Durmaj stands head bowed, to the left.

16 · Pearl

On April 28, five weeks after Diamond Joe died:

Chicago (the movie) opened at the Granada and the Mabro in the city. Both theaters were equipped to show the newest talkies; both offered stage shows as well as movies; both bought big ads. Their ads had photographs of Phyllis Haver in her role as:

"Roxie Hart—Chicago's most beautiful murderess . . . a provocative creature of treacherous kisses and whims and vamping ways . . . a shallow vagabond, fascinating but venomous as a serpent . . . a vixen wife who got away with murder and laughed at the law. She gloried in her notoriety as 'the jazz slayer' and laughed, unrepentant."[1]

Chicago opened on Saturday. On Sunday, *Red Hair*, starring Clara Bow, opened in nearly a dozen other theaters in the city and the suburbs. (Bow was the Marilyn Monroe of her day; before movie audiences could hear Mae West make suggestive remarks, they could see Bow make them with her eyes and her smile.)

On Sunday night, more than two thousand people bought tickets to see Bow flirt with three middle-aged men (guardians of a younger man to whom Bow was actually attracted) on the screen of the Ritz Theater on Roosevelt Road in suburban Berwyn.[2] The Ritz's nine o'clock show had sold out, but dozens of people were still arriving, trying to buy tickets, as late as 9:15. A car—a new, flashy convertible—pulled up across the street; three young men jumped out and ran across to the ticket booth. The driver stayed at the wheel. Gertrude, the Ritz's cashier, looked up. She and Pearl Eggleston had been talking about boyfriends. Trying to talk, despite the latecomers. Pearl had a new beau. Pearl was seventeen, an usherette, part time, visiting on her night off.

The young men ran straight at them. Gertrude knew what was coming: They'd try to sweet-talk her, wheedle their way in. They were good-looking, well dressed, drove a nice car. None of that mattered, though: they might be able to get past Gertrude, but not past Ernie, the doorman, or Mr. Bilba, the manager. Gertrude and Pearl watched as the young men charged the booth.

Gertrude was right about the guys not having tickets. They weren't there to see the show, though. The guy in the gray suit had a sawed-off shotgun; the one in the overcoat had a .38; the one in the dark suit had a .45.

The one with the shotgun pointed it at Ernie Speizer's head; the one with the .38 stepped to the back of the booth and pulled open the door. The one with the .45 stopped short and shoved his gun through the ticket window. Gertrude raised her hands; Pearl screamed; the .45 went off. The guy with the gun froze, then snapped out of it. He stepped to the back, swept the money Gertrude had been counting into a sack: $700. Mr. Bilba heard Pearl's scream, heard the shot, came running from the lobby. Back in March, a gang had stuck up the Annetta Theater in Cicero. They stole $500. Mr. Bilba feared the worst.

The bullet from the .45 hit Gertrude's cash register, ricocheted, then hit Pearl in the stomach. As Mr. Bilba came running, the guy with the shotgun fired both barrels at the theater's doors. One of the loads just missed Mr. Bilba. The robbers ran back to their car. The driver made a U-turn; the car headed east. Back to Chicago. Pearl died thirty minutes later, in the hospital.

Heavily armed police from Oak Park, Berwyn, and Chicago searched the scene. Charles Levy, Berwyn's chief, found a .45 casing on the sidewalk. A passerby remembered the car's license plate—New York, 9-N-435. The next day, two Chicago motorcycle cops found the car, abandoned, in the badlands, southwest of the city's limits. The car had been stolen in early April.

Berwyn's City Council announced a $500 reward for information. Chicago's City Council passed a resolution:

"Whereas the entire city is stunned with horror at the wanton and cold blooded slaying of Miss Pearl Eggleston, the Commissioner of Police is hereby authorized to offer a reward of $500 for her slayers."[3]

Berwyn's mayor wasn't mollified. "I wish they'd keep their crooks in Chicago,"[4] he said. Berwyn was a peaceful place. Everyone had jobs; everyone owned their own homes. New brick bungalows lined new streets. People worked hard, went to Mass on Sunday, went to the movies Sunday night. "The fact that they found the slayer's car where they did shows where the slayers came from."[5] Chicago—and Cicero—were the sinkholes and fleshpots to the east. If people in Chicago wanted to watch movies about themselves killing each other—let them. People in Berwyn didn't live that way.

Hundreds of mourners came to Pearl's funeral. The Reverend Robert Devine spoke to the crowd: "If it were possible that the murder of this innocent girl could result in a clean-up that would make similar crimes impossible, then her death would not be in vain. . . . But I fear that this is impossible. Lawlessness is too firmly rooted."[6] Police from Berwyn and Oak Park and Cicero—even police from Chicago—walked in ranks as escorts to Pearl's hearse. Bloodletting in the papers, bloodletting in the movies, now bloodletting on Sunday, in a place like Berwyn.

Two weeks passed. A Berwyn police informant overheard two young men arguing in a west-side pool hall in Chicago. The two had played a game; the loser couldn't pay up. The winner shouted at him: "What have you done with the money from that last job?!"[7] The pool hall was a hangout for small-time thieves. The father and son who ran the place loaned weapons to customers for a percentage. The informant knew the two who'd been arguing; he also knew their friends, knew their names, knew their addresses. Reward money for Pearl's killers had reached $3,900. The informant contacted a Berwyn police lieutenant.

The lieutenant contacted the Chicago police sergeant who'd been assigned Pearl's case. The lieutenant and the sergeant went looking for the young men from the pool hall.

First they arrested a young car thief named Stanley Thomas, then they arrested two of Thomas's friends—another car thief named Albert Mas and a Polish immigrant named Stanley Durmaj. Durmaj was a semipro baseball player. An out-of-work semipro baseball player.

Thomas wouldn't talk. Neither would Mas.

Durmaj did. He told the police everything—including the name of their driver, a young man named John Tulacz who went by the name of Tulip. When the lieutenant and the sergeant went to the pool hall to arrest Tulip, he jumped out a back window and ran.

"I didn't mean to kill her," Durmaj said. Shooting the girl had been an accident. He'd never handled a .45 before. Never owned one. He and Mas got their guns from the pool hall.

"I was broke and needed money," Durmaj said. He hung his head. "I'd been out of a job for some time. I was riding along with a friend of mine . . . when we met Thomas and Mas. They told me they were stick-up men. They asked me if I'd like to join them. . . . We pulled some ordinary stick-ups . . . then we stepped out in a real job. We held up the Annetta in Cicero. It looked like soft money—so we decided to rob the Ritz.

"Thomas had a shotgun. We needed more guns so we went to the pool hall on West 23rd. It was run by the father of a fellow we knew. We borrowed two revolvers . . . a .38 and a .45 Army gun. . . . Thomas stole an automobile for us. . . .

"Something went wrong so we decided to wait. . . . We planned for two weeks before we finally did it. . . . We drove up to the front of the theater. . . . All of us were nervous. . . . At last we decided to get it over with. . . ."

As Durmaj spoke, he began to cry.

"I had my gun in my pocket. Thomas had a shotgun. I walked up to the cashier's cage and shouted, 'Stick 'em up.'

"One of the girls screamed and I pulled the trigger—I didn't know the gun was cocked. I saw her stagger. I didn't mean to kill her. I stepped over her, grabbed the dough, then we beat it to the machine. . . . Later that night, we all got drunk."[8]

Once Durmaj confessed, Thomas did. "You'll find the shotgun I used . . . behind a radiator in my room."[9] Mas was the last to talk. He told police how they'd spent hours wiping down the car they'd stolen, wiping it clean, so police didn't have anything—not even fingerprints—to use against them.

"I read in the papers that we got $1,400," Durmaj said. He wanted police to know the truth. "All we got was $700—which gave us only $175 apiece when we split to four ways. I hated knowing that I'd killed a girl and we didn't get enough to make it worthwhile. I'm glad it's over now. I suppose it means the chair for us."[10]

The next morning a squad of Chicago police detectives took Durmaj, Thomas, and Mas to Berwyn and ordered them to reenact the crime while they watched. A crowd gathered.

News photographers took pictures. The marquee read:

PAT O MALLEY HOUSE OF SCANDAL

SAT + SUN VAUDEVILLE FIVE ACTS.[11]

Assistant state's attorneys with Gertrude Plante, cashier, Ritz Theater

Durmaj wept as he pushed his empty .45 through the cashier's window. He wore a cloth cap and a college letter sweater. He looked gaunt. He pantomimed sweeping cash into an empty sack.

Thomas stood by the Ritz's front door and clicked both triggers of his empty shotgun. He spun around; he and Durmaj ran back across the street. In the absence of Tulip, Mas sat at the wheel of an empty police car—ready to take his friends back to Chicago.

After the three of them did what they were told to do, police handcuffed them, then stood them against the wall in the lobby. Mr. Bilba, Ernie, and Gertrude identified them on the spot.

A Chicago coroner's jury indicted them—and Tulip—the next day.

Stanley Thomas asked Attorney W. W. O'Brien to defend him and his friends. O'Brien had long ago recovered from the wounds he'd received when he'd been caught in the ambush that killed Hymie Weiss. O'Brien took the new case for nothing. The crime was sensational—the case was hopeless. Publicity was worth more than attorney fees. (Remember Beulah Annan?)

O'Brien and two experienced assistant state's attorneys (Harold Levy and Emmet Byrne) spent a week arguing over prospective jurors. Five hundred men passed before them. Claims, excuses, and challenges resulted in only one man being accepted—tentatively—by both sides. Pearl's death had been so upsetting, public opinion was so outraged—everyone had the same opinion: the defendants deserved to die.

O'Brien took advantage of the slow pace of jury selection: he advised his clients to plead guilty and "throw themselves on the mercy" of the court. Judge Comerford accepted their plea. He would be their jury and their judge.

O'Brien asked Comerford to sentence his clients to life. He argued that Pearl's death had been an accident: Durmaj had intended only to frighten Gertrude by pointing his gun at her. The .45 had discharged accidentally. The bullet that killed Pearl had hit what was in front of it—not Pearl, not Gertrude, only Gertrude's cash register. The bullet had broken apart; a ricochet had killed Pearl.

Comerford asked "state alienist" William Herschfield to interview and evaluate the four defendants (Herschfield had been doing such things since the Wanderer case in 1920 and the Leopold and Loeb trial in 1924). Herschfield concluded that:

Albert Mas "had a pronounced dementia praecox make-up . . . Mas has such an air of bravado that he wouldn't think of the consequences of his acts."[12] Mas was dangerous, but he wasn't legally insane.

As to Stanley Thomas: Thomas may have been able to steal cars; he may even have had enough sense to hire attorney O'Brien—but in Dr. Herschfield's opinion Thomas was "somewhat mentally defective."

John Tulacz: "A definite psychopathic personality." Tulip had a criminal mind.

Only Stanley Durmaj was "a normal boy." (Durmaj was twenty.) According to Herschfield: Durmaj expressed remorse, showed depression. "His contrition was genuine. He entirely lacked the bravado frequently exhibited by the criminal type."[13]

Judge Comerford delivered his verdict on July 23, 1928. "It was so quiet in the courtroom when the judge, in his black robe, ascended the bench that, despite the crowd that packed even the courtroom aisles, the ticking of the great clock above the jury bench could be heard. . . .

"The four boys[14] were clean, neatly dressed, and sat motionless in their chairs, their panicky eyes focused on the judge as he began to speak. . . .

" 'The testimony shows,' said Judge Comerford, 'that the bullet fired by the defendant, Durmaj, struck the cash register and was deflected from it into the body of the deceased. . . .'

"There were tears in the eyes of two of the boys as the judge continued reading his sentence. . . .

" 'Witnesses for the state testified here that Durmaj said in their presence and in the presence of the prosecutor that at the time he fired the fatal shot he was very nervous and that the revolver went off accidentally when it touched the glass of the cashier's cage and that he did not plan to shoot anyone. When Durmaj made these statements, he was in the custody of the police. He was alone so far as his friends were concerned. He did not have counsel. His grief was deep and sincere. . . .'

"Durmaj produced a handkerchief and wiped away tears that were slipping down his cheeks. The relatives of the boys, ranged along the inner railing, sat motionless, their eyes fixed on the judge whose voice sounded clearly throughout the courtroom. . . .

" 'The facts show clearly,' said the judge, 'that there was no cold blooded, deliberate intent to kill, and, while these facts are no defense to the charge of murder, they are proved circumstances of mitigation that I am duty bound to consider in fixing punishment.' "[15]

Comerford sentenced the four "boys" to life. The same sentence that Judge Caverly had imposed on Leopold and Loeb. (At what age do boys become men?)

"As Judge Comerford finished reading . . . the look of fear on Durmaj's face gave way to one of relief. . . . Durmaj uttered a low 'Thank you.' "[16]

So much for getting away with murder and laughing at the law.

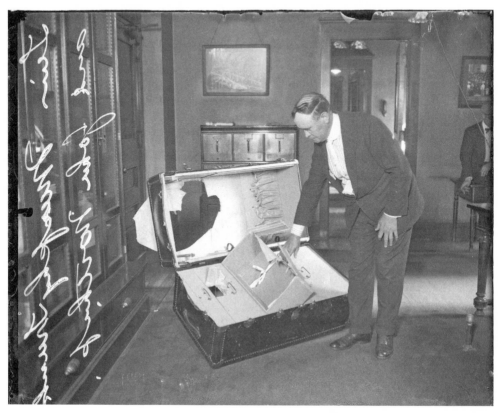

John E. Northrup examining the trunk of "Big Tim"

17 · Three Murders

The year 1928 ended with three professional murders—if blasting a man with shotguns then breaking him with baseball bats could be called professional.

The first to go was Big Tim Murphy. Murphy was the cleverest man to die since Dean O'Banion was killed in his flower shop. Murphy died on his front lawn late one evening. He'd been listening to the radio broadcast of the Democratic Convention in Houston. Someone rang the doorbell. Murphy didn't live to hear Al Smith accept the nomination.

The next to go was Tony Lombardo. Capone had installed Lombardo as president of the *Unione Siciliane*, then had him change the *Unione*'s name to the Italo-American National Union. Lombardo had the bad luck of being alive and in office when Capone had Frankie Yale killed in New York. Yale's people—aided by brothers named Aiello, who'd tried to kill Capone and failed—waited two months, then killed Lombardo during rush hour in the Loop. Lombardo had been walking to a restaurant, accompanied by a bodyguard and a man who wasn't as good a friend as Lombardo thought. Lombardo went down with two bullets behind his left ear.

The last to die was a well-to-do sewer contractor named Ole Scully. Scully had been baptized "Oliverio Scalzetti." Scully's new name and his own hard work had made him rich. When Scully's godson was kidnapped and held for ransom by an old-fashioned Black Hand extortionist named Angelo Petitti, Scully testified against him before a grand jury. Petitti's men caught Scully having drinks with three of his friends after a funeral. The place where they were drinking was a speakeasy patronized by sewer contractors who were all from the same town in Italy. Scully tried to escape, but shotguns took him down. He may or may not have been alive when Petitti's men broke his skull and obliterated his face. Scully's friends were lined up, facing the wall, then beaten senseless. Police were able to identify Scully only because they found a subpoena in his pocket. Petitti's kidnapping and extortion trial had begun that morning. Scully was to have been the prosecution's principal witness, the next day.

BIG TIM

Mount Tennes, the telegraph "Gambling King" of Chicago, had been Tim Murphy's mentor. Tennes's first telegraph switchboard—located in a train station in Forest Park—received race results from tracks in Illinois, Kentucky, and New York. Tennes had a monopoly on that information. In return for 50 percent of the profits, Tennes's operators sent the results by "race wire" to hundreds of bookie joints, gambling parlors, and pool halls all over the city. Since Tennes and the professionals who subscribed to his wire knew race results before most other gamblers placed their bets, Tennes and his clients grew rich and then they grew richer. "Big money from inside information" was the lesson Tim learned from Tennes.

Big Tim was a genial man—tall, handsome, open-faced, well spoken. Big Tim was everyone's friend. After his time with Tennes, Tim went into politics and then into "union organizing." First, Tim got himself elected to the state legislature from the working-class, Irish Catholic Fourth Ward ("Elect Big Tim—he's a cousin of mine" was his slogan), then he made a deal with an important man, an organizer at the American Federation of Labor. With the federation's blessings, Tim organized gas station attendants, then garbage collectors, then street sweepers. Strikes, wage increases, and higher union dues followed. Tim kept a percentage of everything. An ordinary man would have been content to take his cut every month, but Tim was too restless, too imaginative, and too greedy to sit back and let the small change roll in.

In 1920, Tim organized his first mail robbery. In 1921, he organized his second. The first robbery was clever. Understated, elegant. Bloodless. The second was all that—and more. As witty an undertaking as O'Banion's changing barrels of whiskey into barrels of water. A robbery as smooth as a card trick.

Murphy's 1920 Pullman robbery began when two informants told him about a phone conversation they'd overheard. The head cashier of the Pullman Trust and Savings Bank had called the Merchants Loan and Trust Bank in Chicago to request a transfer of $125,000. (All amounts cited in this chapter would be worth ten times as much today.) The cash was to be sent by insured, registered mail, in two locked letter sacks. The sacks would be on the Illinois Central's afternoon local, due to arrive in Pullman at 2:02 on August 30.

When the 2:02 pulled into the station, a bank messenger named Minsch was waiting on the platform. He signed for the letter sacks. He tossed them onto a mail chute. Three boys with a cart knew they could earn a quarter by loading whatever Minsch tossed down the chute, then pushing it over to his car. The boys were waiting, but this time they had trouble lifting the sacks. Two men who had been standing nearby, waiting for someone, noticed the boys and walked over to help. The men picked up the sacks. "Where you boys want them?" The boys pointed at Minsch's car. The men carried the bags over. The boys followed them with their pushcart. The men passed Minsch's car and kept walking. They threw the sacks into the backseat of another car, got in, then drove away. One of the men was Big Tim; the other was Tim's partner, Vincent Cosmano.

Someone squealed. A grand jury indicted both men. Murphy needed money for lawyers. He decided to rob another mail train to get it.

This time, Murphy bribed a mail clerk in Indianapolis named Teter. Teter had worked for the post office for twelve years. He sorted mail on a train—Train 31, the Monon—that ran between Indianapolis and Chicago, then back again. Teter had been a steady, well-respected, hardworking employee. Then he got sick. The post office laid him off. When Teter worked, he earned $90 a month but he hadn't worked for three months. He needed money for food, for rent, for doctors.

Murphy was sympathetic. He cracked the seal on a bottle of scotch, poured Teter a drink, poured one for himself. "You've been in the service of the government for a hell of a long time," Murphy said. "You've given it the best years of your life; now your health is broken. They ought to pension you. I need money and so do you. Come along with me and give me a tip—just a tip, that's all I want—and I'll lay $10,000 in front of you."[1]

Teter refused. "I'd always been on the level and didn't want to go crooked. But Murphy kept arguing. He told me I wasn't taking a chance."[2]

"There ain't nobody in this job that can double cross you," Murphy said. "If they do, I've got enough to hang the lot. If they squeal, I've got friends that'll bump them off and they know it. You won't have to figure in the job at all. All I want is the tip on when they ship the coin."[3]

"The coin" Murphy wanted was a weekly shipment of cash and government bonds—Liberty Bonds—shipped in locked, "red stripe" registered mail sacks that went, by train, Train 31 in fact, from the Federal Reserve in Chicago to a Federal Reserve member bank in Indianapolis. During the twelve years Teter had sorted mail on the Monon, millions of dollars had passed through his hands. Teter knew that the shipments happened on Wednesdays, but he'd just returned to work; he wasn't certain when on Wednesdays the money traveled. "I'll give you $200 just to come to Chicago and go to the depot with me," Murphy said.[4] Teter had another drink. He agreed.

On March 22, Teter and Murphy, Murphy's partner, Cosmano, Murphy's longtime driver, Ed Guerin, and three other men walked into a soft drink parlor across from the Dearborn Station on Polk Street. Two of the men with Murphy were brothers—Frank and Peter Gusenberg—the pair who later shot up "Machine Gun" Jack McGurn while he was standing in a phone booth. The third man was a two-hundred-pound giant named "Fat Mike" Corrozzo. Murphy, Cosmano, and Teter sat at a table, facing the street. Guerin, Fat Mike, and the Gusenbergs sat at another, watching them.

Mail trucks, baggage trucks, parcel and delivery trucks came and went. Then a mail truck with #4212 stenciled on it pulled up to the loading platform. Teter nodded at Murphy. Teter nodded again when the first red-striped, locked canvas mail sack landed on the loading dock. Murphy and Cosmano looked at their watches: three o'clock, Train 31, the Monon, the money train for Indianapolis, was loading coin.

On April 6, Murphy's crew did the job:

First Guerin stole a car. Not just any car. A big, black, high-powered Cadillac. Not just any Cadillac, big or black, but a Cadillac that belonged to a particular man—a rich man who'd made a name for himself by posting big rewards for crooks.

Guerin drove the car to a garage behind a grocery store. Murphy and the rest of the men were waiting. The crew climbed in; Murphy stayed behind. The grocery store would be their rendezvous after the robbery.

Three blocks from the depot, the Cadillac pulled over, and Teter climbed out. His job was to walk over to Clark and Polk. No rush. Just walk over there, then wait. Stand in the corner. When the mail truck with the money in it passed by, all Teter had to do was raise his hat. As simple as that.

There was an empty lot across the street from the station. Next door was a printing plant. Guys who worked there liked to play ball in the lot on their breaks.

Guerin parked the Cadillac in an alley; the crew climbed out. They had a bat and a ball. They had gloves. They started a game. It was two o'clock.

At four-thirty Teter raised his hat.

The men threw down their gloves and pulled out revolvers. They charged the loading dock. "Throw up your hands," they shouted at the men on the platform.[5] One of the Gusenbergs pointed his gun at the driver of the mail truck. "Toss out the registered mail!" The sacks were too heavy to lift. The driver and the bank clerk who rode with him kicked the bags out the back of the truck. Fat Mike lifted the biggest sack, and carried it in one hand, across the street. The Gusenbergs grabbed two more mailbags and followed him. Guerin was waiting. The Cadillac roared off.

A cop on the corner of Federal and Taylor knew something was wrong as soon as he saw the car. He fired two shots at it, then it was gone. It had taken two minutes to steal $380,000.

Murphy was back at the grocery store. "Eddie," he said to Guerin, "take the car and ditch it somewhere out of the neighborhood. The rest of you, beat it. Come around tonight and we'll make the split." As the men were leaving, Murphy spoke to Guerin. "Eddie," he said, "you don't need to worry about your end. I'll see you're taken care of."[6]

Teter was the first to be arrested and the first to confess. Guerin was the second. Teter confessed because—he said—late one night, alone in his cell, he heard another man weeping. "I got down on my knees," Teter said, "and gave myself to God. . . . Next day, I told the Warden to send for the postal inspectors. . . . I was ready to plead guilty."[7]

Guerin talked because Big Tim never did look out for him. A week went by before Murphy contacted him. He handed Guerin an envelope with $2,000 in it. "You've got ten more grand coming as soon as I can cash the bonds." Guerin believed him. "I didn't know at the time," Guerin said, "that the grab amounted to $380,000. I thought $2,000 was pretty good profit for an afternoon's work. . . . Two or three days later, I ran into Cosmano and asked him what he got. He said $20,000 in cash. That made me sore."[8]

By then, Teter had confessed. A judge issued a search warrant for the house where Murphy's father-in-law lived. Postal inspectors found a trunk in the attic. It was so heavy—so full of cash and bonds—that it took four men to haul it out. As soon as Guerin read about the trunk in the papers, he called the police. "I knew Tim had double crossed me—and all the rest of us."[9]

Big Tim Murphy's funeral

The trunk had $112,000 in it. The bills were new. The Federal Reserve had a list of their serial numbers. Those serial numbers, plus the two confessions, sent Murphy to Leavenworth for four years. A judge issued search warrants for four of Tim's safety deposit boxes as well as the house where he'd lived before the Pullman robbery in 1920. Police never found anything. Which is why, when Tim was released in 1926, as genial as ever, there were more than a few people, outside the law, who held grudges against him.

Tim was an optimist. He thought he could take up where he'd left off. Maybe not mail robbery, but labor organizing. Tim tried organizing tire dealers; when that didn't work, he tried jelly manufacturers. After that, he tried gasoline dealers, then cookie jobbers, then garage workers. No go.

Tim wasn't discouraged. There was money to be made, and Tim was the man to make it. He floated a scheme to start banana plantations in Texas. He came up with the idea of a new kind of grocery wagon—fleets of them, in fact. Stocked with everything a modern homemaker might need. Talk about convenience! No need to go to the butcher shop, then the fruit stand, then the baker. No need to go anywhere! Tim's wagons would come to the little ladies! Grocery stores on wheels! No one was interested.

Tim kept trying. He loved a challenge. How about a dog track? How about a travel agency? Not your old-fashioned kind of travel agency. No sir! Tim's new agency would sell one ticket—a universal ticket—good for travel anywhere, at any time, anywhere in the world. No luck.

Three weeks before Tim died, he hit on a sure thing: he'd take over the Cleaners and Dyers Union. The union had 10,000 members. Each and every one of them paid $2 a month dues. All Tim had to do was get himself elected president.

Maybe Tim had been away too long. Maybe he was too optimistic, or too greedy, or too desperate. The Cleaners and Dyers had long ago attracted some very serious people. People who worked for Al Capone. The union didn't need a new president.

Police sent eight squads of detectives to Tim's house after he was shot. Detectives searched the yard, questioned a few neighbors. Police never arrested anyone. Tim was a great guy. He had a lot of enemies. He'd be missed.

ANTHONY LOMBARDO

The news about Frankie Yale reached Chicago quickly. Early in July, people began leaving Little Italy; whole families fled like war refugees. People knew—blood for blood. What had happened in Brooklyn would happen in Chicago. "For Rent" signs began appearing in places that had been settled, cheek-to-jowl, for as long as anyone could remember. Alky cookers closed their stills; fewer people walked the streets; mothers kept their children close. The nuns at St. Philip's noticed something unusual when school opened in September: they had two hundred fewer children in their classes. The teachers at Jenner Elementary noticed it too: they had four hundred fewer students than before. Outsiders who came and went from the district noticed something peculiar: one by one, every butcher shop began to close. People who knew—and were willing to talk—said it was because all the butchers came from the same village—from Bagheria. The butchers knew something very bad was about to happen.

That "something" had begun in 1925, when Mike Genna died, kicking and cursing, after his shootout with police. Until then, the Gennas, the Terrible Gennas, had controlled Little Italy like dukes. Everyone in the Twelfth Ward, civilian or policeman, worked for the Gennas—cooked alcohol for them or took money from them. After Mike Genna died—and after Torrio and Capone raised money to have Anselmi and Scalise acquitted—a struggle began.

Capone believed he had the right to bestow the district on a man of his own choosing. Capone decided Anthony Lombardo—a sugar wholesaler, a commodities dealer, a man of probity—would take over the Gennas' stills.

Five brothers—the Aiellos—disagreed. Joseph, the eldest, was their leader. Joseph knew that Lombardo's effort to broker a truce with Hymie Weiss had been a charade. Tony Lombardo wasn't his own man: he was Al Capone's dog. Dog and master ate from the same bowl. Let them eat, thought Joseph. He'd poison them both.

Joseph kidnapped the chef of the Bella Napoli (Diamond Joe's restaurant), where Capone and Lombardo liked to eat. Aiello offered the cook $35,000 to poison his two most important customers.[10] Poison them with prussic acid. One drop in each of their soup bowls. The scent of bitter almonds. Both men, dead. Take the money and kill them, said Aiello. Don't take the money and die. The cook took the money—and told Capone. Capone sent a crew of machine gunners to Aiello's store on West Division. They fired two hundred rounds into Joseph's shop as a warning.

Joseph persisted.

He imported two assassins from St. Louis. He offered them $50,000—twenty-five for Lombardo; twenty-five for Capone. The only people who died were the assassins. Capone's people dumped them near Melrose Park.

In 1926, Capone had had Hymie Weiss killed in an ambush. Aiello decided to use Capone's methods against him and Lombardo. He set up a machine-gun nest across from Lombardo's home on Washington Boulevard.[11] Capone's people found out. They informed the police. The police raided the post and arrested the gunmen.

Aiello tried once more. This time, he stationed machine gunners in a hotel across from a cigar store on South Clark Street. First Ward politicians and big-time crooks—Capone himself—used the place as a rendezvous.[12] Capone's people found out again. They called the police. This time, though, they told the police to arrest Aiello and hold him for questioning. Hold him, they said, until they got there.

The police did almost everything right. Except they released Aiello just as Capone's gunmen arrived at the station. To avoid embarrassment—an assassination in the lobby, a gunfight on the front steps—the police locked everyone up. Aiello in one cell; Capone's men in another. Aiello pleaded for his life. Capone's men told him he was a dead man, walking.[13] Aiello's lawyer got him out before Capone's lawyers did the same thing for their clients. Joseph asked the police for protection. The police made him an offer—leave town now and live. Go to New York, they said. Then leave the country.

That night, Joseph and two of his brothers left the city. They reached New York, then kept going. They stopped when they got to Trenton. They set up shop. They and Frankie Yale became the very best of friends. Which is why, when Yale was killed in Brooklyn, Joseph and his brothers decided to return the favor; they sent four men to Chicago to kill Lombardo.

In Little Italy, the Feast of Our Lady of Loreto had begun. In good times, crowds filled the streets. This time, there were more people in the parade than on the sidewalks, watching them. There were paper garlands and lanterns, fried cakes and grilled sausages—but few people to enjoy them. Those who were out walked quickly and averted their eyes. There was one banner, though, that everyone saw, that everyone noticed. It hung above the doors of the church of San Fillippo Benzi, above its parish hall:

FRATELLI

PER RISPETTO A DIO IN CUI, CREDETE

PER ONORE DELLA PATRIA E DELLA UMANITA

PREGATE

PERCHE CESSI. L'INDEGNA STRAGE

CHE DISONORA IL NOME ITALIANO

DINANZI AL MONDO CIVILE

"BROTHERS!" it read. "For the respect of your American country and humanity—PRAY that this ferocious manslaughter which disgraces the Italian name before the civilized world may come to an end."

Anthony Lombardo didn't see the parade or the banner. He was downtown in his office, the office of the Italo-American Union, in the Hartford building, on South Dearborn, in the Loop. The only formal appointment Lombardo had that day was to hear the petition of a man named Ranieri—a sewer contractor whose son had been kidnapped and was being held for ransom. The kidnappers wanted $60,000 for the boy. Ranieri wanted Lombardo to negotiate with them. Of course, Lombardo knew the kidnapper: an extortionist named Petitti. Petitti would settle for less than what he asked. Doing Ranieri a favor wouldn't be difficult—but it was all very tiresome.

At four-thirty Lombardo decided to go out for lunch. Get some food in his stomach before Ranieri began his weeping and moaning. Joseph Ferraro and Joseph Lolordo went with him. Ferraro was a bodyguard. Lolordo was a friend.

The sidewalks and the streets were crowded with people. Lombardo's office was next door to the Hamilton Club, across the street from the Union Trust Bank. A fine address. Three blocks from City Hall. One block from what Chicago liked to call "The World's Busiest Corner."[14]

On the corner across from Lombardo's office was the Boston Store, a department store famous for its size and promotions. On that day, the store was installing an airplane—a mail plane—in its sixth-floor showroom. The plane hung, suspended from cables, attached to a crane, which was guiding it, nose first, through the store's upper windows. Down below, the crowd stopped to watch. Ferraro, Lolordo, and Lombardo stood and watched along with everyone else. "Would you look at that thing!" were Lombardo's last words.

The men the Aiellos sent used dumdum .45s—a good choice for shooters who wanted their slugs to spread out and stay inside their target. Ferraro was shot twice in the back; Lombardo twice in the head. Lolordo didn't have a mark on him. (Lolordo died four months later, just after New Year's, while he was having dinner in his own home. His dinner guests shot him eleven times in the head, neck, and shoulders, while he was raising his glass to toast their health.)

Ferraro lived for two days after he was shot. He refused to answer any questions. The only thing police knew for certain was that Ferraro wasn't his real name. The only address they had for him was Capone's old headquarters in Cicero, the Hawthorne Hotel. (Capone had just moved to the Lexington Hotel at Twenty-second and Michigan in Chicago.) Rumors, not evidence, connected Ferraro to only one crime: the shotgun assassination of Ben Newmark, one of Mr. Crowe's investigators. (Newmark had been the man who'd interrogated—and broken—Harvey Church.)

Capone sent an enormous heart of red roses to Lombardo's funeral. At

Floral display in front of Tony Lombardo's home following his death

the center of the heart, white carnations spelled out the words "My Pal." Thirty of Capone's bodyguards, some in cars, some on foot, stood watch at Lombardo's house. The ones in cars wrapped their machine guns in brown paper and lay them at their feet. Eventually, Capone came to pay his respects. Police investigators watched the crowd and wrote down the license plate of every car they saw. Albert Anselmi and John Scalise made an appearance. So did Machine Gun Jack McGurn; so did Mops Volpe, an old friend of the late Diamond Joe.

The front of Lombardo's house was draped with garlands. Banners of flowers spelled his name. Hundreds of people filled the street to watch. The cortege assembled: twenty cars of flowers; pallbearers dressed in tuxedos; a parade of mourners in Cadillacs and Lincolns and Chryslers, two miles long. At Mount Carmel, a quartet sang "Nearer My God to Thee." Lombardo's casket was carried into a mausoleum. The church refused him consecrated ground.

Reporters were permitted to gather around Capone. "Honest," Capone said, "it's all a puzzle to me. Tony and Frankie Yale were good friends. . . . I don't know who killed either of them. . . . It all seems to me like a dream."[15]

OLE SCULLY

Two men kidnapped Billy Ranieri while he was playing kick-the-can all by himself, in the school yard across from his home. Billy was ten years old, but he was small for his age, and frail. Little Billy. The men hit him in the head, threw him onto the floor of their car, kicked him until he stopped moving. They drove him to a farm run by a family named Cappellano. The Cappellanos locked Billy in a room.

Billy's father, Frank Ranieri, went to see Angelo Petitti the next day. Frank's cousin Ole Scully told him to do that. Petitti had been extorting money from Scully—and everyone else Scully knew—for years. Petitti ran a soft drink parlor—but, as a police detective named Burns later testified, there were no bottles of anything, soft or hard, in the place.[16] Just Petitti and his notebook, full of names and sums.

Petitti told Frank to go home and wait for a phone call. Frank's phone rang ten minutes later. "If you want your boy back alive, it'll cost you $60,000." Frank went back to see Petitti. To ask for advice. Petitti told him not to come back again unless he had the $60,000 with him. Then what? Then the two of them would go for a little walk. Someone would approach them; Frank would hand the money to the man. Little Billy would come home.

Frank made an appointment to see Tony Lombardo.

Lombardo didn't live long enough to be of any help, so Frank went back to see Petitti. "I don't have $60,000," he said. "How about $5,000?" Petitti glared at him. "What are you bargaining for?" Petitti said. "If you can get $5,000 you can get $7,000."[17]

Petitti and Frank made a deal; Frank's brother, Nick, would come back with $5,000. After Little Billy came home, Petitti would get the other $2,000. Not for Petitti, himself. For the kidnappers.

Frank borrowed the $5,000 from his cousin Ole Scully. Scully went to see the grand jury. He told the jury everything he knew about Petitti. Police arrested Petitti immediately. The next day, when Petitti appeared before Judge Frank Comerford, the judge explained a new fact of life to him: there would be no bail. Petitti would stay in jail until Little Billy came

Angelo Petitti

home. Robert Crowe was no longer state's attorney. The facts of life had changed.

Petitti sent word to the Cappellanos. They took Billy for a ride. They handed him a $10 bill and told him to walk down the road. His father was waiting. Billy wandered around until he found a gas station. The owner called the sheriff.

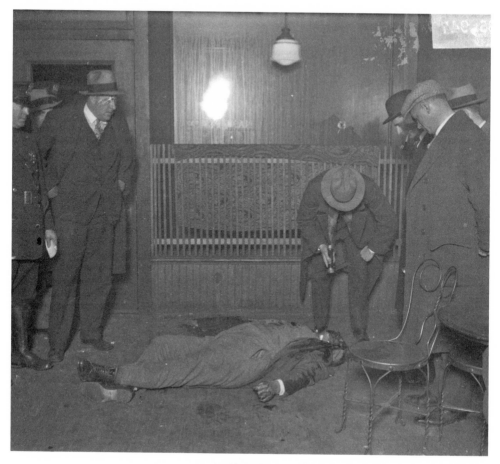

Ole Scully

Judge Comerford ordered Petitti held on the charge of kidnapping for ransom. The Cappellanos were arrested the next day. They said Petitti had forced them to do what they did.

It took three weeks to assemble a jury. Everyone knew jury service in a Black Hand trial could be lethal. Prosecutors asked for the death penalty.

On December 13, as prosecutors were making their opening arguments, Petitti's men found Scully and killed him. Assistant State's Attorney Sam Hoffman and Hoffman's assistant Charles Mueller received death threats. Handwritten notes. Simple, straightforward, ominous. Hoffman sent his wife and children out of town. He and Mueller moved into a hotel. They ate and slept, came and went under guard.

Judge John Swanson was the new state's attorney. He issued a statement.

"If Scully was murdered because he was a witness in the Ranieri case, I construe it as an open challenge to all law enforcement officials. . . . As public prosecutor of the county, I accept the challenge."[18]

The state announced that the Ranieris—father and son—would replace Ole Scully as prosecution witnesses. Frank Ranieri got a letter in the mail: "You better save your money and don't be crazy. If you do not do it . . . you won't live to see the end of the trial. We see you every day. You'll get it soon. Last chance. Remember the boy."[19] Little Billy got a letter of his own. State's Attorney Swanson ordered fifty police officers to guard the Ranieris, day and night.

The presiding judge, Robert Genzel, was threatened. The note he received was nearly illegible: Quit the trial or die. Genzel ordered bailiffs to search and question all spectators. He issued a statement:

"It is high time that private citizens are protected properly from these undesirable aliens. Something must be done on behalf of our respectable Italians so they may have proper protection from these vicious killers. The federal government must step in to deport these aliens. It is deportation they fear more than penitentiary cells."[20]

Three more prosecution witnesses received death threats. Swanson ordered additional police protection for them.

On December 23, prosecutor Hoffman made his closing argument to the jury:

"You men," he said, "have lived through a terrible drama. . . . If you hadn't heard the story here, you probably wouldn't have believed that this kind of thing could happen in this country in 1928.

"You have the opportunity today to make history. For Chicago. For the nation. Some 230 million eyes are watching you men today."[21]

The jury deliberated until two-thirty in the morning. Petitti and his lawyers said the kidnappers had forced him to do what he did. He'd only been trying to help. He had kids of his own. He knew what Frank must have been going through.

The jury compromised: Petitti had been guilty of something—but not guilty enough to die. Twenty-five years. Justice was done.

Afterword

During the 1920s, Chicago was the scene of three perverse—and enduring—homicidal dramas: Leopold and Loeb's killing of Bobby Franks, their little neighbor boy;[1] the St. Valentine's Day massacre of members of the Moran gang by a firing squad of Capone men dressed as police detectives and patrolmen;[2] and the two man killers who became "Velma" and "Roxie Hart" in Maurine Watkins's play *Chicago*.[3]

Chicago in the twenties may not have been Sophocles' Thebes, and the nightmare fables its most grotesque murders became may have had characters more twisted than tragic, but the city and its homicides—now almost ninety years in the past—have become as much a part of America's bloody mythology as Kennedy in Dallas, Custer at Little Bighorn, and the fall of the Twin Towers.

One city, in one decade, produced three Grand Guignol, theater of cruelty dramas. Dramas that have endured.

How did that happen?

Consider these facts:

In 1924, the year of Leopold and Loeb *and* of "Velma" and "Roxie Hart," Chicago's homicide rate, measured in homicides per 100,000, was 24 percent higher than the national urban average.[4]

By April of 1924, the *Chicago Tribune* had begun to print a strange kind of clock face on the inside pages of its weekday editions. The *Tribune*'s clock had three hands, "The Hands of Death": one hand was labeled "Moonshine"; one hand was labeled "Guns"; one hand was labeled "Autos." Death by automobile was a new phenomenon. Death caused by cars driven by people who had never driven before, or by people who had never driven while impaired by alcohol, was also a new phenomenon.[5]

There were other cities—Birmingham and Memphis, Nashville and New Orleans—that had homicide rates many, many times higher than Chicago's. But Chicago was America's second largest city—after New York. The comparison—and the rivalry—between the two cities had an effect on the way America perceived Chicago. In 1924, the year Chicago's homicide rate was 24 percent higher than the national urban average, New York's was 31 percent *below* that average.

Since New York was the intellectual, entertainment, and communications capital of the country, whatever its opinion makers thought was true soon became the "common knowledge" of their counterparts elsewhere. When New York writers, reporters, and intellectuals walked the streets of their city, then looked up and away at their distant rival to the west, they came to believe that the place they inhabited was far more civilized than the slaughterhouse that had turned from killing hogs to murdering its own citizens.

The statistical disparities between Chicago and New York never lessened during the decade: New York's homicide rate was always at least thirty (or even more) points lower than the national average. Of course, New Yorkers— ordinary people *and* opinion makers—didn't see things from a "national average" point of view. Since the life they lived was "normal," Chicago was a place depraved—a Bedlam, a City of Mayhem, and a Throne of Blood.

Numbers and New York hauteur weren't the only reasons Chicago became "Murder City."

Chicago's own newspapers told their own bloody stories to their own readers. William Randolph Hearst bought his way into a very competitive Chicago newspaper market in 1900, first with the raw headlines of his *Chicago American*, then, in 1902, with his *Chicago Examiner*.

"A Hearst paper," said Arthur Pegler, a Chicago reporter, "is like a screaming woman running down the street with her throat cut." Robert Casey, another Chicago reporter, described the newsroom of Hearst's *American* this way: "Nobody moved even to the water cooler except at a dead run. . . . The city editor yelled at his copy readers, the copy readers yelled at the copy boys, and the copy boys yelled at each other. Each story, from a triple murder to a purse snatching in the ghetto, was a big story and greeted with quivering excitement by everybody who had anything to do with it."[6]

By 1910, a series of circulation wars had begun between Hearst's *American* and the McCormick family's *Tribune*. Both papers hired thugs to threaten newsboys, newsdealers, and even subscribers who read one newspaper instead of the other. Dean O'Banion, the bootlegger (who was assassinated the same year Leopold and Loeb committed their less than perfect crime), got his start hijacking *Tribune* delivery trucks for the *American*. In 1912, three gunmen on the *American*'s payroll boarded a trolley. They shot and killed the conductor, and then they shot and killed two passengers. The passengers had been foolish enough to be caught reading copies of the *Tribune*. The McCormicks hired their own killers: Max Annenberg and his younger brother, Moe. The Annenbergs were brilliant mercenaries, switching from one side to the other, depending on who offered them the most money, the best protection, and the most power.[7]

Between 1913 and 1917, as many as twenty-seven people—civilians, newspaper employees, and newspaper thugs—died.[8] The newspapers responsible for the attacks and counterattacks of the circulation wars reported them as "labor disputes" caused by striking employees. When William Hale Thompson, elected mayor in 1919, cast around for a dependable police chief, he settled on a man—Charles Fitzmorris—whose primary qualification for the job was his experience as city editor for Hearst's *American*.

Ring Lardner wrote for the *Tribune*; Carl Sandburg and Ben Hecht wrote for the *Daily News*; Charles MacArthur worked for the *American*. Chicago's newspapers employed gifted writers and critics, and reporters of talent. But: the same newspapers that reported the bloodletting of the twenties were themselves soaked with blood. The stories they told in columns under two-inch headlines—stories that continued for months, even years, one unnerving homicide overlapping with another—were chanted in unison, sung in antiphonal chorus. These stories, point and counterpoint, these recitations of anger, greed, hunger, fear, cruelty, avarice, cunning, and deceit—floated in the public air like a bloody haze, a fog of droplets, a mist that colored the light. The people who read these stories shared a common history: a world war followed by a pandemic; a postwar depression punctuated by upheavals and strikes. The people who read the stories retold in this book read them, one day after another, one week to the next, like chapters from a novel, published in installments. The strange thing was that the novel appeared to be true.

There are two other facts to consider about Chicago and its murders:

In 1927, Al Capone's gross annual income (as estimated by the U.S. Attorney's office in Chicago) was $105 million.[9] That sum would be worth ten times as much today.[10]

Capone's income was enormous—but like everything, it had a past, a lineage. It had grown, from one criminal generation to the next. Capone inherited an enterprise that had been making money for thirty years.

The enterprise was based on sex work and on gambling. Alcohol, legal and illegal, fueled it.

This was its genealogy:

In 1921, Capone was brought to Chicago from Brooklyn by a very smart man named John Torrio. Torrio and Capone were cousins. They were both Neapolitan crooks—crooks whose incomes were traditionally based on pimping, extortion, and gambling.[11] Syphilis—mixing business with pleasure—was an occupational hazard of such work.

The man who brought John Torrio to Chicago (in 1910) was a brothel owner named "Big Jim" Colosimo. Colosimo had grown rich—very rich—by running brothels, first in the city's vice district, then scattered, here and there, big and small, all over the city.[12]

From Capone to Colosimo, the lineage was purely criminal. *But*: The man who was Colosimo's mentor wasn't a crook, or a pimp, or a brothel owner. Colosimo's mentor was a local politician, a city council alderman named "Bathhouse John" Coughlin. The link between Bathhouse and Big Jim had something in common with the link between Big Jim and John Torrio.

The ward Bathhouse represented was the city's vice district. Its First Ward. Also known as "the Levee." Bathhouse knew talent when he saw it. Big Jim became one of Bathhouse's precinct captains. He also became one of Bathhouse's "collectors."

Bathhouse—along with nearly everyone else on the city council—was a "boodler." A boodler took bribes—big bribes—from contractors. Contractors who wanted exclusive licenses—monopolies—to do things like lay track and operate trolleys or lay pipe and deliver natural gas to city neighborhoods.[13] The bribes such "public" utility contractors paid were generous; the profits such contractors made—if and when they provided the services for which the city paid—were enormous.[14]

The tidal flows of money that passed through the bank accounts of city council boodlers like Bathhouse John were sizable—but those funds met and mingled with another tide of illegal money—money from the city's vice district, its Levee. The Levee lived and grew inside the city's First Ward like a parasite inside its host.

By 1910, the city's Vice Commission estimated that there were 1,020 brothels in the Levee, run by 1,880 pimps and madams, employing 4,000 prostitutes.[15] The Vice Commission estimated that the Levee's enterprises—its brothels, bars, and betting parlors—generated a collective gross annual income of $60 million.[16] The commission estimated the Levee's annual profits to be $30 million.[17]

The difference between the Levee's gross and net incomes wasn't the result of salaries paid to bouncers, cooks, piano players, and whores:

Large sums—over time, huge sums—were paid for "protection." Paid to precinct captains/collectors like Big Jim Colosimo. Collectors who took something for themselves, then passed the cash to Bathhouse and other aldermen, who took what they needed, then passed the money upstream—to police officers at all levels and all ranks, to court clerks and bailiffs, to prosecutors and judges, to fellow city servants, to . . .

Every favor had a price: $1,000 stopped an indictment for pandering; $2,000 stopped a complaint for "harboring a girl." Saloons paid fees; bookies paid fees; after-hours clubs paid fees. Fees and fees and fees.

For thirty years, vice-money bribes commingled with public utility bribes. The city's courts, police, and politicians had been taking bribes for a generation by the time Al Capone began to buy the protection he needed to do business in Chicago and elsewhere. By 1929, the parasite that had once been the Levee had begun to consume the city that had once been its host. The stories that resulted from this became the crime dramas that Americans have been consuming ever since like salted nuts at a bar. Criminals killed criminals, but their deaths only added to Chicago's unprecedented homicide rate. It wasn't just the professionals who were painting the town red.

There is one last set of historical circumstances to consider. They provide perspective to the murders committed by the plucky heroines of Maurine Watkins's *Chicago*.

Before Maurine Watkins, playwright, wrote *Chicago*, she had been Maurine Watkins, police reporter for the *Chicago Tribune*. Watkins didn't so much invent "Velma" as transpose what she'd reported about the arrest, trial, and acquittal of a middle-aged, former cabaret singer named Belva Gaertner. *Chicago*'s "Roxie Hart" had the same newsprint lineage: the beautiful Beulah Annan had shot her boyfriend in the back less than a month after Belva Gaertner had shot her lover during an alcoholic blackout. The murders both women committed—and the acquittals they enjoyed—were part of a pattern of crime and criminal justice dating back nearly fifty years.

The number of murders committed by women in Chicago between 1875 and 1920 increased by 420 percent.[18] Men did most of the killing in the city: murders committed by women during the period the stories in this book begin accounted for only 6.6 percent of the total. But: very, very few of the women who killed their husbands during that time ever went to jail. "Every white woman who killed her husband between August, 1905 and October, 1918, was exonerated or acquitted, totaling 35 consecutive cases."[19] *Thirty-five consecutive cases.*

"A woman, by marrying, does not become the slave or chattel of her husband," said a judge instructing a jury, just before the jurors passed sentence on a husband killer named Jessie Hopkins. Mrs. Hopkins shot her husband on New Year's Day, 1905, after he'd hit her once too often, following years of abuse. Said the judge: "If a woman is unfortunate enough to marry a brute whose favorite pastime is to mistreat her, she has the same right as her husband. . . . She has the right to kill her husband in self-defense if she is in imminent danger of bodily harm."[20]

The jury that acquitted Jessie Hopkins was an entirely male jury—as was every jury that acquitted the women who killed their husbands or their lovers from 1905 until the very end of the 1920s. Every lawyer who defended a woman who'd killed a man, married to him or just having an affair with him, argued—true or not—that their client was innocent, either because she'd acted in self-defense or because she'd been overwhelmed: emotions and intoxicants had impaired her judgment. The jurors who heard such arguments agreed with them because they believed two things. First: Women—especially white women—were innocent and not responsible, by reason of their gender. Second: Men, white or black, rich or poor, native born or immigrant, were, by their very nature, brutes. The jurors were usually right about the men.

One final note:

The stories in this book have been told in chronological order. Their progression forms a sequence; that sequence has patterns, explicit and implicit. These patterns have a variety of meanings. The story of Leopold and Loeb and the story of St. Valentine's Day were part of that sequence of meanings. They have been omitted from this book for two reasons: they are at the center of so much research and writing that there was little I thought I could add; second, I wanted to retell stories that were part of Chicago's own bloody mythology. Stories that reveal as much (or more) about Chicago's collective consciousness as they do about America's troubled soul. The story of Belva and Beulah turned out to be far more local—and the facts about these women more obscure and more revealing—than *Chicago* and its iterations have made known.

There is one story in this book—a 1926 murder in Wisconsin—that appears to be out of place. The Chicago papers gave that story the same coverage and the same headlines as they did the 1920 murder that begins this book. There were two reasons for such coverage: the victims in both stories were young, pregnant women; the men who murdered them were the fathers of the children they carried. When the first such crime was reported, it seemed so strange that everyone who read about it, investigated it, prosecuted it, and defended it began to question what was sane and what wasn't—what was normal and what was pathological. When the second such murder happened, in Wisconsin, it seemed to confirm people's worst fears: the bloody fog that covered Chicago had drifted north and settled over the countryside. Whatever was infecting the city had spread.

Notes

CHAPTER 1 · Carl Wanderer

1. *Chicago Daily News*, July 10, 1920.
2. *Chicago Daily News*, March 15, 1921.
3. *Chicago Tribune*, July 10, 1920.
4. *Chicago Daily News*, July 10, 1920.
5. Ibid.
6. *Chicago Tribune*, March 9, 1921.
7. *Chicago Daily News*, July 13, 1920.
8. *Chicago Tribune*, July 11, 1920.
9. *Chicago Daily News*, July 10, 1920.
10. Ibid.
11. *Chicago Daily News*, July 13, 1920.
12. *Chicago Tribune*, July 10, 1920.
13. Ibid.
14. *Chicago Daily News*, July 9, 1920.
15. *Chicago Daily News*, July 10, 1920; *Chicago Tribune*, July 10, 1920.
16. *Chicago Tribune*, October 4, 1920.
17. *Chicago News*, July 10, 1920.
18. Ibid.
19. *Chicago Tribune*, July 10, 1920.
20. Ibid.
21. Ibid.
22. Ibid.
23. *Chicago Daily News*, July 10, 1920.
24. Ibid.
25. *Chicago Tribune*, July 10, 1920.
26. *Chicago Tribune*, July 11, 1920.
27. *Chicago Daily News*, July 10, 1920.
28. *Chicago Daily News*, July 12, 1920; *Chicago Daily News*, March 15, 1921.
29. *Chicago Daily News*, July 12, 1920.
30. *Chicago Herald Examiner*, July 14, 1920.
31. *Chicago Tribune*, July 14, 1920.
32. *Chicago Herald Examiner*, July 14, 1920.
33. *Chicago Tribune*, July 20, 1920.
34. *Chicago Tribune*, October 4, 1920.
35. Ibid.
36. *Chicago Tribune*, October 21, 1920.
37. *Chicago Tribune*, October 21, 1920.
38. *Chicago Tribune*, October 22, 1920.
39. Ibid.
40. *Chicago Tribune*, October 26, 1920.
41. *Chicago Tribune*, October 30, 1920.
42. Ibid.
43. *Chicago Tribune*, October 31, 1920.
44. *Chicago Tribune*, October 30, 1920.
45. *Chicago Tribune*, March 2, 1921.
46. *Chicago Tribune*, March 8, 1921.
47. *Chicago Tribune*, March 9, 1921.
48. *Chicago Tribune*, March 11, 1921.
49. *Chicago Tribune*, March 12, 1921.
50. *Chicago Tribune*, March 16, 1921.
51. *Chicago Tribune*, March 17, 1921.
52. *Chicago Tribune*, March 19, 1921.
53. *Chicago Tribune*, March 20, 1921.
54. *Chicago Tribune*, July 29, 1921.
55. Ibid.
56. Ibid.
57. *Chicago Tribune*, August 6, 1921.
58. *Chicago Tribune*, September 30, 1921.
59. *Chicago Tribune*, October 6, 1935.

CHAPTER 2 · Cora Isabelle Orthwein

1. *Chicago Tribune*, March 2, 1921.
2. Ibid.
3. *Chicago Tribune*, June 16, 1921.
4. *Chicago Daily News*, June 21, 1921.
5. *Chicago Daily News*, June 17, 1921.

6. Ibid.

7. Ibid.

8. *Chicago Tribune*, March 2, 1921.

9. *Chicago Tribune*, March 3, 1921.

10. *Chicago Daily News*, June 22, 1921.

11. *Chicago Tribune*, March 2, 1921.

12. Ibid.

13. *Chicago Daily News*, June 22, 1921.

14. *Chicago Herald Examiner*, March 4, 1921.

15. *Chicago Daily News*, March 1, 1921; June 22, 1921.

16. *Chicago Herald Examiner*, March 1, 1921.

17. *Chicago Daily News*, March 1, 1921.

18. *Chicago Daily News*, June 22, 1921.

19. *Chicago Daily News*, March 1, 1921.

20. *Chicago Herald Examiner*, March 1, 1921.

21. *Chicago Daily News*, March 1, 1921.

22. Ibid.

23. *Chicago Herald Examiner*, March 1, 1921.

24. *Chicago Daily News*, March 1, 1921.

25. *Chicago Herald Examiner*, March 1, 1921.

26. *Chicago Tribune*, March 2, 1921.

27. Ibid.

28. *Chicago Tribune*, March 3, 1921.

29. *Chicago Herald Examiner*, March 2, 1921.

30. Ibid.

31. *Chicago Herald Examiner*, March 4, 1921.

32. Ibid.

33. "Jurors returned guilty verdicts for only seven of the eighty white husband killers (8.8%), and the judge quickly remitted the sentence of one of the seven . . . of the eighty white husband killers in the city from 1875–1920, only two were found guilty and sentenced to prison terms of more than one year." Jeffrey Adler, "I Loved Joe But I Had to Shoot Him," *The Journal of Criminal Law and Criminology*,

vol. 92, nos. 3 and 4, pp. 883–84. Northwestern University School of Law, Chicago, 2003.

34. Ibid., p. 876.

35. *Chicago Herald Examiner*, March 5, 1921.

36. *Chicago Tribune*, June 21, 1921.

37. *Chicago Tribune*, June 22, 1921.

38. *Chicago Daily News*, June 21, 1921.

39. Ibid.

40. Ibid.

41. *Chicago Tribune*, June 21, 1921.

42. *Chicago Daily News*, June 21, 1921.

43. *Chicago Daily News*, June 22, 1921.

44. Adler, "I Loved Joe . . . ," *Journal of Criminal Law and Criminology*, p. 891.

45. Quoted by Jeffrey Adler, *First in Violence, Deepest in Dirt* (Cambridge: Harvard University Press, 2006), p. 111.

46. *Chicago Daily News*, June 21, 1921.

47. *Chicago Tribune*, June 22, 1921.

48. Ibid.

49. Ibid.

50. *Chicago Tribune*, June 22, 1921.

51. *Chicago Daily News*, June 25, 1921.

52. Ibid.

53. Ibid.

54. Ibid.

55. Ibid.

CHAPTER 3 · Harvey Church

1. *Chicago Daily News*, September 9, 1921.

2. Ibid.

3. *Chicago Tribune*, September 11, 1921.

4. *Chicago Tribune*, September 12, 1921.

5. Ibid.

6. *Chicago Daily News*, September 12, 1921.

7. Ibid.

8. Ibid.

9. Ibid.

10. *Chicago Tribune*, September 13, 1921.

11. Ibid.

12. *Chicago Daily News*, September 13, 1921.

13. *Chicago Tribune*, September 14, 1921.

14. *Chicago Daily News*, September 13, 1921.
15. *Chicago Daily News*, September 14, 1921. There was no such factory and no such address.
16. Ibid.
17. Ibid.
18. *Chicago Daily News*, September 13, 1921.
19. *Chicago Tribune*, September 17, 1921.
20. *Chicago Daily News*, September 16, 1921.
21. *Chicago Tribune*, September 18, 1921.
22. Ibid.
23. Ibid.
24. *Chicago Tribune*, December 1, 1921.
25. *Chicago Tribune*, December 24, 1921.
26. *Chicago Tribune*, February 21, 1922.
27. *Chicago Tribune*, February 22, 1922.
28. *Chicago Tribune*, March 2, 1922.
29. *Chicago Tribune*, March 4, 1922.

CHAPTER 4 · Catherwood

1. *Chicago Daily News*, November 23, 1921.
2. Ibid.
3. Ibid.
4. Ibid.
5. Ibid.
6. Ibid.
7. Ibid.

CHAPTER 5 · Roach and Mosby

1. *Chicago Tribune*, April 22, 1922.
2. Three years before, in July 1919, a race riot had begun when whites stoned a black teenager whose raft had drifted into their territory along a beach on Lake Michigan. The riot lasted a week. Street fighting and arson killed thirty-eight people, injured more than five hundred, drove at least one thousand people from their homes. Nine hundred of those homeless were Lithuanians who'd fled a fire of suspicious origin that had gutted their neighborhood near the Union Stockyards.

3. *Chicago Daily News*, April 21, 1922.
4. *Chicago Tribune*, April 21, 1922.
5. Ibid.
6. Ibid.
7. *Chicago Tribune*, July 5, 1922.
8. *Chicago Tribune*, July 6, 1922.

CHAPTER 6 · Arthur, Eleanor, and Kate

1. "Mitchell" was Kate's maiden name. "Elois" quickly turned back into "Eleanor."
2. *Chicago Daily News*, December 14, 1922.
3. Ibid.
4. *Chicago Tribune*, December 14, 1922.
5. *Chicago Daily News*, December 14, 1922.
6. Ibid.
7. Ibid.
8. Ibid.
9. *Chicago Tribune*, December 17, 1922.
10. *Chicago Tribune*, December 15, 1922.
11. *Chicago Daily News*, December 15, 1922.
12. *Chicago Tribune*, December 15, 1922.
13. *Chicago Daily News*, December 15, 1922.
14. *Chicago Tribune*, December 23, 1922.
15. *Chicago Daily News*, December 26, 1922.
16. Ibid.
17. Ibid.
18. *Chicago Daily News*, December 27, 1922.
19. Ibid.
20. *Chicago Daily News*, January 26, 1923.
21. *Chicago Daily News*, January 27, 1923.
22. *Chicago Tribune*, February 14, 1923.
23. *Chicago Tribune*, May 13, 1923.
24. Ibid.
25. *Chicago Tribune*, July 26, 1923.
26. *Chicago Tribune*, July 29, 1923.

CHAPTER 7 · The Banker

1. Please multiply this dollar figure by ten to determine its current value.

2. Comptroller.

3. *Chicago Tribune*, March 15, 1923.

4. *Chicago Tribune*, March 13, 1923.

5. *Chicago Tribune*, March 10, 1923.

6. Photographs of June that appeared in the papers after Mr. Popp died weren't flattering. Heartbreak might have aged her.

7. One was a doctor; one was a vice president of Inland Steel.

8. *Chicago Tribune*, March 14, 1923.

9. *Chicago Tribune*, March 16, 1923.

10. *Chicago Tribune*, March 13, 1923.

11. Ibid.

12. *Chicago Tribune*, March 18, 1923.

13. Ibid.

CHAPTER 8 · Leighton Mount

1. *Chicago Tribune*, May 9, 1923.

2. J. Z. Jacobson, *Scott of Northwestern* (Chicago: Louis Mariano, 1951), ch. 8.

3. *Chicago Tribune*, May 9, 1923.

4. *Chicago Tribune*, June 3, 1923.

5. Ibid.

6. Ibid.

7. Ibid.

8. Ibid.

9. Ibid.

10. *Chicago Tribune*, May 15, 1923.

11. Please multiply all dollar figures in this chapter by ten to determine their current value.

12. Robert R. McCormick and James Medill Patterson.

13. *Chicago Tribune*, May 5, 1923.

14. *Chicago Tribune*, May 10, 1923.

15. *Chicago Tribune*, May 15, 1923.

16. Ibid.

17. *Chicago Tribune*, May 5, 1923.

18. Ibid.

19. *Chicago Tribune*, May 1, 1923.

20. Ibid.

21. *Chicago Tribune*, May 1, 1923.

22. Ibid.

23. *Chicago Tribune*, May 2, 1923.

24. *Chicago Tribune*, May 7, 1923.

25. Ibid.

26. *Chicago Tribune*, May 10, 1923.

27. Ibid.

28. *Chicago Tribune*, May 11, 1923.

29. Ibid.

30. Ibid.

31. Ibid.

32. *Chicago Tribune*, May 14, 1923.

33. *Chicago Tribune*, May 11, 1923.

34. *Chicago Tribune*, May 13, 1923.

35. Ibid.

36. Ibid.

37. Ibid.

38. Ibid.

39. *Chicago Tribune*, May 15, 1923.

40. Ibid.

41. Ibid.

42. Ibid.

43. *Chicago Tribune*, June 14, 1923.

44. *Chicago Tribune*, June 17, 1923.

45. *Chicago Tribune*, June 21, 1923.

CHAPTER 9 · Fred-Frances

1. *Chicago Tribune*, June 22, 1923.

2. Ibid.

3. *Chicago Daily News*, June 6, 1923.

4. *Chicago Tribune*, June 7, 1923.

5. Ibid.

6. Ibid.

7. Appointed by newly elected, reform Mayor William Dever. Dever entered office pledging to clean up the corruption that had permitted bootleggers to become multimillionaires. Dever's reform efforts destroyed arrangements that had kept the peace, satisfied demand, and made many civil and police officials rich. Dever's reforms spawned power struggles, assassinations, and acts of terror and counterterror that transformed the city.

8. *Chicago Tribune*, June 13, 1923.

9. *Chicago Tribune*, June 16, 1923.

10. Ibid.

11. Ibid.

12. Ibid.

13. Ibid.
14. *Chicago Tribune*, June 20, 1923.
15. Ibid.
16. Ibid.
17. Ibid.
18. Ibid.
19. *Chicago Tribune*, June 23, 1923.
20. Ibid.
21. Ibid.
22. *Chicago Tribune*, June 22, 1923.
23. Ibid.
24. Ibid.
25. *Chicago Daily News*, June 23, 1923.
26. Ibid.
27. *Chicago Tribune*, June 24, 1923.
28. Ibid.
29. Ibid.
30. *Chicago Tribune*, June 28, 1923.
31. *Chicago Daily News*, October 2, 1923.
32. Ibid.
33. Called "puffs" or "transformations."
34. *Chicago Herald Examiner*, October 4, 1923.
35. *Chicago Daily News*, October 2, 1923.
36. *Chicago Herald Examiner*, October 3, 1923.
37. Ibid.

CHAPTER 10 · Duffy Double Murder
1. Illinois Association for Criminal Justice, *The Illinois Crime Survey* (Chicago, 1929), p. 1031.
2. Herbert Asbury, *The Gem of the Prairie* (New York: Knopf, 1940), p. 344.
3. *Chicago Tribune*, July 9, 1924.
4. *Chicago Tribune*, February 23, 1924.
5. Rose Keefe, *Guns and Roses* (Nashville, Tenn.: Cumberland House, 2003), p. 162.
6. *Chicago Tribune*, February 29, 1924.
7. Ibid.
8. Ibid.
9. Ibid.
10. *Chicago Tribune*, February 27, 1924.
11. *Chicago Tribune*, February 28, 1924.
12. *Chicago Tribune*, March 7, 1924.

13. *Chicago Tribune*, February 28, 1924.
14. Ibid.
15. Ibid.
16. Ibid.
17. *Chicago Tribune*, March 1, 1924.
18. Ibid.
19. *Chicago Tribune*, March 3, 1924.
20. *Chicago Tribune*, March 5, 1924.
21. *1929 Illinois Crime Survey*, p. 914.
22. Laurence Bergreen, *Capone: The Man and the Era* (New York: Touchstone/Simon and Schuster, 1996), p. 87.
23. Ibid., p. 235.
24. *Chicago Tribune*, March 7, 1924.
25. *Chicago Tribune*, March 8, 1924.
26. *Chicago Tribune*, March 10, 1924.
27. *Chicago Tribune*, March 12, 1924.
28. *Chicago Tribune*, March 15, 1924.
29. Ibid.
30. *Chicago Tribune*, March 14, 1924.
31. Ibid.

CHAPTER 11 · Belva and Beulah
1. *Chicago Tribune*, April 5, 1924.
2. *Chicago Tribune*, March 14, 1924.
3. *Chicago Tribune*, March 12, 1924.
4. Gilbert Geis and Leigh Bienen, *Crimes of the Century* (Boston: Northeasern University Press, 1998), p. 14.
5. Sheldon Abend, president of the American Play Co., cited by Andy Seller, *USA Today*, March 25, 2003.
6. *Chicago Tribune*, March 12, 1924.
7. *Chicago Tribune*, July 10, 1920.
8. *Chicago Tribune*, March 3, 1924.
9. *Chicago Tribune*, March 13, 1924.
10. *Chicago Tribune*, June 5, 1924.
11. *Chicago Tribune*, March 13, 1924.
12. Ibid.
13. Ibid.
14. *Chicago Tribune*, March 13, 1924.
15. *Chicago Tribune*, April 14, 1924.
16. *Chicago Tribune*, May 24, 1924.
17. *Chicago Tribune*, April 14, 1924.
18. *Chicago Tribune*, May 24, 1924.
19. *Chicago Tribune*, April 4, 1924.

20. *Chicago Tribune*, April 5, 1924.

21. *Chicago Tribune*, May 9, 1924. Mrs. Unkafer's conviction was unusual. Between 1906 and 1935—according to figures published in the *Tribune* in March 1935—only two out of every nine women, charged with murder in Cook County, had ever been convicted. By contrast, during that same period in Cook County, four out of every five men charged with murder were convicted.

22. *Chicago Tribune*, June 7, 1924, and March 28, 1935.

23. *Chicago Tribune*, June 7, 1924. Besides Mrs. Unkafer and Mrs. Crudelli, there were three other women in jail, accused of murder, when Belva and Beulah were arrested: Lela Foster was a nondescript white woman who'd killed her husband for the usual reason: self-defense. Minnie Nichols and Rose Epps were African-American women, both charged with murder. Mrs. Nichols's and Mrs. Epps's presence in jail was evidence of a persistent homicidal phenomenon, linked to both class and race: Between 1870 and 1920, African-American women committed 22 percent of all "husband killings" in the city. Further, during that same fifty-year period, African-American women committed 24 percent of all murders committed by all women in Chicago—this at a time when African Americans were less than 5 percent of the city's population—and when African-American women were an even smaller percentage of the city's female population. See Adler, "I Loved Joe . . . ," *Journal of Criminal Law and Criminology*, pp. 867–97.

24. Sam Hamilton—the same man who'd won a guilty verdict against Arthur Foster, back in 1922.

25. *Chicago Tribune*, June 6, 1924.

26. *Chicago Tribune*, June 7, 1924.

CHAPTER 12 · Assassins

1. Bergreen, *Capone*, p. 129.

2. Keefe, *Guns and Roses*, pp. 114–15; *Chicago Tribune*, November 3, 1925.

3. Ibid.

4. A sum equivalent to $3 million today. All amounts cited in this chapter would be worth ten times as much today.

5. Bergreen, *Capone*, p. 131.

6. John Bender, *The Chicago Outfit* (Charleston, S.C.: Tempus publishing, 2003), p. 6.

7. Keefe, *Guns and Roses*, pp. 182–83.

8. Bergreen, *Capone*, pp. 132–33; Keefe, *Guns and Roses*, pp. 196–98.

9. Keefe, *Guns and Roses*, pp. 208–9. Other details: Illinois Association for Criminal Justice, *The Illinois Crime Survey* (Chicago, 1929), p. 1,029; Bergreen, *Capone*, pp. 136–37.

10. Bergreen, *Capone*, pp. 136–37; Keefe, *Guns and Roses*, p. 210; Illinois Association for Criminal Justice, *Crime Survey*, p. 1,030.

11. Illinois Association for Criminal Justice, *Crime Survey*, p. 923.

12. Bergreen, *Capone*, p. 137. Cited by Bergreen. Kenneth Alsop, *The Bootleggers and Their Era* (New York: Doubleday, 1961), p. 87.

13. Keefe, *Guns and Roses*, p. 220.

14. Bergreen, *Capone*, pp. 143–44; Keefe, *Guns and Roses*, pp. 220–23.

15. Keefe, *Guns and Roses*, p. 226.

16. *Chicago Daily News*, June 15, 1925.

17. *Chicago Tribune*, May 27, 1925; *Chicago Tribune*, January 11, 1926.

18. Bergreen, *Capone*, p. 147; Keefe, *Guns and Roses*, pp. 226–27.

19. The Army had used Hupmobiles as ambulances and staff cars in the First World War. They weren't fast, but they were tough.

20. Loaded, one shell in each chamber, each shell packed with .00 shot, each pellet equivalent to a .30 caliber round.

21. Loaded, one shell in the chamber, two or three shells in each magazine.

22. *Chicago Tribune*, June 15, 1925.

23. Ibid.

24. *Chicago Tribune*, June 14, 1925.

25. A "flivver" was a class of car—a small, cheap, lightweight car.

26. *Chicago Tribune*, June 15, 1925.

27. *Chicago Tribune*, June 14, 1925.

28. Ibid.

29. *Chicago Tribune*, June 15, 1925.

30. *Chicago Tribune*, November 1, 1925.

31. *Chicago Tribune*, November 3, 1925.

32. *Chicago Tribune*, November 1, 1925.

33. Bergreen, *Capone*, pp. 278–81.

34. *Chicago Tribune*, March 3, 1925.

35. *Chicago Tribune*, March 31, 1929.

36. *Chicago Tribune*, November 12, 1925.

37. Ibid.

38. Ibid.

39. Ibid.

40. Ibid.

41. *Chicago Tribune*, March 3, 1929.

42. Ibid.

43. *Chicago Tribune,* December 24, 1926.

44. *Chicago Tribune,* June 10, 1927.

45. *Chicago Tribune,* June 18, 1927.

46. Ibid.

47. *Chicago Tribune,* June 23, 1927.

48. Bergreen, *Capone*, pp. 286–90.

49. Ibid., pp. 305–8.

50. Keefe, *Guns and Roses*, pp. 265–66.

CHAPTER 13 · Hymie Weiss

1. He and Dapper Dan McCarthy had been sentenced to six months for helping Dean O'Banion during the Corning Distillery hijacking back in 1924.

2. Keefe, *Guns and Roses*, pp. 235–36.

3. Capone shot the man soon after Capone's own brother Frank had been killed by a posse of Chicago detectives, sent to Cicero to "oversee" the elections there. The man Capone killed had made the mistake of calling one of Capone's closest friends "a dirty kike." The man made things worse by insulting Capone. "Go back to your girls, you dago pimp." Capone had the last word: he shot the man four times in the face.

4. Illinois Association for Criminal Justice, *Illinois Crime Survey*, 1929, p. 832.

5. *Chicago Tribune*, May 5, 1926.

6. *Illinois Crime Survey*, pp. 837–38.

7. Ibid., p. 829.

8. Bergreen, *Capone*, p. 204.

9. Keefe, *Guns and Roses*, p. 236.

10. Ibid.

11. Bergreen, *Capone*, p. 206.

12. Keefe, *Guns and Roses*, p. 238.

13. See "Assassins," Ch. 12.

14. Bergreen, *Capone*, p. 207.

15. Ibid.; Keefe, *Guns and Roses*, p. 239.

16. *Chicago Tribune*, October 14, 1926.

17. *Chicago Tribune*, October 20, 1926.

18. Saltis and two other men, armed with shotguns, had ambushed a bootlegger named Mitters Folley. Folley died with sixty holes in him. They left him on the street for his mother to find. Saltis had grown so careless, and was in such a hurry, that he'd killed Folley in front of witnesses. Saltis and his men went into hiding—like Capone, they left town. Distance didn't do *them* any good. A crew of Chicago detectives, led by William Shoemaker, surrounded Saltis's hunting lodge on a lake in Wisconsin and brought him and his men back to Chicago to stand trial.

19. *Chicago Tribune*, October 14, 1926.

20. *Chicago Tribune*, October 12, 1926.

21. Ibid.

22. Ibid.

23. Ibid.

24. *Chicago Tribune*, October 15, 1926.

CHAPTER 14 · Christ's Dream

1. *Chicago Tribune*, December 3, 1926.
2. *Chicago Tribune*, December 7, 1926.
3. Ibid.
4. Ibid.
5. Ibid.
6. Ibid.
7. *Chicago Tribune*, May 19, 1929.
8. Ibid.
9. Ibid.
10. *Chicago Tribune*, December 2, 1926.
11. *Chicago Tribune*, December 7, 1926.
12. Ibid.
13. *Chicago Tribune*, December 3, 1926.
14. *Chicago Tribune*, December 7, 1926.
15. *Chicago Tribune*, May 19, 1929.
16. Ibid.
17. Ibid.
18. *Chicago Tribune*, December 7, 1926.
19. The girl believed she was pregnant; the college boy was accused of poisoning her with cyanide. The body of the girl had been found in a snowy clearing in a park in February 1916. The boy's trial began in May and ended in July. Chemists, pathologists, and psychiatrists testified; sixty love letters were introduced as evidence; friends and relatives testified about the girl's mental health; the boy told one intricate, foolish, and obvious lie after another. News reports began from the day after the girl's body was discovered to the day after the jury delivered its verdict: The girl had killed herself with poison she'd stolen from her high school chemistry lab. She wasn't pregnant but thought she was. She believed the boy planned to marry someone else. She'd swallowed the poison after a final meeting with the boy in a park.
20. *Chicago Tribune*, December 6, 1926.

CHAPTER 15 · Diamond Joe

1. There were sixty-four bombings in Chicago between October 1927 and April 1928. Sometimes the people who threw the bombs worked for bootleggers; sometimes they worked for racketeers (crooks who took over unions or trade associations by doing damage, then offering protection); sometimes they worked for politicians. More often than not, those politicians were Republicans. Chicago had been a bombers' town for decades. During the Bomb War of 1907, big-time bookmakers bombed each other to gain control of the city's gambling business. Twenty years before that, there'd been the Haymarket Riot: Chicago police attacked a rally, organized by anarchists in support of workers, on strike against the McCormick Harvester Company. Someone in the crowd threw a dynamite bomb at the police. Sixty officers were wounded; one died at the scene. Six other officers died, later, of their wounds.
2. *New York Times*, February 18, 1928.
3. *Chicago Tribune*, March 15, 1922.
4. *Chicago Tribune*, March 23, 1926.
5. *Chicago Tribune*, March 9, 1926.
6. *Chicago Daily News*, March 22, 1928.
7. Ibid.
8. *Chicago Tribune*, March 28, 1928.
9. Ibid.
10. *Chicago Tribune*, March 22, 1928.
11. *Chicago Tribune*, March 23, 1928.
12. All excerpts reproduced in the *Chicago Tribune*, March 23, 1928.
13. *Chicago Tribune*, March 27, 1928; *New York Times*, March 27, 1928.
14. *New York Times*, March 27, 1928.
15. *Chicago Daily News*, March 28, 1928.
16. Ibid.
17. Ibid.
18. Ibid.
19. *New York Times*, March 27, 1928.
20. *Chicago Daily News*, March 27, 1928.
21. Ibid.

22. Deneen had imported a professional political organizer and strategist from Detroit named Jacob Allen.
23. *Chicago Daily News*, March 27, 1928.
24. *New York Times*, March 28, 1928.
25. Ibid.
26. *New York Times*, March 29, 1928.
27. Ibid.
28. Ibid.
29. *New York Times*, March 30, 1928.
30. Ibid.
31. Ibid.
32. *Chicago Tribune*, March 31, 1928.
33. *New York Times*, April 5, 1928.
34. *New York Times*, April 11, 1928.
35. *Chicago Tribune*, April 13, 1928.
36. *Chicago Tribune*, April 11, 1928.

CHAPTER 16 · Pearl

1. *Chicago Tribune*, advertising copy, April 27, 1928.

   Phyllis Haver began as a Mack Sennett bathing beauty. Sennett said he thought Haver had cute knees. Haver worked her way through two-reeler after two-reeler until Cecil B. DeMille cast her as Roxie in his production of *Chicago*. *Chicago* was a big hit; Haver became an international star. In 1929, she broke her contract to marry a millionaire named William Seemen. The story was: Haver invoked the "act of God" clause in her contract as the reason she breached it. "If marrying a millionaire ain't an act of God—I don't know what is," she said. Haver's marriage to Mr. Seemen lasted until 1945. She died of an overdose of barbiturates in 1960.

2. Hollywood produced more than eight hundred movies in 1928—enough movies for theaters in cities to change their shows every day. In Chicago, more than a hundred theaters posted daily ads in the *Tribune* and the *Daily News*. Huge, four-thousand-seat theaters like the Chicago on North State Street always advertised their shows; three-thousand-seat theaters, like the Tivoli on South Cottage Grove, and two-thousand-seat theaters like the Riviera on Broadway bought daily ads as well. There were other theaters, though, medium-size neighborhood theaters like the Ritz in Berwyn, that simply posted their shows on their marquees, then relied on neighborhood traffic, reviews, and word-of-mouth to fill their seats.

   On May 9, 1928, the *Tribune* published a photograph of a crowd gathered in front of the Ritz in Berwyn. The photo included the Ritz's marquee: *House of Scandal* was playing that day. If a historian were to compare this information with movie ads posted in the *Tribune* that same day, then, if that historian were to note which theaters showed which movies ten days earlier, on Sunday, April 29, he might be able to make an educated guess about which movie packed the house at the Ritz the night of the twenty-ninth. His guess: *Red Hair*.

3. *Chicago Tribune*, May 2, 1928.
4. Ibid.
5. Ibid.
6. *Chicago Tribune*, May 3, 1928.
7. *Chicago Tribune*, May 19, 1928.
8. Ibid.
9. Ibid.
10. Ibid.
11. The actual name of the movie was *House of Folly*. Mr. Bilba or Ernie had it wrong.
12. *Chicago Daily News*, July 22, 1928; *Chicago Tribune*, July 22, 1928.
13. *Chicago Tribune*, July 22, 1928.
14. Thomas was twenty-one; Mas was twenty-one; Tulacz was twenty-two. *Chicago Daily News*, July 18, 1928.

15. *Chicago Daily News*, July 23, 1928.
16. Ibid.

CHAPTER 17 · Three Murders
1. *Chicago Daily News*, November 2, 1928.
2. Ibid.
3. Ibid.
4. Ibid.
5. *Chicago Tribune*, April 7, 1921.
6. *Chicago Daily News*, June 17, 1921.
7. *Chicago Tribune*, March 4, 1923.
8. *Chicago Daily News*, June 17, 1921.
9. Ibid.
10. *Chicago Tribune*, September 8, 1928.
11. Ibid.
12. Bergreen, *Capone*, pp. 238–39.
13. Ibid.
14. *Chicago Tribune*, September 8, 1928.
15. *Chicago Tribune*, September 11, 1928.
16. *Chicago Tribune*, December 22, 1928.
17. *Chicago Tribune*, December 19, 1928.
18. *Chicago Daily News*, December 18, 1928.
19. *Chicago Tribune*, December 18, 1928.
20. Ibid.
21. *Chicago Tribune*, December 23, 1928.

AFTERWORD
1. See Hal Higdon's *Leopold and Loeb: The Crime of the Century*, reissued in 1999 by the University of Illinois Press.
2. Crime historians are still arguing about the who, what, and why of that ambush.
3. Watkins's play opened on Broadway in 1927.
4. Chicago's 1924 homicide data were collected just before a five-year war of criminal revenge began. That war began in November 1924 and ended—more or less—in February 1929. Complete data describing Chicago's homicide rates can be found in the U.S. Department of Commerce,

Bureau of Census, *Mortality Statistics* for 1924. See also: *Mortality Statistics* for 1925, 1926, 1927, and 1930.
5. Between 1920 and 1929, automobile registrations in Chicago grew from 90,000 to 400,000—an increase of 400 percent during a time when the city's population grew by 22 percent. Fatal automobile accidents created a new kind of common jeopardy. In 1926, there were 889 auto fatalities in and around Chicago; in 1927, there were 987. See: Leigh Bienen and Branden Rottinghaus's essay, "Learning from the Past," in *The Journal of Criminal Law and Criminology*, vol. 92, nos. 3 and 4, 2002, pp. 533–34.
6. Higdon, *Leopold and Loeb*, pp. 27–28.
7. Moe's son, Walter, became a distinguished publisher and philanthropist. In 1989, Walter sold every newspaper, magazine, and television station he owned to Rupert Murdoch. The price was in the billions.
8. Higdon, *Leopold and Loeb*; Keefe, *Guns and Roses*, pp. 67–99.
9. Fred Pasley, *Al Capone: The Biography of a Self-Made Man* (Garden City, NJ: Garden City Publishing, 1930), p. 60; Bergreen, *Capone*, p. 236.
10. Samuel H. Williamson, "What Is the Relative Value?" Economic History Services, April 2004, http://www.eh.net/hmit/compare.
11. Bergreen, *Capone*, pp. 25–26, 81.
12. In 1912, Colosimo's monthly income was estimated to be $50,000. Cited by Bergreen, *Capone*, p. 81. One dollar in 1912 would be worth a little more than $19 today. See Williamson, "What Is the Relative Value?"
13. Lloyd Wendt and Herman Kogan, *Lords of the Levee* (Evanston: Northwestern University Press, 2005).
14. Charles Tyson Yerkes, Chicago's greatest "traction magnate," made

$30 million (in old money) from 1882 to 1897, building and operating trolley lines in the city. Yerkes bribed half a generation of politicians and civil servants. He even bought a newspaper—the highbrow *Inter Ocean*—to shape public opinion in his favor.

15. Wendt and Kogan, *Lords of the Levee*, p. 294.

16. Equivalent to the staggering sum of $1.2 billion today. See Williamson, "What Is the Relative Value?" for conversion factors.

17. Wendt and Kogan, *Lords of the Levee*, p. 294. For an earlier historical investigation of the Levee and its enterprises, see William Stead, *If Christ Came to Chicago* (Chicago: Lord and Lee Publishers, 1894). Stead's book reports on the Levee at the moment it changed from a local vice district to an enterprise with a regional and national clientele. A change caused by the huge influx of American tourists, attracted by the 1893 World's Columbian Exposition.

18. Adler, *First in Violence*, pp. 88–89.

19. Ibid., p. 113.

20. Ibid., pp. 110–111.

List of Illustrations

Acknowledgments

Martha Lincoln was working at a film archive in Chicago when I asked her to be my researcher. Martha was on her way to graduate school. She wanted to study anthropology. In the meantime, she agreed to scout the public records and newspaper archives I'd need to write this book.

For six months, Martha sent me dispatches from Chicago. Then, in June 2004, as Martha searched databases at her computer in Chicago, and I trolled the Web, sitting in my office in Amherst, we both stumbled on a site that made our jaws drop.

A writer, lawyer, and legal scholar named Leigh Buchanan Bienen, on the faculty at the Northwestern School of Law, had just launched a site called the Chicago Historical Homicide Index (http://www.homicide .northwestern.edu). The site had taken Leigh and her staff years to build. It was—and is—unprecedented.

Based on more than eleven thousand homicide cases, entered, by hand, in logs maintained by the Chicago Police Department, from 1870 until 1930, Leigh's Homicide Index is an interactive, searchable treasure trove of information, not just about the crime of murder but about the world in which that crime was embedded. Like a watering hole or a salt lick or a bird feeder, the site quickly attracted a variety of visitors: historians, legal scholars, sociologists, anthropologists, urban geographers; scholars interested in race, class, and gender relations; scholars interested in public health. . . . Within its first year, 250,000 people had visited the site. Eventually, I had the chance to meet Leigh and thank her for her work. Leigh and I became colleagues, then friends. As I wrote each chapter of this book, I sent it to Leigh; I asked her to critique it. I am in her debt.

In July 2004, I moved to Chicago to research the sources Martha had found. That meant reading microfilm. I lived in a single room, facing an alley. Every day, I woke up before dawn, came back late every afternoon. Each morning, I'd stand with the same group of homeless men, outside the doors of the Harold Washington Public Library, waiting for the guards to let us in. Once they did, we'd surge past them, up the escalators; many of us were headed for the same place: the library's Newspapers and Periodicals reading room. We all wanted the same thing: a place to sit for the rest of the day.

The Harold Washington Library's microfilms were old—brittle, scratched, and torn; some were misfiled, some were missing. The machines that displayed and made copies from the films were heavily used; they were often in disrepair. Reading microfilm, even under the best circumstances, is never easy. I'm very grateful to the clerks, research staff, and repair staff who helped me. In particular, I want to thank: Margaret Kier, then unit head of Newspapers and Periodicals; William Cliff, a senior clerk in the archive's reading room; Frankie Palerico, a repair and service tech who fixed what he could, when he could.

During the months I read microfilm at the Harold Washington, the only online service that could access and search old issues of the *Chicago Tribune* was an imperfect instrument vended by a company called Newsbank. Newsbank's results were hit and miss—when and if it produced results. Access to Newsbank and its searches was available only to research librarians. The public's demands on them were so constant and the results produced by Newsbank were so inconsistent, I want to make particular mention of those professionals who found the time to help me: Jesus Calprepra, Christian Matera, Susan Puterko, and Lynn White. My thanks.

All this text-driven research existed only because of the *Chicago Daily News* photographs I first saw posted online by the Chicago Historical Museum. (The entire *Chicago Daily News* collection can be seen on the Library of Congress's *American Memory* Web site. Go to: http://memory. loc.gov/ammem/ndlpcoop/ichihtml/cdnhome.html.) Robert Medina, rights and reproductions coordinator at the museum, gave me excellent advice and assistance throughout the course of my research and writing. Robert's cordiality and kindness, his goodwill, helped make this book possible. My thanks to him, his staff, and to the museum they serve.

Other than the homeless men I saw every day and the Mexican grill crew who worked in the chicken joint where I liked to eat, I didn't know many people in Chicago. One of the people I did know—had known for years—

was a very public person named Ira Glass. Ira is the host of a nationally broadcast radio show called *This American Life*. Ira and his producers collect and tape other people's stories; they edit the stories, then group them around themes: ideas or questions or situations or encounters that everyone listening to Ira's show—maybe two million people at a time—recognizes. Droll, sweet, sad, tragic, grand, quotidian. True. Ira loves Chicago. He works relentlessly. He and I talked now and then. I told Ira what I was discovering. He was suitably skeptical. Eventually he came to believe me. I want to thank him for his skepticism, his kindness, and his support.

I also want to thank Ira for introducing me to a fellow named Tim Samuelson. Tim is the cultural historian for the city of Chicago. Tim knows the city's past and present, its neighborhoods and buildings, its citizens and their histories. He knows the city, talks about it, understands it as if Chicago was a grand, sprawling novel, never completed, always in draft form. As I'd write each chapter of this book, I'd ask Tim where a place was located, what type of people lived there, who had come and gone from it. Tim saved me from many mistakes: misspellings, false attributions, erroneous conclusions. What errors remain exist only because I didn't have the wit to ask Tim the right questions.

In September 2004, I came back to Amherst with eighty pounds of documents. Within a few months, I realized that the time I'd set aside to master the material, then write about it, was inadequate. I'd been on the faculty at Hampshire College for years; the college had granted me paid and unpaid leave to research and write this book. The time the college had granted me was generous but the book had its own ideas about when it would be done.

In Amherst I was working the same hours I'd worked in Chicago: up before dawn, back late in the afternoon. Six days a week. Writing this book was like riding a horse that had never been ridden: if I stayed in the saddle, I'd crack my back; if I fell off or jumped, I'd break my skull. The horse didn't care: it wanted to get away.

The college decided to let me ride. The book took eighteen months to finish. I could never have done it if two people at Hampshire hadn't given me the time I needed. I want to thank Aaron Berman, the college's dean of faculty; I also want to thank Bill Brayton, the dean of the School of Interdisciplinary Arts, the place that is my academic home.

In the early stages of the writing, I asked colleagues of mine at Hampshire if they'd be willing to read sample chapters, then tell me what they thought. I felt like a cook testing recipes. Jim Miller and Eric Schocket read a few chapters; Steve Weisler read many more. Everything they said was helpful—I'm grateful to them.

As I made my way through the documents I'd brought back from Chicago, I'd notice gaps in the information. Fortunately, between the time I sat and read microfilm at the Harold Washington and the time I was back in my office in Amherst, trying to write this book, an information service company called Pro Quest had launched an online, keyword searchable database for what it called "The Historic Chicago Tribune." Pro Quest's service was easy to use and accurate—qualities that the Harold Washington's Newsbank service didn't have. Pro Quest's service wasn't free; at first, only a few public libraries in the Chicago Metro Area subscribed to it. One of those public libraries was in Skokie, Illinois.

For the first fourteen months of my writing, I'd make long-distance phone calls to Skokie's reference desk. Each time I'd explain my project, then ask the librarians to search Pro Quest's *Tribune* database using a specific name and specific dates. I'd ask the librarians to please e-mail PDF files of whatever articles they found. The librarians at the reference desk in Skokie were very kind—patient, forbearing, and helpful. I want to thank them by name: Bruce Brigell, Skokie's coordinator of information services; the librarians, Gary Gustin, Michaela Haberkern, Cheryl Sachinoff, and Pam Weinberg. The information they sent me—the articles and citations—were of critical importance. I thank them for their help and their goodwill.

I must confess: I never learned how to type. When I was fourteen, my parents enrolled me in a secretarial class taught by nuns. I passed the course—but every book I've ever written, I've written by hand. Libby Reinish typed this one. My thanks.

None of this—the research, the phone calls, the typing, the writing—would have been possible if I hadn't been married to Lisa Stoffer. Lisa underwrote this project. She worked a high-stress, high-stakes job, while I spent two years of my life sitting in small, single rooms, writing about seventy-year-old murder cases. I had saved some money before I began this project. Hampshire College and W. W. Norton helped pay some of the bills. But I could never have afforded to write this book—*we* could never have afforded for me to write this book—if Lisa hadn't said, "OK, I believe in you. I'll help. We can manage. This is worth it."

Lisa not only tolerated my obsession, she shared it. Read what I wrote, talked about it, critiqued it. There are ideas folded into this book, narrative strategies and moral architectures, that exist only because Lisa told me what she thought.

There are two other people responsible for this book.

First: Jim Mairs, my editor at W. W. Norton. I wrote every chapter because I knew Jim would read it. Every month, I'd send Jim an installment and he'd reply, quickly and emphatically. It was as if I were the publisher and he was the one and only subscriber to a very strange sort of periodical news service. What fun we had! We had the same, dark sense of humor; we shared the same sorrow for the same dreadful and despicable things. We were both beset by the same sort of ruefulness and impatience. We also loved many of the same things: cars in Jim's case; cars and guns in mine. Best of all, we both loved the photographs. Jim and I have done three books together. Perhaps we have a future.

Finally, I want to thank Carl Brandt. Carl is a distinguished literary agent. I've been his client since 1985. When I told Carl I was headed for Chicago, he put me in touch with his daughter: she knew every coffee shop, laundromat, and bookstore in the neighborhood where I'd found a room. After reading just the first few chapters of this book, Carl understood everything: "This is just like *Wisconsin Death Trip*," he said. "Expanded, updated. Opened up. But it's the *Death Trip*." Thank you, Carl.

Index

Page numbers in *italics* refer to pictures.